THE NAZI ROCKETEERS

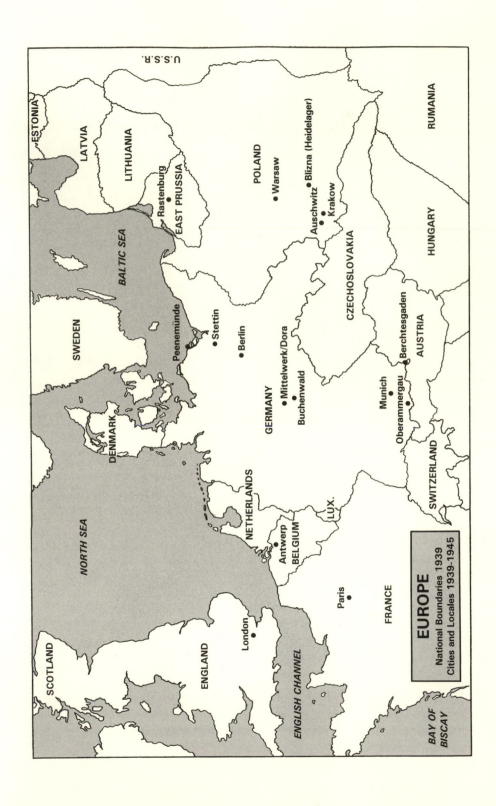

EUROPE
National Boundaries 1939
Cities and Locales 1939-1945

U.S.S.R.

ESTONIA

LATVIA

LITHUANIA

EAST PRUSSIA

• Rastenburg

POLAND

• Warsaw

• Blizna (Heidelager)

• Auschwitz • Krakow

BALTIC SEA

SWEDEN

Peenemünde •

• Stettin

• Berlin

CZECHOSLOVAKIA

DENMARK

GERMANY

Mittelwerk/Dora •

• Buchenwald

HUNGARY

Berchtesgaden
• Munich

AUSTRIA

NORTH SEA

Oberammergau

SWITZERLAND

RUMANIA

NETHERLANDS

LUX.

BELGIUM

Antwerp •

• Paris

FRANCE

SCOTLAND

ENGLAND

London •

ENGLISH CHANNEL

BAY OF
BISCAY

THE NAZI ROCKETEERS

Dreams of Space and Crimes of War

DENNIS PISZKIEWICZ

 PRAEGER

Westport, Connecticut
London

Library of Congress Cataloging-in-Publication Data

Piszkiewicz, Dennis.
    The Nazi rocketeers: Dreams of space and crimes of war
  / Dennis Piszkiewicz.
       p.   cm.
    Includes bibliographical references and index.
    ISBN 0–275–95217–7 (alk. paper)
    1. Von Braun, Wernher, 1912–1977. 2. World War, 1939–1945—
Technology. 3. Rocketry—Biography. 4. World War, 1939–1945—
Atrocities. 5. War crimes.   I. Title.
D810.S2P57   1995
629.4′092—dc20   95–10102
   [B]

British Library Cataloguing in Publication Data is available.

Library of Congress Catalog Card Number: 95–10102
ISBN: 0–275–95217–7

First published in 1995

Praeger Publishers, 88 Post Road West, Westport, CT 06881
An imprint of Greenwood Publishing Group, Inc.

Printed in the United States of America

The paper used in this book complies with the
Permanent Paper Standard issued by the National
Information Standards Organization (Z39.48–1984).

10 9 8 7 6 5 4 3 2 1

For the victims of the Nazi rocketeers:

Those who were killed by the V-weapons in London and Great
Britain, in Antwerp and on the Continent,

and

Those who died in the Dora and Nordhausen concentration camps
while building the V-weapons.

Contents

Photo essay follows chapter 17

Preface

Wernher von Braun entered the consciousness of America as its prophet of space travel on a Sunday evening in 1955. He had been hired by Walt Disney to develop a series of stories for his Disneyland television program. The show itself was designed to plug Disney's new amusement park in California, which had a space-travel-oriented section called Tomorrowland; and von Braun appeared on the program to explain the intricacies of space travel. True, von Braun had appeared on television earlier, and he had written many magazine articles; but Disney gave him one of the new medium's most popular hours as a podium to sell his ideas and himself. With his smooth German accent, von Braun came across as foreign as outer space; yet with Disney as his patron, he became as familiar as Mickey Mouse and he seemed as squeaky clean as Snow White.

Some Americans still remember von Braun's appearances on television. They are in their late forties or older, and many of them are career scientists, like myself. We were influenced by von Braun and others of that era who told us that education was important, and that scientific education was necessary if we ever wanted to participate in the great adventure of exploring space. We eventually learned—if we did not know already—that von Braun had designed the V-2 missile that had rained terror on London during World War II, a war many of us did not remember. According to his story, von Braun had little choice but to let his genius be exploited by the Nazis. Now, in the mid–1950s, he was working for the United States Army to build rockets that would defend us from the Communists.

About a decade ago, as many government documents dating from the end of World War II were declassified, von Braun's true story began to emerge. The documents told of the Nazi activities of von Braun and many other German scientists who came to the United States after the war. It was no longer credible for them to say that they were not dedicated Nazis and only did what they did to protect their jobs and secure their personal safety. Yet, some still cling to the post–World War II myth. They claim that any scientist in the same position would have been a willing collaborator in Nazi war crimes. They would have us believe that von Braun and his contemporaries were made by their age, where, in fact, their age was made by them.

While Wernher von Braun may be the best known of the Nazi rocketeers, there were others, equally brilliant and dedicated to their own personal causes and ambitions, who collaborated in the development of missile warfare and in the creation of the space age. In addition to von Braun, the Nazi rocketeers were Hermann Oberth, the theoretician; Army General Walter Dornberger, the career soldier; Albert Speer, the technocrat; and SS General Hans Kammler, architect of death camps and director of the rocket war. There were also others who were less well known, like Arthur Rudolph, who with von Braun traded the dream of space travel for the obsession of building a weapon with the blood of concentration camp slaves.

In the final analysis, any debate of whether von Braun and his partners in developing modern rocketry were dedicated Nazis is semantic. They belonged to the Nazi party, the SS, and other Nazi organizations. They were honored by the Nazis generally and by Hitler specifically. They dressed in Nazi uniforms; and, most damning of all, they behaved like Nazis. They were indirectly—and in some cases directly—responsible for the deaths of thousands of concentration camp slave laborers. The damage and deaths caused by their creation, the V-2 rocket, was slight in comparison.

ACKNOWLEDGMENTS

I found ready access to the historical records on which *The Nazi Rocketeers* is based through many fine, mostly public, institutions and several individuals who unselfishly shared with me their time and resources. I thank the staffs of the following institutions for their help in unearthing this story: the Los Angeles County Public Library, the Orange County Public Library, the library of California State University at Fullerton, and the library of the Simon Wiesenthal Center in Los Angeles. Additionally, I was aided by the staffs at the Library of Congress and the National Archives in Washington.

Special thanks for assistance in locating historic photographs goes to the National Archives Still Pictures Branch, to the National Air and Space Museum of the Smithsonian Institution, and to NASA.

I especially wish to thank the following individuals for their generosity in helping me piece together the lives and times of the Nazi rocketeers: Peter Rosenwald of the Los Angeles County Library, Duarte branch, and Aaron Breitbart of the Simon Wiesenthal Center. Marvin Kaylor, rocket engineer and pilot, helped me keep technical details correct; Lyn Chevli, Wilma Kaylor, and Lucy Malarkey generously critiqued the manuscript. Michael Larsen gave me regular doses of reality and encouragement; and Dan Eades, my editor, guided me in the final stages of this project. I sincerely appreciate their help. Above all, I thank P. J. Kaylor for her unselfish encouragement and patience with my many moods as I wandered through library stacks and various archives and then wrote this book.

I

DREAMS AND ILLUSIONS

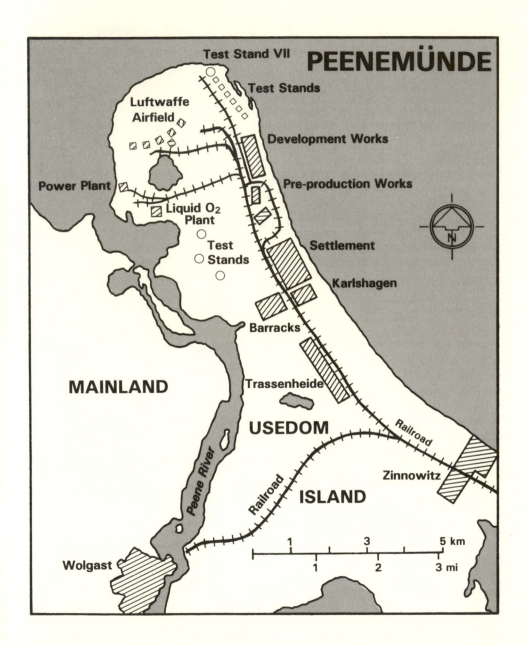

CHAPTER 1

When Space Travel Was Science Fiction

---

15 OCTOBER 1929

"Noch zehn Sekunden zum warten!"
The rocket ship stands in the blaze of spotlights under a starry sky.

"Neun."
It is shaped like a bullet resting on four massive fins, each almost as large as the bullet itself.

"Acht."
The spacecraft carries six passengers: four men, a woman, and a stow-away, a boy.

"Sieben."
They are bound for the moon,

"Sechs."
A new world of wonder and treachery,

"Funf."
Of riches and death.

"Vier."
The crowd of thousands surrounding the rocket ship are dwarfed by it. They are pins in a table top.

"Drei."
The numbers flash in descending order.

"Zwei."

The audience freezes in silence,

"Ein."

As time comes to an end,

"Null."

And tension becomes . . .

"Feuer!"

A flame bursts from the tail of the rocket ship, lifting it and its passengers into the mysterious sky.

The audience watching the silver screen in the Berlin theater did not mind the deception. They had suspended their disbelief. Rocket ships did not exist. A trip to the moon was impossible. The counterfeit rocket on the theater screen swung across a painted sky on its way to an improbable, imaginary moon. The audience at the premiere of *Frau im Mond* (The Girl in the Moon) loved the film.

One man sat sullenly in the darkened theater contemplating the fraudulent rocket ship. It was his own creation, yet he felt a sense of failure. He was none of the things he longed to be. Hermann Julius Oberth was not a German, not recognized as a legitimate scientist, and, on that cold and wet evening in Berlin, he was not a builder of rockets. Although the events that preceded the movie premiere appeared to argue against it, Oberth would leave his mark. He was the founding genius of rocket science in Germany; and he would soon become the teacher of the man who would be most responsible for the expeditions to the moon 40 years later, Wernher von Braun.

Hermann Oberth was a high school mathematics teacher on leave from his school in Transylvania, a district of Rumania. In 1923, he had published a small book on his lifelong interest, rockets and space travel. To his surprise and delight, his book was widely read. Its success catapulted him to the position of Germany's—and possibly the world's—leading authority in a field that did not and would not exist for another 30 years: travel by rocket through space. The rocket had appeared on the screen only because Oberth had dreamed of it, and he had told the world how it could take men to the moon; and only Hermann Oberth cared that the flight of the rocket ship they were watching was just an illusion.

The man who had orchestrated the illusion that thrilled the audience in the Berlin theater on that October evening was Fritz Lang, arguably Germany's greatest and most successful film director. Although Lang was only of medium height and build, he was an imposing figure. He had a sharp profile with a long, straight nose. The forward thrust of his chin and the way he combed his hair straight back accentuated the angularity of his face. A monocle tucked under his left eyebrow and a cigar wedged between the middle and forefinger of his right hand gave him the appearance of an aristocrat or a Prussian general. His air of self-confidence and authority was justified. Two years earlier he had completed his masterpiece *Metropolis*, a highly stylized and darkly prophetic story about exploitative masters and the enslavement of men in a subterranean factory. He followed that triumph with another futuristic tale titled *Frau im Mond*, the script for which was written by Lang's wife and collaborator, Thea von Harbou.

The new story was about travel to the moon. Lang needed a rocket ship for his film, and he called on the world's leading authority on rockets and space travel to build it. So in the fall of 1928 Hermann Oberth packed up his ego and dreams, kissed his wife and children good-bye, and left Rumania by train for Berlin.

Hermann Oberth may have been impressed by Fritz Lang, but he was not intimidated. After all, Lang had invited him to Berlin because he was the expert on rocket ships. At the age of 35, Oberth was a gangling man with unruly black hair and a trim moustache; dark, brooding eyes peered over his somewhat hooked nose. Those who knew him would describe him as proud, introverted, eccentric, and focused to the point of obsession on space travel. Oberth was also an experienced teacher, a professor. He had spent three years teaching unruly adolescents, and if he could keep them under control while lecturing them on a subject as tedious as mathematics, educating a movie director should be child's play. The battle of wills began as soon as Oberth saw the script.

"This isn't acceptable, Herr Lang. We can't have the travelers walking around inside the spaceship. They would float around freely in zero gravity"

"It must be that way, Herr Professor. The actors would look ridiculous floating all over the motion picture screen."

"And, Herr Lang, there is no atmosphere on the moon. The travelers would need to wear suits and helmets like deep sea divers so they could breathe. We must be realistic."

"Don't worry about it, Herr Professor. We're making art, not science. We don't have to be realistic."

"The issue was settled."

To anybody interested in building rockets, a movie about space travel meant two things: publicity for the cause and money. Oberth worked with a popular young science writer named Willy Ley to remove the most embarrassing scientific errors from the script and to design the props that would counterfeit a rocket flight to the moon. The rocket itself was based on the Model B design which Oberth had described in his book. Both Oberth and Ley would be credited as technical advisors for *Frau im Mond*. Both wanted more. They wanted to build a working version of Oberth's rocket, and they wanted the UFA Film Company, which was producing the film, to pay for it.

Fritz Lang was sympathetic to Oberth's and Ley's plan. He saw publicity value in a rocket launch that coincided with the premiere of his film, and he tried to get the UFA Film Company to support the enterprise. In the end, however, it was Lang and Oberth who paid for the fiasco.

Oberth took up residence in a workshop at the UFA studio as the clock began to tick down the time to the premiere of *Frau im Mond* and the projected launch of his rocket. Oberth could not do all of the work by himself, so he placed a classified advertisement for assistants in the daily newspaper. He was rewarded with his first recruit, a World War I combat pilot with a record of downing 11 planes. Although Rudolf Nebel had no relevant experience, he had a diploma in engineering, and he was anxious to work. Oberth then hired Alexander Borissovitch Shershevsky, a Russian aviation student and displaced Bolshevist. Shershevsky was no better qualified than Nebel, and he was more interested in talking about the project than actually working on it.

Oberth then addressed the problem of fuels. He had theorized that liquid fuels, gasoline or alcohol and liquid oxygen, would generate more power than solid fuels; therefore, they would be the choice for an interplanetary rocket. Until that time, nobody—at least nobody in Germany—had shown that it was possible to burn liquid fuels in a controlled manner. Oberth demonstrated that it could be done by burning a fine stream of gasoline squirted into a dish of supercooled, liquefied air. Unfortunately, the control of combustion was not always reliable. A delay in ignition would result in an explosion, and one such explosion had left Oberth shellshocked and had temporarily affected the sight in one of his eyes.

Finding a site from which to launch the rocket also proved to be difficult. Oberth wanted to fire his rocket from a tiny island in the Baltic called the Greifswalder Oie. When the rocket had consumed the last of its fuel, it would fall harmlessly into the sea. However, he was denied permission to launch from the island by the authorities who feared that the rocket might damage the lighthouse on the island when it returned from its flight—if it ever got off the ground.

Finally, the project was doomed by the design of the rocket itself. As the calendar approached 15 October, Oberth realized that his Model B was too complex a machine to finish in time. He switched over to a simpler design that he hoped would at least demonstrate the feasibility of a liquid-fueled rocket. The simpler model proved not to be so simple, and it was not finished.

On 15 October 1929 Hermann Oberth, the world's leading authority on travel through interplanetary space, went to the premiere of *Frau im Mond*, his rocket not built, his dream still a fantasy. The cream of German intellectual, literary, and political life was there that night. They poured congratulations and accolades on Lang for creating another masterpiece. Hermann Oberth, ignored, disillusioned, and broke, went back home to Rumania.

*   *   *   *

The dream was as old as mankind. The world was in two parts: the earth that held the animals man hunted and the cave where he slept, and above the earth the forbidden sky that held the unknown. The vision crept into man's mind as he watched the buzzards soaring high in the midday sky and as he watched the moon creep into the heaven at night. The dream was to go into that world, to be as free of the earth as the birds, to soar as high as the moon.

Dreamers came and went, but the vision remained. Man developed the tools of civilization, science, and art; and his dream slowly, incrementally approached reality. The astronomers defined the concepts of space and stars and planets. Leonardo da Vinci designed and built models of flying machines. The Montgolfier brothers devised the hot air balloon, and F. Pilatre de Rozier used it to lift man above the earth. The Wright brothers built the first powered aircraft and made air travel practical. It was only a matter of time before someone asked the question: What kind of machine could take man into the heavens, to space, and to the moon?

Three men who lived in different worlds and never met came up with the same answer. The men were a Russian, Konstantin Eduardovitch Tsiolkovsky, an American, Robert H. Goddard, and a German-speaking Rumanian, Hermann Oberth. They had little in common except that they all had the same dream, and as children they all had read the works of Jules Verne. They all admitted to having been inspired by Verne's book *From the Earth to the Moon*, which had been published in 1865.

What Verne possessed in the way of imagination—they all quickly figured out—he lacked in scientific practicality. Verne's characters rode to the moon in a projectile that was fired from a cannon. Tsiolkovsky, Goddard, and Oberth needed only an intuitive understanding of physics to realize that the force of acceleration would squash the projectile's passengers—like a ripe tomato slammed by a sledgehammer. Acceleration would have to be gradual to be compatible with life; therefore, it would have to be integral with the vehicle. It would also have to operate in the vacuum of extraterrestrial space. Only one machine created by man met these criteria: the rocket.

The science of astronautics had its first stirrings in tsarist Russia in the mind of Konstantin Eduardovitch Tsiolkovsky, an obscure high school teacher. At the age of ten, he became almost deaf as the result of scarlet fever. Because of his hearing impairment, he turned inward and became a scholar. Tsiolkovsky supported himself by teaching mathematics and physics in high school for 40 years, but he spent his free hours theorizing about and designing ways of being free of the earth. He designed and built a model of a flying machine powered by flapping wings. He designed dirigibles.

In 1883 Tsiolkovsky began to think seriously about space travel. Twenty years later, in 1903, he finally described his studies in a paper titled "Investigation of Cosmic Space by Reactive Machines," which he published in the Russian journal *Scientific Survey*. A reactive machine exploited Isaac Newton's third law of motion, which states that for every action there is an equal and opposite reaction. In Tsiolkovsky's mind, a reactive machine was a rocket. His later work included the modern concepts of the multistage rocket and a rocket motor fueled by liquid hydrogen and liquid oxygen. Unfortunately, because of his virtually nonexistent financial resources, Tsiolkovsky never built a rocket. His theoretical studies and speculations were all published in Russian. They were untranslated, unavailable, and unread outside his native land.

With the exception of a brief but humiliating moment in the public eye, Robert H. Goddard was equally obscure during his lifetime. As a member of the faculty of Clark University in Worcester, Massachusetts, he began a systematic study of rockets and their possible application to space travel. "I began to realize," he observed dryly, "that there might be something after all to Newton's laws." Goddard built rudimentary rockets to test his theories. By 1914, he had received patents for several components of liquid-fueled rocket motors and for multistage rockets. In 1919 he wrote a summary of his studies that was published by the Smithsonian Institution under the title *A Method for Reaching Extreme High Altitude*. In the last chapter of this report, he indulged in a little speculation. The chapter was titled "Calculation of Minimum Mass Required to Raise One Pound to an 'Infinite' Altitude." "Infinite Altitude" meant flight into space, and Goddard's last chapter explored the requirements for sending a rocket to the moon with enough flash powder to allow its impact to be seen from the earth.

Goddard's monograph was seen by the editors of the *New York Times* who, in an editorial titled "A Severe Strain on Credulity," condescendingly criticized what they viewed as his lack of understanding of Newton's laws. The *Times* was wrong, of course, but Goddard had been publicly and outrageously ridiculed. His life's work had been simplified to what he viewed as a derogatory term, "moon-rocket." After the humiliating incident, Goddard continued his experiments, but he worked in self-imposed silence and anonymity.

Almost ten years after the *New York Times*'s moon-rocket incident, Goddard unexpectedly found an influential ally and patron. Charles A. Lindbergh, the Lone Eagle, who had made the first non-stop, transatlantic airplane flight in 1927, learned of Goddard's work and was intrigued by the possibilities of rocketry. The two men met on 23 November 1929, little more than a month after Hermann Oberth's failure and Fritz Lang's brilliant success with *Frau im Mond*. Lindbergh opened doors for Goddard. The rocket scientist soon received a $50,000 grant from the Guggenheim Fund for the Promotion of Aeronautics and a smaller grant from the Carnegie Institution for the purpose of acquiring a test facility. Goddard then embarked on the most productive phase of his career, building rockets and testing them in the vast open spaces near Roswell, New Mexico. Regrettably, Goddard's innovations and successes remained virtually unknown and unappreciated in his own country during his lifetime.

Goddard's admirer and patron, Charles Lindbergh, would see rockets again 16 years after he befriended Goddard. He would find them in a subterranean metropolis where the dream of space flight had become a nightmare of terror and death.

The last of the three pioneers of astronautics was Hermann Oberth. Oberth was born in Transylvania, the Saxon backwater of the Austro-Hungarian empire known primarily and erroneously as the home of vampires. Oberth was the son of a doctor. He was enrolled at the University of Munich as a medical student when World War I put him on a new career track. After a brief stint in the infantry, he was assigned to a field ambulance unit. There, amid the carnage of battle, he discovered that he was not cut out for a career in medicine.

When the war ended, Transylvania was ceded to Rumania, and Oberth became a foreigner to his own culture, if not his own country. Upon his return to university in Germany, he was treated not just as a citizen of another country, but also as an enemy Rumanian. Nevertheless, he plodded along, passing his teaching examination and earning the credentials of a *professor secundar* in mathematics and physics. Oberth also wrote a doctoral thesis on his overpowering interest, space travel. The professors of the University of Heidelberg incredibly, inexplicably rejected it. Was it rejected because the science was bad, the writing poor, the author an enemy Rumanian? Who could tell? All that was clear was that he would not become a doctor of philosophy and that he had failed.

When the pain of rejection subsided, Oberth converted his thesis into a book. He presented theoretical calculations on rocket propulsion, plans for a liquid-fueled rocket, the Model B, and speculations about travel in space. Oberth submitted his book to six publishers with the same result: rejection and failure. He finally paid a publisher to print the short volume of unintelligible mathematics, fanciful illustrations, and fascinating speculation under the title *Die Rakete zu den Planetenraumen* (By Rocket to Interplanetary Space). Then the most amazing thing happened: the rejected thesis became a best seller.

Although Oberth's treatise was widely read, the scientific and engineering establishment had no use for this nonsense about traveling through interplanetary space. Its author was no more credible than Jules Verne, who had written about travel to the moon, or Robert Goddard, who had encountered the editors of the *New York Times* four years earlier. Oberth's disciples came from a part of the German-speaking world that was less impressed by conventional wisdom and authority. They were young and imaginative men who saw the obscure Rumanian as the leading theoretician of the future. They actually wanted to build rockets that could take men into space. Why rockets and space travel should have captured the imagination of the young at that time is open to speculation. Perhaps the economic depression and political chaos in Germany that followed World War I opened the door to this most outrageous form of escapism. Perhaps technological advances had brought the concepts of rockets and space travel to the brink of possibility—at least for the imaginative.

It was inevitable that the young enthusiasts would organize and seek out Oberth for his ideas and his company. One group that was to become the most influential began with less than ten members. It incorporated itself in Breslau in 1927 under the name of Verein fur Raumschiffahrt (Society for Space Travel), or VfR. Oberth was invited to join, which he did; and in 1929 he became president of the group. By September of that year, the VfR had 870 members. That same month Oberth was building a rocket for Fritz Lang. Opportunity was his at last. Anything was possible.

As Hermann Oberth began to hammer his dreams into reality, fate found him unprepared and inept. His attempts to build a real rocket floundered, and only the counterfeit rocket he had created took off on its imaginary journey to the moon. Fritz Lang had given Oberth the opportunity to assault space, but Oberth remained earthbound.

17 MAY 1930

Others in Germany were also experimenting with rockets and experiencing varying degrees of success and failure. The untimely death of rocket pioneer Max Valier was a tragic footnote to the history of rocket development.

Valier was a member of the VfR, a researcher, and writer who wanted quickly and publicly to demonstrate the applications of rocket propulsion. A public and spectacular success was, in his mind, the fastest way to gain support—both moral and financial—for rocket development. While many members of the VfR were building liquid-fueled rocket motors, Valier bought solid-fueled, or "powder," rockets off-the-shelf and focused on applications.

The invention of powder rockets is lost in history. The Chinese are generally given credit for inventing them. Europeans made modest improvements, using them for fireworks and occasional military bombardments. By World War I, the powder rocket had been surpassed in accuracy and efficiency by artillery and was, therefore, all but ignored as a weapon. Nevertheless, the device was simple and reliable enough to lift signal flares into the sky and to fire lines for the purpose of rescue at sea. The powder rocket worked.

Max Valier had joined Fritz von Opel, an automobile builder who knew the commercial value of a good stunt, in building a rocket-propelled automobile. They raced it in front of cameras and awestruck spectators. They also talked a glider designer named Alexander Lippisch into mounting small rocket motors to the rear of the fuselage of one of his aircraft. The glider made two successful flights of 35 and 70 seconds each. On the third flight, the rocket exploded, setting the aircraft on fire; but the pilot escaped unharmed.

In the spring of 1930 Valier made a fateful decision. He abandoned the reliable solid-fueled rocket for the theoretically more powerful liquid-fueled motor. Valier built a crude engine, fueled by gasoline and liquid oxygen, and attached it to the frame of a racing car. As he was testing the motor, it exploded, sending shrapnel everywhere. A metal splinter pierced his chest, cutting his aorta. Within minutes he bled to death in the arms of his associates Walter Riedel and Arthur Rudolph.

The death of the man who had courted publicity brought on a public outcry against the dangerous endeavor. A bill intended to ban further rocket experimentation was introduced into the Reichstag. The Reichstag, suffering the multi-party paralysis that would lead to its demise a few years later, failed to take action. Still, the rocket enthusiasts would be more discreet about publicizing their activities in the future.

While Max Valier's life and career came to an abrupt end, those of his co-workers were just beginning. Aircraft designer Alexander Lippisch and Valier's assistants, Walter Riedel and Arthur Rudolph, were young, imaginative, and ambitious. For good and for evil, they would make unique contributions of their own to the development of rockets.

SPRING 1930

Fate gave Hermann Oberth a second chance. Oberth and his former assistant Rudolf Nebel, under the auspices of the VfR, had been trying to raise funds from industry and government organizations to continue their rocket development work. The hunt for money in an economy rapidly slipping into depression was, not surprisingly, unsuccessful; but it did turn up an unexpected opportunity. Nebel contacted Oberth at his home in Mediasch, Rumania, to tell him of an offer by the government-sponsored institute called the Chemisch-Technische Reichsanstalt (Reich Institute for Chemistry and Technology) to use a workshop and its facilities to assemble and test a rocket motor. The institute served a purpose similar to that of the United States Bureau of Standards; and, in addition, it evaluated new industrial inventions and processes. In May 1930, Oberth returned to Berlin resolved to succeed in building a liquid-fueled rocket.

23 JULY 1930

When Hermann Oberth returned to Berlin—no doubt with his *Frau im Mond* disaster painfully in mind—he set for himself the modest goals of building, firing, and measuring the performance of a liquid-fueled rocket motor. He would complete construction of the engine he had designed to power the rocket that he had failed to launch as the climax of the movie project. Oberth gave this rocket motor the name "Kegelduese," or "cone jet."

In addition to Rudolf Nebel, two young members of the VfR offered Oberth their assistance in the Kegelduese project. They were a young engineer who worked for the Siemens Company named Klaus Riedel (no relation to Max Valier's associate Walter Riedel) and an ambitious 18-year-old engineering student from the Berlin Institute of Technology named Wernher von Braun. Oberth and his three assistants worked through the summer building their earthbound rocket.

The combustion chamber of the Kegelduese was a hollow cone of steel with an exhaust vent bolted to its base. Two crude inlet ports for fuel and liquid oxygen, pointing toward the center of the combustion chamber, were also part of the base. Pieces of quarter-inch copper tubing led to these inlet ports from a small gasoline tank and a Dewar flask of liquid oxygen. The liquids in both containers were pressurized to ten atmospheres with nitrogen gas. The Kegelduese was affixed inside a metal bucket with its cone apex pointing downward and its exhaust vent pointing upward. The bucket was filled with water to cool the motor, and the entire assembly was placed on a grocer's scale to measure the rocket motor's thrust.

The rocket was to be tested out of doors in a clearing among the pines. It had rained the day before, and it was still pouring the day of the test. The clouds were so low that they hid the tops of the trees. It was a miserable day, but at least the rain could be counted on to put out any fires. Oberth, Nebel, Riedel, and von Braun were joined by Dr. Ritter, director of the Chemisch-Technische Reichsanstalt, who would verify the results of the test. Also present were press photographers. Undoubtedly they remembered the demise of Max Valier a little over two months earlier and were aware of moves to ban the testing of rockets. No matter how the day turned out, the reporters could return to their offices with a story and, although somewhat blurred by the rain, pictures.

It was Oberth's show, his last chance to salvage success from his encounters with the dreamers and dilettantes he had met in Berlin. His mood matched the gloom of the day. He watched as his team prepared the equipment, and he made an occasional sarcastic comment. His assistants plodded on, their senses of humor no doubt dampened by the continuing downpour and Oberth's sullen mood.

Oberth, being the senior scientist on the project and having been shell-shocked the previous year by exploding rocket fuel, left the hazardous job of ignition to Klaus Riedel. Oberth and the others watched from a safe distance. As the gasoline and liquid oxygen squirted into the Kegelduese from the pressurized tanks, Riedel threw a burning, gasoline-soaked rag over the upward-pointed exhaust nozzle. He dove for the protection of a shield some distance from the equipment as the rocket burst to life with an ear-shattering roar. A three-foot-long spear of flame shot straight up from the Kegelduese. The roar of the engine continued for ten seconds, thirty, sixty, a minute and a half.

The director of the institute, Dr. Ritter, presented Oberth with a certificate stating that his Kegelduese "had performed without mishap on July 23, 1930, for 90 seconds, consuming 6 kilograms of liquid oxygen and 1 kilogram of gasoline, and delivering a constant thrust of about 7 kilograms."

Hermann Oberth had succeeded at last; he had built a certified, working, liquid-fueled rocket motor. Future advances would be left to others. Oberth turned his back on the disappointments of the past and happily got on the train to return to Rumania. He still had a wife and family to support, and he still had a job teaching mathematics to high school students.

CHAPTER 2

The P. T. Barnum of Rockets

27 SEPTEMBER 1930

When Hermann Oberth returned to Rumania, Rudolf Nebel became the dominant figure among the German rocket enthusiasts. Although another man became president of the VfR after Oberth resigned, Nebel, who was secretary of the group, preempted the leadership in the area of rocket development. He was not interested in organizational politics or the slow, methodical building of rockets. He was an activist. He set about turning the VfR into an energetic organization that would lead mankind into interplanetary space. Rudolf Nebel became the P. T. Barnum of German rocketry.

Nebel's first tiny step on the road to space was to find a home for the VfR, a permanent facility for building and testing rockets. After surveying many vacant parcels of property in and around Berlin, he found exactly what they needed in Berlin's northern suburb of Reinickendorf. He immediately began to negotiate a lease with the owners of the land, the city of Berlin. The property, which covered about two square miles, was in a hard-to-find location, down a bad road, and surrounded by a wire fence. It had been an ammunition dump during World War I and had not been used since then. The compound contained about a half-dozen ammunition storage buildings, each surrounded by earthen walls 40 feet high and 60 feet thick at the base. Single, narrow passages cut through the walls allowed access to the buildings. According to the terms of the lease, the VfR would have the use of one of these buildings and a smaller administrative building near the main gate. The VfR was not to enter any of the other buildings, to modify either of the buildings it occupied, or to bring in any equipment that could not be removed on 48-hours notice. Despite the restrictions, the price was right: a nominal ten marks per year.

They took possession of the property on 27 September, and as the ambitious young men began cleaning out the long-disused buildings and clearing away the weeds and brush, Nebel mounted a sign at the entrance. It read "RAKETENFLUGPLATZ BERLIN." *Raketenflugplatz* translates as "rocket airdrome."

FALL 1930–SPRING 1931

The hard times of the deepening economic depression and the promise of adventure and accomplishment combined to give the *Raketenflugplatz* a resident staff. Rudolf Nebel and Klaus Riedel soon made homes of two small rooms in the administrative building. In time, about 15 unemployed draftsmen, mechanics, metal workers, and electricians also took up residence in the growing technological commune. They received a rent-free place to live and had the opportunity to continue working at their crafts. Nebel, Riedel, Willy Ley, Wernher von Braun, and the rest were soon blissfully at work building prototypes of the vehicles that would someday take them into space.

Nebel's entrepreneurial approach soon began to bring in materials and money. The VfR published a mimeographed newsletter for distribution to its membership. Two members, previously not known to be wealthy, were sufficiently impressed by its contents to contribute significant sums for building and testing rockets. The leadership began a letter-writing campaign to industrial concerns asking not for money, but for materials and equipment. The industrialists, eager to buy into the dream of space travel, quickly donated the components of a complete machine shop, an inventory of metal stock, fittings, tubing, paints, office furniture, and supplies. When one industrial patron came through with a large donation of welding wire for which they had limited use, Nebel traded it to a welding shop for the services of a skilled welder, which they needed more. Buoyed by their success, they asked for and got a waiver on gasoline tax, which reduced its cost by over 80 percent. They were soon ready to take the next step after Hermann Oberth's Kegelduese.

Rudolf Nebel had two guiding principles that significantly influenced the design of the early rockets. First, he believed and preached that all of the components needed to build liquid-fueled rockets were already available as off-the-shelf items. Second, he preached that, even though funds might be available, they should never buy anything but should rely on donations. The first principle made engineering sense in the days when designs were primitive, and the second was mandated by the hard economic times.

The first project of the *Raketenflugplatz* group was to build a rocket designed by Nebel. It was named "Minimumrakete," abbreviated "Mirak," and it was the material incarnation of Nebel's principles. The Mirak looked like an all metal version of a common fireworks skyrocket. It had a bullet-shaped headpiece with the rocket motor at its rear and a long, thin aluminum tube trailing behind like a guiding stick. The combustion chamber was made of copper, and it was a small version of Oberth's Kegelduese design. The bullet-shaped main body was filled with liquid oxygen at −183°C. It capped the motor and was intended to cool the motor as it burned fuel. The trailing aluminum tube was the gasoline fuel tank. It was pressurized by a carbon dioxide cartridge of the type commonly used to pressurize seltzer bottles. The strange trailing fuel tank was not designed to fulfill any engineering requirement but to utilize some aluminum tubing which Nebel had obtained for free—as usual. In a few brief months, the group perfected the rocket and established a system for safely firing it into the sky above the *Raketenflugplatz*.

When Rudolf Nebel had been soliciting funds to support the *Raketenflugplatz*, he had promised to invite the donors to observe demonstrations of the rockets. Now that they had the Mirak, a rocket that actually flew, he invited the observers: past contributors, engineering societies, and potential contributors. Of course, gasoline and liquid oxygen had to be paid for, so they charged admission. If the rocket did not clear the top of the launching rack, well, they were rocket scientists, not performers in a circus. There were no refunds.

FALL 1931

The *Raketenflugplatz* had not only survived its first year of existence, navigating through the economic depression on the waves of contributions, it had actually prospered. Nebel and his group of enthusiasts had turned the abandoned ammunition dump into a functioning rocket-testing and -firing range. By Willy Ley's account, they had done 270 test-stand firings of rocket motors, and had launched 87 complete rockets, not counting the early primitive Miraks.

The *Raketenflugplatz* group had given many demonstrations of its rockets, and news of their fantastic and spectacular machines began to spread through Berlin. Two years after Oberth's *Frau im Mond* fiasco, and one year after the *Raketenflugplatz* began to operate, the UFA Film Company sent a crew to record their activities for its weekly newsreel. Rockets were news.

The climax of the newsreel segment was to be a demonstration firing of a rocket. The rocket would be their most advanced creation, which they named the "One-Stick Repulsor." The Repulsor was a bizarre contraption; but, in the early days of rocket research, any rocket appeared strange. It was a "nose-drive" machine: the rocket motor, encased in a bullet-shaped jacket filled with cooling water, was at the extreme front end. Below it and connected to it by two curved pipes that fed it oxygen and fuel were the liquid oxygen and gasoline tanks. A single shaft ("one-stick") ran through the axis of the rocket, connecting and supporting the two tanks. A sheet metal cone atop the tanks sheltered them from the blast of the rocket engine. Four aluminum fins intended to stabilize the craft were attached to its stern. A compartment at the bottom end of the rocket held a parachute to bring the fragile craft safely back to earth after its flight. The whole assembly was 12 feet long, had a diameter of 4 inches, weighed 22 pounds when empty and 45 pounds when loaded with fuel.

UFA's camera was rolling.

With the roar of a locomotive, the Repulsor rose on its blue flame, swiftly clearing the launch tower and climbing into the sky. Its flight was perfect; its landing was not. The parachute that was supposed to return the Repulsor gently back to earth tore off. The rocket fell, trailing wisps of flame that were fueled by the last few drops of gasoline. It landed on the roof of a shack across the road from the test site and set the shack on fire. The shack was old, and little of value was stored in it. Unfortunately, it was the property of the local police garrison. Before anyone realized it, the *Raketenflugplatz* was invaded by uniformed officers who wanted all experimentation with those dangerous toys stopped. Permanently. Now.

After much discussion between the police and the *Raketenflugplatz* group, an agreement was worked out that was surprisingly reasonable. The *Raketenflugplatz* group would place several sensible restrictions on their equipment and operations, and the police would let them resume their experiments. Rockets again flew over the *Raketenflugplatz*.

And UFA had a very entertaining newsreel.

SPRING 1932

To dream of flying into interplanetary space or to the moon by rocket was one thing; to actually do it would be something else entirely. The theory was there, put there by the Russian Tsiolkovsky, the American Goddard, and the Rumanian, Oberth; it was as solid as it could be without being tested. Giant liquid-fueled rockets would be needed, but they did not exist, and might not exist for decades. For the young adventurer, impatient to explore the skies, there was only one way to go: on wings.

Wernher von Braun had taken his first glider lessons at the Grunau Training School in Silesia the previous year and was back to take an advanced course. One of his classmates was a diminutive girl with an infectious smile and a well-developed sense of daring named Hanna Reitsch. It was inevitable that the two would become friends. Both were from solid, prosperous families. Von Braun's father was a landowner and bureaucrat; Reitsch's father was a doctor. They were the same age; von Braun was born on 23 March 1912, and Reitsch six days later on 29 March. Most important, both were ambitious adventurers and dreamers. Reitsch wanted to become a missionary doctor in Africa who flew to her charges, and von Braun wanted to fly to the moon.

Having developed the skills to fly gliders, both Wernher von Braun and Hanna Reitsch were ready for new challenges. Within a year both of them would be at the controls of propeller-driven aircraft. They attacked the future with the optimism of youth. Anything was possible.

ALSO IN SPRING 1932

In one of his continuing efforts to raise capital for the operation of the *Raketenflugplatz*, Rudolf Nebel wrote a technical treatise titled "Confidential Memo on Long-Range Rocket Artillery," which he personally delivered to Colonel Doctor Karl Becker, chief of ballistics and ammunition for the Reichswehr. The memo, according to Willy Ley, was technically inadequate to the point of embarrassment. The absurdity of taking it to Becker was compounded by the fact that Becker was one of Germany's leading authorities on ballistics, having co-authored the most widely used handbook on the subject. Nevertheless, Becker was receptive to Nebel's interest in rocket artillery. Unknown to the *Raketenflugplatz* group, the army had already begun to explore the possibilities of rockets as bombardment weapons. Their motivation was wholly practical. The Treaty of Versailles, which ended World War I, had severely restricted the German Army and, among other limitations, denied it the use of heavy artillery. The treaty, however, had failed to mention rockets, which had fallen into disuse as weapons. The German Army now saw in rockets a means of evading the treaty's restrictions and re-establishing its heavy and long-range bombardment capability.

Soon after Nebel's encounter with Colonel Becker, three men dressed in civilian clothes visited the *Raketenflugplatz*. There was no reason to advertise the fact that they or the organization they represented, the German Army, had an interest in the developing technology of rockets. The men were Colonel Karl Becker, Major Ritter von Horstig, Becker's ammunition expert, and Captain Walter Dornberger, who was in charge of developing powder rockets for the army. In time this third man, Walter Dornberger, would become a dominant figure in rocket development.

Walter Dornberger was a career officer in the German Army. He came from a solid middle-class background; his father was a pharmacist. Dornberger had wanted to become an architect, but custom dictated that, as the second son in the family, he would make a career for himself in the military. He enlisted in the German Army in August of 1914, just before his 19th birthday and just as Germany declared war on France. Within months he was a second lieutenant with the heavy artillery on the western front. His luck was good in that he survived the war and bad in that he was captured before the armistice in 1918. Dornberger spent the following two years in a prisoner-of-war camp in France. After his return, he remained in the army. In 1925 he went on an extended leave to study engineering at the Berlin-Charlottenburg Technische Universitat. He returned to active duty five years later with both bachelor's and master's degrees. The Army put him to work in its ballistics branch to examine the potential of rockets. Captain Walter Dornberger was 34 years old, of medium height, clean shaven, with blue eyes, and thinning brown hair. He was self-assured, opinionated, and assertive—the stereotypical German officer.

The *Raketenflugplatz* group was, as usual, enthusiastic about showing off its toys for its visitors. They were prepared to launch a Mirak I for the edification of their visitors. The visitors were not interested. They showed some interest in the Mirak II, an enlarged version of the Mirak I, but it was not yet ready to fly. The three army officers wanted to see instrumentation and data. They watched a static firing of a rocket engine, but they concentrated on the thrust balance rather than on the rocket motor. They got a briefing on current test and flight activities as well as plans for the future. The army contingent was impressed by how much developmental work had been done, but disappointed with how poorly the performance of the rockets had been documented. They were interested in systematic development and scientific analyses, not in fireworks displays, which seemed to be—under the leadership of Rudolf Nebel—what the *Raketenflugplatz* group did best.

The site visit by the army would have been thoroughly disappointing if, at its end, they had not proposed that the *Raketenflugplatz* group build a rocket of advanced design and launch it at the army's Versuchsstelle Kummersdorf-West (Experimental station Kummersdorf West), 17 miles south of Berlin. The army would pay them 1,360 marks upon the successful firing of the rocket. Nebel signed the agreement on behalf of the VfR.

AUGUST 1932

Two cars pulled out of the *Raketenflugplatz* in the dark, predawn hours. Atop the lead car was the rocket; the second carried liquid oxygen, gasoline, and tools. The cars also carried Rudolf Nebel, Klaus Riedel, and Wernher von Braun. At five o'clock they rendezvoused with Captain Dornberger in the forest south of Berlin. Dornberger then led the procession to the army's artillery firing range at Kummersdorf.

The testing range was a revelation. It held measuring equipment—ballistic cameras, chronographs, photo-theodolites—that were common to artillery specialists but unknown to the novice rocket builders. These tools were intended to track artillery shells; but that day they would, for the first time, measure the performance of a rocket. The young men erected the launcher, set up and fueled the rocket, and by two o'clock in the afternoon, they were ready to launch it. The rocket was a One-Stick Repulsor modified to meet the army's requirements. The compartment at the bottom end of the rocket held, besides the parachute, a flare to be released at the peak of its trajectory.

With dreams of glory and hopes of funding from the army, they launched the Repulsor. The rocket rose rapidly to a height of about 100 feet, then tipped over and flew horizontally until it crashed in the nearby forest. The flare was not released at the top of the trajectory; the parachute did not open. The Repulsor's flight was, as Walter Dornberger described it years later, a "great disappointment." Their measurements were inadequate and their rocket unreliable. There would be no money coming from the army to the *Raketenflugplatz*.

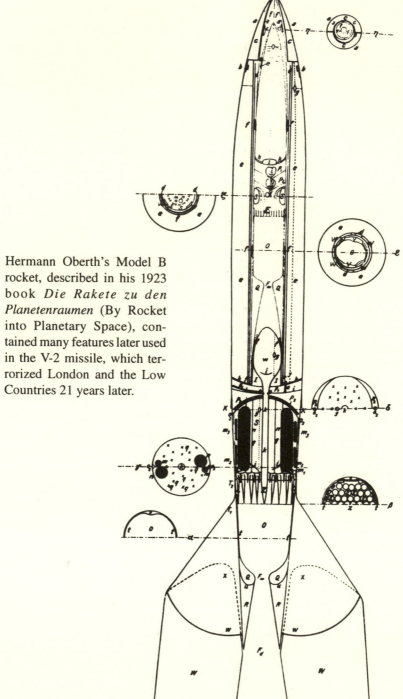

Hermann Oberth's Model B rocket, described in his 1923 book *Die Rakete zu den Planetenraumen* (By Rocket into Planetary Space), contained many features later used in the V-2 missile, which terrorized London and the Low Countries 21 years later.

Modell B.

CHAPTER 3

The Baron's Son and the Soldier

SUMMER 1932

Wernher von Braun, until then a college student, an apprentice rocket builder, and a follower, took the initiative.

The young man was the son of an aristocrat, descended from a long line of aristocrats. The first von Braun stepped into the history book in 1245 by leading a defense against the invading Mongols. His descendants became Prussian Junkers, the land barons who ran the affairs of state. Wernher was the second of three sons born to Baroness Emmy and Baron Magnus von Braun. The baroness had descended from old Swedish-German aristocratic lines. The year Wernher was born, 1912, the baron was the *Landrat*, the provincial councilor, of the old Prussian province of Posen and owner of extensive land holdings. The cession of Posen to Poland at the end of World War I caused the von Brauns to relocate to Silesia. The von Brauns also had a residence in Berlin where the baron served as minister of agriculture in the last days of the Weimar Republic. As Wernher grew up, he had the benefit of private and boarding school educations. Baron von Braun once remarked that he did not know where his son had developed his interest in rocketry. Wernher's interest, if not his aptitude, had developed early. In his early teens he had conducted several imaginative but reckless experiments with skyrockets, much to the baron's chagrin.

Willy Ley gave a concise description of the young man: "Physically he happened to be a perfect example of the type labelled 'Aryan Nordic' by the Nazis during the years to come. He had bright blue eyes and light blond hair and one of my female relatives compared him to the famous photograph of Lord Alfred Douglas of Oscar Wilde fame. His manners were as perfect as rigid upbringing could make them." At six-foot-one, young Wernher looked the part of the aristocrat. Apparently, he also acted the part. When he was a member of the board of directors of the VfR, he was known as Count von Braun. He had lived all his life among the rich and powerful, and it is likely that he viewed figures of wealth, power, and authority with no special solicitude. After all, he was an aristocrat; he was one of them.

Like Tsiolkovsky, Goddard, and Oberth before him, von Braun had been inspired by Verne's *From the Earth to the Moon*; however, he selectively accepted the book as an inspiration for space travel and ignored its lesson as a savage satire of weapons builders when he sought support for rocket development. According to the story he told years later, he decided "to beard the lions in their den." He scooped up what little data the *Raketenflugplatz* group had been able to gather on their rockets, and carried it with him to a meeting with Colonel Becker, chief of ballistics and ammunition for the Reichswehr. To von Braun's surprise, he received a warm welcome from the man Nebel had led him to believe was, at best, narrow minded.

"We are greatly interested in rocketry," Becker told von Braun, "but there are a number of defects in the manner in which your organization is going about development. For our purposes, there is far too much showmanship. You would do better to concentrate on scientific data than to fire toy rockets."

Von Braun replied that they would like nothing better than to generate the data, but they did not have the necessary equipment. As for the business of showmanship—von Braun was still under the influence of the P. T. Barnum of rockets, Rudolf Nebel—they needed the showmanship and publicity to raise money to pay for their rockets.

Colonel Becker did not share these values. As an Army officer and the chief of ballistics and ammunition, he was interested in developing a weapon for long-range bombardment. Becker patiently explained to von Braun that one simply did not develop a new weapon system in public view, much less make it the center of attraction in a pyrotechnic circus.

Von Braun saw the colonel's point.

Colonel Becker made von Braun an offer of financial support for rocket development. His decision was based, no doubt, on the young man's enthusiasm, intelligence, and persuasive ability. Of course, von Braun's membership in the aristocratic elite may have simplified Becker's decision. The colonel was, no doubt, aware of the young man's father's title and position as minister of agriculture; and, according to one account, the two men were friends. The only string attached to Becker's offer was, not surprisingly, that all of the work was to be done in the discreet privacy of an Army installation. At barely 20 years of age, Wernher von Braun had succeeded in doing what Nebel and the others before him had failed to do: he got the army to offer financial support to the *Raketenflugplatz* group.

Nebel wanted no part of von Braun's deal with the army. His service during World War I had soured him on any dealing with the military. Furthermore, the string the army would tie firmly to the deal, that all research would be done in total secrecy behind the walls of some military base, would strangle rocket development, those involved, and Nebel in particular. Von Braun recalled Nebel's dread of "ignorant people who would hinder the free development of our brain child." One can only wonder if Nebel's intransigence was not also firmly rooted in pride. He was the man with the military experience, the engineer with the degree, the driving force behind the *Raketenflugplatz*. He was being asked to follow a lead developed by a 20-year-old student who, although very bright, had as qualifications for leadership only his aristocratic heritage, unbounded self-confidence, and a natural aptitude for self-promotion that rivaled Nebel's. Nebel would not deal with the army; von Braun could take it or leave it.

Wernher von Braun would leave it. When the *Raketenflugplatz* group would not accept the army's offer, Colonel Becker made a second offer, an offer the young man could not refuse. Von Braun was about to graduate from the Berlin Institute of Technology, and Becker offered him a way to simultaneously pursue his interest in rockets and continue his education. He would go to work for the army under the supervision of Captain Walter Dornberger and develop a rocket motor. Formally, he would experimentally and theoretically study the combustion process in a liquid-fueled rocket motor. Becker, who held a full professorship at the University of Berlin, would arrange for the study report to be accepted as a doctoral thesis.

For von Braun and all those who would follow him accepting the army's deal was simply a matter of youthful and innocent opportunism. "We needed money for our experiments, and since the army was ready to give us help, we didn't worry overmuch about the consequences in the distant future. . . . We were interested in only one thing—the exploration of space. And our main concern was how to get the most out of the Golden Calf." With the army's money, anything was possible.

The story Wernher von Braun told to his colleagues in 1932 about his departure to join the army had some striking differences from the tale just recounted. To begin with, he led his colleagues in the VfR to believe that he had been conscripted. Then late in that year, he leaked pieces of information about the army's rocket program and his experience with it. First, according to von Braun, the army had given up on the use of liquid fuels because of the difficulty in storing them. Second, the army had fired a rocket—presumably solid fueled—a distance of 30,000 yards; whether this distance was vertical or horizontal was unclear. Third, von Braun claimed that the army had ended its rocket research and given him a boring job that he disliked. Much of what he told his young colleagues was accepted as fact; but none of it, as time would eventually reveal, was true.

SUMMER–FALL 1932

The year 1932 was eventful for Walter Dornberger. He was promoted to the rank of colonel, and he was given the command of Versuchstelle Kummersdorf West. On 3 September he was married. Less than a month later, his first recruits were reporting to work at Kummersdorf. Dornberger's life was apparently filled with success and promise.

One intriguing report of an incident that happened to Dornberger, however, hovers over that year like the angel of death. According to the story, Dornberger was impatiently disassembling a solid-fueled rocket. Contrary to good safety procedures and his own regulations, he was using a steel hammer and chisel. The steel sparked and ignited the propellant. The explosion left Dornberger with hideous burns over his face and arms. He was not expected to live, but he did. He spent a year in a military hospital recovering from his wounds. To minimize disfigurement, an orderly would patiently smear the scarred areas with butter, then with tweezers remove the black powder embedded in his skin, particle by particle. The treatment was such a success that, in later years, those who were not aware of the accident would never guess that scar tissue was responsible for his unwrinkled skin.

How this episode influenced Dornberger's thinking about solid-fueled versus liquid-fueled rockets is not recorded. In view of Dornberger's other activities that year, one might wonder if his injuries were as serious as reported. Perhaps the description of the event and its aftermath, which were told decades later, were grossly exaggerated; perhaps it never happened. All that can be said about the story with certainty is that it accurately portrays rocket research in 1932 as a very dangerous business.

*   *   *   *

On 1 October, Walter Dornberger's first technical assistant, twenty-one-year-old Wernher von Braun, reported for work. He was soon followed by an enthusiastic mechanic named Heinrich Gruenow. On 1 November, a month after von Braun arrived, Dornberger hired Walter Riedel. Riedel was one of the two engineers who had been assisting rocket pioneer Max Valier when the explosion of a rocket motor took Valier's life. Riedel was von Braun's complement both in physical appearance and in temperament. Von Braun was tall, young, self-taught in rocketry, relatively inexperienced, and temperamental. Riedel was short, sedate, dignified, had practical engineering experience, and was even tempered.

The newly formed rocket team set to work to build its first rocket motor under the direction of Colonel Walter Dornberger at Kummersdorf.

21 DECEMBER 1932

Walter Dornberger stood ten yards from the open door of his new test stand at Kummersdorf. The night was clear, and the cold cut through his short fur jacket and ate through the soles of his boots. The flame of the rocket motor that was about to be fired would melt the ice.

The test stand was the first built for rocket motors in Germany, and it was state of the embryonic art. Three concrete slabs, 18 feet long and 12 feet high, formed three walls of the square enclosure; folding metal doors were the fourth. The roof was made of tar-paper-covered wood mounted on rollers so that it could be retracted when a rocket engine was tested. A 12-foot-long control and measurement room was built up against the back wall. The roof had been rolled back, and the folding doors had been opened to reveal the rocket motor on the test stand in the brilliant glare of two spotlights. The motor was mounted over a pit in the floor that would deflect the rocket's blast harmlessly out of the enclosure. The rocket motor was the first creation of Dornberger's team. It was a 20-inch-long, pear-shaped block of duraluminum intended to generate 650 pounds of thrust. A maze of pipes, cables, and control rods snaked around the motor and led back to the control room.

Walter Riedel and the mechanic Heinrich Gruenow were safely ensconced in the control room attending to fuel tanks and thrust recorders. Walter Dornberger watched from behind the slim shelter of the four-inch-diameter trunk of a fir tree. Wernher von Braun, the doctoral student, the least experienced and most expendable of the group, stood in front of the test stand holding a 12-foot-long pole with a can of gasoline attached to its end. Riedel called out that the alcohol and oxygen fuel tanks were pressurized. Von Braun lighted the gasoline in the can. A whooshing, hissing sound came from the rocket motor. Liquid alcohol and oxygen were flowing into the combustion chamber, trickling out of the motor's nozzle, and falling into the pit. Von Braun pushed the flaming gasoline at the end of his 12-foot pole under the nozzle of the rocket motor.

A thunderous blast tore through the enclosure and filled the night with a brilliant ball of fire. The flames boiled into the winter sky; then it was dark. The test stand was in ruins, the enclosure's doors had been wrenched from their hinges, and the spotlights had been shattered. Shards of metal were embedded in the trunks of the surrounding fir trees. Random flames hissed, crackled, and sputtered, burning the last of the fuel and the insulation off cables. The air was full of the black fumes of burnt rubber.

Riedel and Gruenow came sprinting out of the control room at the back of the enclosure expecting the worst. They found Dornberger and von Braun miraculously unharmed.

It did not take long to figure out what went wrong. The alcohol and liquid oxygen had been pouring out of the rocket motor for wasteful seconds before they ignited. Then the rocket fuels went off in a spectacular fraction of a second. They would have to repair the test stand and the rocket motor, and perhaps they would develop an improved ignition system.

January 1933

A small, water-cooled rocket motor was in place on the repaired test stand at Kummersdorf. To the amazement of those who knew about the earlier test, the new engine performed flawlessly. It generated 310 pounds of thrust for 60 seconds. The new motor's performance was impressive, but later tests did not live up to the promise of the first. There were more explosions at ignition, random fires, and chronic malfunctions. Failure became the disease. Trial and error were the only cures.

CHAPTER 4

The Birth of the Third Reich and the Death of Conscience

5 MARCH 1933

Representative democracy in Germany was ended by a 44 percent minority vote for Nazi representation. The election was held little more than a week after the fire that gutted the building that housed the Reichstag, Germany's parliament. The fire was blamed on the Communists, although it was later revealed that the fire had been started by the Nazis themselves. The Nazis immediately set to work to amplify their minority representation in the Reichstag. They excluded enemies and forged temporary alliances to gain control. Then Hitler asked the emasculated Reichstag for an "enabling act" that would give him and his cabinet all legislative powers for four years. The Reichstag dutifully delivered the two-thirds majority necessary to make this change legal according to the constitution. After the four years had passed, nobody bothered to mention that the enabling act had expired.

*   *   *   *

When Hitler and the Nazis came to power in Germany, the exodus began.

Albert Einstein had been the most beloved and honored physicist in a country that had nurtured some of the most brilliant physicists since Newton. He had left Berlin in 1932 to spend a semester teaching at the California Institute of Technology. When the Nazis came to power, Einstein was no longer the pride of Germany. He lost his positions as professor and director at the Kaiser Wilhelm Institute, and he was summarily expelled from the Academy of Sciences. All of his property was confiscated, and the Nazis put a price of 20,000 marks (about $5,800) on his head. Of course, it could be said that Einstein had brought his ill fortunes upon himself. He had been politically indiscreet when, in 1933, he had headed the committee that published a treatise titled *The Brown Book of Hitler Terror*. And, of course, he was a Jew.

Berthold Brecht was Berlin's outstanding and outspoken poet and playwright. He was also a Communist and a militant opponent of the Nazis. The day after the Reichstag fire, he packed his bags and left for Vienna. Soon afterward, Kurt Weill, the composer who collaborated with Brecht on "The Three Penny Opera," left with his wife Lotte Lenya for Paris.

The Bauhaus, the intellectual center for architecture and the arts, had been founded by Walter Gropius and directed by Mies van der Rohe. When pressured by the Nazis to dismiss part of its faculty and replace them with Nazis, van der Rohe chose to close the school for good. Gropius, van der Rohe, and many of the leading teachers at the Bauhaus eventually found their way to America.

Joseph Goebbels, the man who had taken the newly created post of minister of propaganda and public enlightenment, had a chilling effect on the fine arts. He bullied the Berlin State Museum to remove from its walls the works of most artists of consequence since Van Gogh, labeling their work as "degenerate art." Germany's leading painters soon left. George Grosz and Lionel Feininger became exiles in America. Max Beckmann went to Holland, and Vasily Kandinsky left for Paris.

Fritz Lang, on the other hand, received the initial favor of the Nazis. Joseph Goebbels, the Nazi arbiter of taste, was a fan of Lang's films. He understood the enormous power films had for defining a way of life and opinions.

Soon after taking office as minister of propaganda, Goebbels invited Lang to visit him at his office. Goebbels told Lang that Hitler was an admirer of his films. Many years before, Goebbels and the Fuehrer had seen *Metropolis* in a small town. Hitler had been very impressed and had said at the time that he wanted Lang to make Nazi pictures. Lang listened politely as Goebbels got to the meat of the matter: he wanted Lang to be head of the German film industry. Lang, who had encountered criticism of his films and obstruction of their production by Nazis, was wary. He asked for 24 hours to think over Goebbels's generous offer.

According to Lang's account of the event, he asked a friend to buy a train ticket for him under a fictitious name. He packed what he could and left that night for Paris. Soon afterward he learned that the possessions he left behind had been confiscated. His wife, Thea von Harbou, divorced him later that year, and then she joined the Nazi movement.

Willy Ley, the writer of popular science who had assisted Hermann Oberth as a technical advisor to Lang for his film *Frau im Mond*, went on an extended vacation from which he never returned. He eventually took up residence in the United States.

Of course, most Germans did not have the ability or opportunity to relocate. They had the responsibilities of family at home, and their futures abroad were frighteningly risky. Einstein, Gropius, Weill, Grosz, and Lang were welcomed with open arms by their foreign patrons, but lesser men would have faced uncertainty. Also, the Nazis did seem to be improving the lot of the German people and giving the country the stability it had lacked since World War I. Perhaps it would all work out for the best.

Baron Magnus von Braun, who had been minister of agriculture during the last days of the Weimar Republic, decided not to participate in the Nazi regime. He turned in his resignation, packed up his household, and shipped it back to the family farm. He invited his son Wernher to join the family in the peace and comfort of distant Silesia. He suggested that his son stay with them until Germany had had its fill of the Nazis and threw them back into the streets, but the young man had other plans.

While he may not have understood, cared about, or subscribed to the Nazi cause, Wernher von Braun was in an excellent position to exploit it and benefit from it. He had joined the Deutscher Luftsport-Verbund (German sport aviation club) in order to learn how to fly powered aircraft, and he earned his pilot's license in the summer of 1933. The club was taken over by the N. S. Fliegerkorps (national socialist aviation corps) in the summer of the following year, but von Braun remained a member until 1935. Von Braun eventually joined several other relatively innocuous Nazi-affiliated organizations: Deutsche Arbeitsfront (DAF, trade union), the NSV (national socialist welfare organization), Deutsche Jaegerschaft (hunting organization), and Reichsluffschutzbund (air raid protection organization). In the fall of 1933, he joined the SS horseback riding school of the Reitersturm I at Berlin Halensee, where he took riding lessons twice a week. His graduate education was being sponsored by the German Army, and he was a leading member of the best rocket research group in the world. Von Braun was in a truly enviable position. At the age of 21, he had climbed onto the back of the eagle of Nazi Germany, and he was positioned for an exciting flight.

The call for German nationalism was heard far beyond the borders of the Fatherland. In distant Rumania, the man who was not a German but longed to be part of the great nation did the next best thing. Hermann Oberth, in 1934, joined the Transylvanian Nazi organization. He then demonstrated

his loyalty to the Nazi cause by denouncing his former colleague Willy Ley
for having communicated with non-Germans about rockets. At the time
Oberth did not realize how much he would give to the Nazi cause and how
little he would get in return.

SOMETIME 1933

Before the German Army decided to do its own rocket development
under Colonel Walter Dornberger at Kummersdorf, it had contracted with
businesses and entrepreneurs across Germany to build liquid-fueled rockets. They had done so with Rudolf Nebel at the *Raketenflugplatz*; and,
although they did not get a satisfactory rocket, they did get Wernher von
Braun. One of the people they had contracted with was a man named
Pietsch, who had submitted a proposal which seemed practicable. The Army
advanced Pietsch substantial sums of money for materials. Then Pietsch
disappeared and left behind his co-worker to deal with the consequences.

The co-worker was 27-year-old Arthur Rudolph, the same man who, with
Walter Riedel, had been assisting rocket pioneer Max Valier when Valier
was killed by the explosion of his own liquid-fueled rocket motor. Rudolph
convinced Dornberger that he was the designer of the motor that Pietsch
had promised to build. Dornberger gave Rudolph access to the facilities at
Kummersdorf and laid out some more money for supplies. Within a few
weeks Rudolph had completed and test fired a rocket motor, fueled by
alcohol and liquid oxygen that produced 650 pounds of thrust for 60
seconds. Dornberger then invited Rudolph to join his growing team of
rocket builders. He remembered Rudolph at the time he was hired as having
reddish-blonde hair and appearing lean, almost starved.

When Arthur Rudolph came to work for the army, he took up residence
at the officers' mess where Wernher von Braun, also a bachelor, was staying.
Rudolph fondly recalled those early days. "We didn't like to get up early;
we liked to work late at night instead . . . at midnight von Braun had his best
ideas. He would expound them on a sketch pad and his ideas led to one
thing: space travel. It was at that time that he developed his flight plan to
Mars. We didn't want to build weapons; we wanted to go into space.
Building weapons was a stepping-stone. What else was there to do but join
the War Department? Elsewhere there was no money."

Two years earlier in 1931, long before such an act would become
fashionable, Arthur Rudolph had joined another organization: the Nazi
party. His reason for joining the party was that Hitler promised to fight
communism. He was aware of Hitler's racial theories and his hatred for the
Jews. Rudolph had read *Mein Kampf*; but, he explained, Hitler's ideas on

the subject of race and the Jews were "far-fetched." There is no way of knowing if Rudolph and von Braun discussed politics when they both lived at the officers' mess. Still, Rudolph was riding the crest of two waves of the future, rocketry and the Nazi movement, and he remained a member of the latter until its end.

Rudolph's employment by the army would turn out to be doubly significant. He would make major contributions to the design and construction of Germany's rockets, and he would play a pivotal role in the sorrow, misery, and deaths of tens of thousands of Nazi Germany's victims.

LATE 1933

Walter Dornberger was a realist. He knew that his group could do nothing significant if it did not get more personnel and more, much more, money. They would have to present the Army with a tangible, flaming, flying progress report. They would build a high-speed rocket that would fly a prescribed trajectory. The rocket would be the sum total of everything they had learned about rocket motors, fuel delivery systems, and the organization of parts. The Kummersdorf group set about designing their first liquid-fueled rocket, the A-1. "A" stood for Aggregate.

Dornberger's team had as their central component the 650-pound-thrust rocket motor, which was durable and approaching reliability. They immediately discarded the nose-drive configuration favored by the *Raketenflugplatz* group as a dead-end design. The exhaust from the large motor could quickly incinerate the fuel tanks being dragged behind, and the rocket would be inherently unstable at high speed. Instead, they designed the A-1 to resemble a huge artillery shell one foot in diameter and 4.6 feet long. The motor would be at the base, with the alcohol and liquid oxygen tanks stacked above it. To give the missile stability, they built an 85-pound flywheel into the nose section. This heavy chunk of steel was to rotate on ball bearings during flight and, like a gyroscope, resist forces that would swing it and the rocket off course.

After six months of building and testing, the A-1 was ready. Even before it was loaded into its vertical launching rack, the Kummersdorf group was having doubts about the design. The A-1 was nose heavy; its center of gravity was too far from the center of thrust. Even with the gyroscope in the nose, it would be unstable during flight. They began thinking about a redesigned rocket with more stable flight characteristics, the A-2.

The A-1 had completed its static tests and was as ready to fly as it ever would be, so the Kummersdorf group decided to go ahead with a test flight. They loaded it into the launching rack, fueled it, and fired the rocket motor.

A fraction of a second later the A-1 disappeared in a ball of flame and shattered metal. They still had not overcome the problem of delayed ignition of fuel and liquid oxygen, which had accumulated in the combustion chamber.

27 JULY 1934

The University of Berlin conferred on Wernher von Braun a Ph.D. degree in physics less than 21 months after he received his bachelor's degree. His thesis, which was obscurely titled "About Combustion Tests," dealt with theoretical and experimental studies of the liquid-fueled rocket motor that were conducted while he was in the employ of the army. The speed with which von Braun completed his studies and wrote his thesis appear to be a triumph of genius, although the latter would be hard to verify since his thesis, as a secret army document, was not published.

Von Braun had the resources of the German Army, the academic prestige, and the time—now that his formal education was complete—to play a major role in the development of rockets for space exploration and for war. He was only 22 years old.

2 AUGUST 1934

Obituary: President Paul von Beneckendorf und von Hindenberg

The 87-year-old anachronistic remnant of the Weimar Republic, died at nine in the morning. Three hours later, Hitler's regime announced that the offices of chancellor and president had been combined. Hitler would be officially known as Reich Chancellor and Fuehrer. He became head of state and chief of the armed forces.

In a move to consolidate his power, Hitler called upon all officers and men of the armed forces to take an oath of allegiance:

I swear by God this sacred oath, that I will render unconditional obedience to Adolf Hitler, the Fuehrer of the German Reich and people, Supreme Commander of the Armed Forces, and will be ready as a brave soldier to risk my life at any time for this oath.

The German officer corps pledged itself to obey the Fuehrer's orders regardless of the moral justification or consequences. It was a matter of personal and professional honor.

SUMMER 1934

Obituary: Raketenflugplatz

The school of amateur rocketry in Germany where many of Germany's finest young engineers had built and tested their dreams succumbed after an uncertain but exciting life. The *Raketenflugplatz* was not killed by the Gestapo as had been widely rumored. It had silently bled to death over the four-year period of its existence. Many of its buildings were unused—buildings the VfR was not allowed to even enter according to its lease—and their plumbing was in disrepair. Four years of leaky taps had resulted in the district of Reinickendorf presenting the tenants with a water bill for about 1600 marks, an enormous sum to the chronically underfinanced VfR. When the bill could not be paid, the lease was canceled.

Without a home, the VfR was all but dead. Klaus Riedel, who knew one of the directors of the Siemens Company, arranged for the VfR's files, equipment, rockets, and models to be stored in a Siemens warehouse where they were eventually forgotten and lost. The dreamers who had lived and worked at the *Raketenflugplatz* had no choice but to find new homes and jobs. Many of the best men went to work for the aircraft instrument division of Siemens and later found their way to the army's rocket development program. Rudolph Nebel, who was for many years the driving force behind the VfR and the *Raketenflugplatz*, started his own engineering business. His experience with the military as a pilot during World War I had soured him to any involvement with it. He feared that collaboration with the military would hinder rather than help rocket development. For its part, the military wanted to avoid the showmanship and publicity that Nebel would bring. Henceforth, all significant work on rockets in Germany would be done by the Army in total secrecy.

4 SEPTEMBER 1934

Triumph des Willens

The bold script lingered on the silver screen, "Triumph of the Will."
"A document of the 1934 Party Rally"

Nobody needed to be told which party.
"Produced by Order of the Fuehrer"
"Directed by Leni Riefenstahl"

The words poured onto the screen accompanied by stirring martial music.
"20 years after the outbreak of the world war"

"16 years after Germany's crucifixion"
"19 months after the beginning of the
German Renaissance . . ."

Hundreds of thousands of German men paraded through the streets and
arenas of Nuremberg. They were all in uniform, the uniform of their
subgroup of the Nazi German state. They were the young workers with
shovels at arms ready to dig a greater Germany, the old SA in their brown
and tan with arms outstretched in *Sieg Heil* salute, and the SS goose-step-
ping in prophetic black.

When night came, thousands of swastika flags flowed onto Zeppelin
Field, flaming in the glare of spotlights. They filed into the arena in orderly
rows, and it was easy not to notice that all one saw were flags, not men and
women. Yet, the Zeppelin Field was filled with 200,000 devout Nazis.

High above the dais a gigantic eagle spread its wings over a hundred feet
and held a swastika in its talons. Around the perimeter of the field at 40-foot
intervals, searchlights pointed their beams directly upward. The columns
of light reached 25,000 feet into the night sky till they blended into a distant
glow. The Zeppelin Field was the "cathedral of light" of the secular god of
National Socialism; and, once again, Adolph Hitler appeared to preach his
gospel of German nationalism.

*   *   *   *

The "Triumph of the Will" was the triumph of illusion. The annual Nazi
Party rally was, in reality, a chance for middle-level and minor party hacks
and hangers-on to get together, drink beer, and talk about the good old days.
They were an embarrassment to those in positions of power in general and
to Hitler in particular. How could the master race be represented by these
pot-bellied, indolent representatives of the lumpenproletariat? They
couldn't even be expected to march into the Zeppelin Field in orderly rows.
How could Germany win the respect of the world if it saw this pitiful
display? How could the German people respect the Nazis? Albert Speer had
the answer: "Let's have them march up in darkness."

Albert Speer was from an upper-middle-class family; he was the son and
grandson of architects. He studied his craft in Berlin; but, in the years after
World War I, commissions were few. His disillusionment with Germany's
post-war economy led him to follow a man who promised change. Speer
joined the Nazi party in January of 1931. He did minor architectural jobs
for the party, and when the Nazis assumed power, found himself doing major
jobs for Joseph Goebbels, the minister of propaganda. Hitler soon noticed

Speer and drafted him for his own projects, which included the settings and decorations for party rallies.

Once the march-up-in-darkness concept was defined and accepted, Speer's ideas for the 1934 party rally began to flow. Lighting of some kind was needed, so why not make it decorative? Why not make it architectural? The party borrowed 130 anti-aircraft searchlights from the military, most of the searchlights in Germany. When the sun set, and the swastika flags paraded into the arena of light, Albert Speer had his first great triumph.

Twelve years later, Albert Speer would return to Nuremberg. And while the event would be even more memorable, it would be anything but triumphant.

DECEMBER 1934

The A-2 had the same dimensions as its predecessor, the ill-fated A-1; it was a foot in diameter and 4.6 feet long. It used the same 650-pound-thrust motor as the A-1. The most significant change in the new model was that the gyroscopic stabilizer had been moved to the middle of the rocket's body, between the oxygen and alcohol fuel tanks.

Two identical rockets were built, nicknamed Max and Moritz after two popular, mischievous cartoon characters. They were taken to the tiny island of Borkum in the North Sea and fired a few days before Christmas. Both Max and Moritz performed admirably, reaching altitudes of about 1.5 miles. Most importantly, Dornberger, von Braun, and the Kummersdorf group had demonstrated to the army's satisfaction that they could design and build a functional liquid-fueled rocket. For their success, the army would reward them with more money for their next project, the A-3.

CHAPTER 5

Rockets for the Reich

JANUARY 1935

The Luftwaffe was one of the worst kept military secrets in Germany. Officially it did not exist. The Treaty of Versailles had forbidden Germany an air force. As minister of aviation—officially civilian aviation—Hermann Goering had spent much of his time the preceding two years putting the Luftwaffe together, arranging for the training of military pilots in the seemingly innocuous League of Air Sports, and contracting for the development of new war planes. Unlike the Army, which had a history of loyalty to Germany rather than to any political movement, the Luftwaffe was unambiguously a creation of the Nazi regime.

One of Goering's subordinates came to Kummersdorf to explore the feasibility of liquid-fueled rocket propulsion for aircraft. Luftwaffe Major Wolfram von Richthofen was the cousin of the late and legendary Red Baron of World War I. Goering himself had also been a flying ace and the last commander of the Richthofen Fighter Squadron. Major von Richthofen quickly evaluated the army's capabilities and offered a contract to the senior military service for the development of a rocket engine to power aircraft. The Kummersdorf group, always short on money to support its work, quickly accepted the offer. Neither the apolitical tradition of the army nor the ethical implications of working with the Nazi-dominated service entered into the decision.

They were to build an engine fueled by alcohol and liquid oxygen that would generate 2,200 pounds of thrust. The device would be tested first as an auxiliary power plant for a propeller-driven aircraft; it would eventually become the sole power source of a yet-to-be-designed rocket plane.

SUMMER 1935

As part of the program to develop a liquid-fueled rocket motor for the Luftwaffe, the Kummersdorf group had received the fuselage of a small aircraft, a Junkers "Junior," to be used as a test bed. They mounted the 650-pound-thrust engine below the fuselage with the fuel tanks inside the fuselage and the control levers and switches on the side wall by the pilot's seat. The wingless plane with the rocket engine was in the arena that surrounded the big test stand when the test pilot climbed behind the controls.

The 650-pound-thrust engine had been around the longest and had a record of being reliable, but one could never predict performance of a rocket motor with 100 percent certainty. The test pilot switched on the controls; and the rocket motor roared to life, throwing out a spear of flame and smoke and shaking the anchored fuselage. When the test ended, Wernher von Braun climbed out of the pilot's seat. His face was pale, but his eyes sparkled. He had piloted the first airplane powered by a liquid-fueled rocket on a flight that went nowhere.

7 MARCH 1936

In the first military action taken by the Third Reich, three battalions of German troops crossed the Rhine at dawn. They began the occupation of the Rhineland, German territory that had become by treaty a demilitarized zone at the end of World War I. The German command was prepared to withdraw their token force immediately if challenged by France. However, France, focused on its internal economic and political problems, did not respond to the German move. Nazi Germany had bluffed its way to its first bloodless military victory.

MARCH 1936

In nearly four years at Kummersdorf, Dornberger's team had made a great deal of progress. They had produced liquid-fueled rocket engines of 650-pound and 3,500-pound thrust that were intended to power the army's missiles. Under contract with the Luftwaffe, they were developing the 2,200-pound thrust motor to power an airplane. But at Kummersdorf, there were limits. Their buildings were small and cramped, the firing range was fine for artillery, but too small for rockets—at least the rockets they wanted to build. There was, also, the problem of secrecy. How could they possibly keep the rocket program a secret at this small camp just 17 miles south of Berlin? If they fired a rocket, it could be seen clearly by anybody standing at the Brandenburg Gate. Already the Berliners could probably hear the rocket engines being test fired on the ground.

The army's group at Kummersdorf needed a new rocket development facility. Walter Dornberger wanted a facility where his team could do everything from research to manufacturing to testing. He wanted plenty of space, the best equipment, and all the resources needed to take the rocket from a crude pencil sketch to a weapon ready for mass production. He and his team had drafted a plan for the new rocket development facility. It was big, remote, and expensive.

Colonel Dornberger and Wernher von Braun fired in succession their three rocket motors with 650, 2,200, and 3,500 pounds of thrust. Major General Werner von Fritsch, commander in chief of the Reichswehr was suitably impressed. How could he not be when he saw, felt, and heard the engines pouring out thunder and the flames of hell? He agreed to support rocket development provided Dornberger and his team would produce an operational weapon of war.

Von Fritsch played out his part of the drama and asked Dornberger, "How much do you want?"

Putting a price tag on his dream made Dornberger uncomfortable; but if he did not say, he would get nothing. So Walter Dornberger said millions.

*   *   *   *

Several days after General von Fritsch had visited Kummersdorf and committed funds for the expanded rocket development facility, Walter Dornberger, Wernher von Braun, and Walter Riedel began planning seriously for the future. They laid out plans for their new facility, its workshops, and test stands. But what they really needed to bring the whole project together, to give it a focus in both their own minds and that of the German Army's command, was a rocket. They would design, then build, a rocket that would be synonymous with their new facility and with themselves.

Colonel Walter Dornberger, as the officer in charge of rocket development for the army, took the lead in defining the project. Unlike von Braun and Walter Riedel, he did not have the dream. He was not interested in travel to the moon or manned exploration of space. Space, if he thought about it at all, was just an area above the earth that a projectile might touch on its way to the target. Dornberger had memories of service with the heavy artillery at the end of World War I and of the following two years in a prisoner-of-war camp in southern France.

As Dornberger planned his new project, he vividly recalled the Paris Gun, which he viewed as artillery's highest achievement. Its official name was the Kaiser Wilhelm Geschutz. It had been developed by Germany during World War I and renamed by the German troops "die Pariserin" after its intended target; in English it was known as the Paris Gun. The weapon had been used, albeit ineffectually, to hurl shells from the forest of Crepy to the city of Paris during the spring of 1918. It could fire a 210-mm shell carrying about 23 pounds of explosives—a distance of 80 miles. Offsetting these deadly specifications were the weapon's tactical disadvantages. It was an enormous and ungainly piece of equipment that required rail transport and a lot of ground support to be fired. It had the more subtle disadvantage in that state-of-the-art ballistics left it virtually ineffective against its targets. An acceptable accuracy for artillery at the time was a "dispersion" of 4 to 5 percent. In layman's terms this meant that 50 percent of shells would fall within a distance from the target of 4 to 5 percent of the firing range. Thus, for the Paris Gun with a range of 80 miles, only 50 percent of the shells would be expected to fall within 3.2 to 4 miles of the target. This performance might be acceptable if the target was as big as Paris, but it was worthless if one wanted to bombard a point of enemy strength or vulnerability.

Dornberger laid out for Wernher von Braun and Walter Riedel his concept of a bombardment rocket. It should have dimensions that would allow it to be transported over roads or, if by rail, through any railroad tunnel. It should carry a ton of explosives 160 miles, twice the distance the Paris Gun could throw a shell. The rocket should have a dispersion of 0.2 to 0.3 percent, 20 times better than conventional artillery. Even with this degree of accuracy and a ton of explosives, an effect on a target would be improbable. The area impacted, however, could be increased greatly with the use of the right warhead. Although Dornberger did not specify it, a warhead containing a ton of incendiary material or poison gas of the type used by Germany during World War I could have a devastating effect over a broad area that had a fair probability of including the target.

Von Braun and Riedel pulled out their slide rules and came up with their first preliminary description of the rocket. It would be over 45 feet long with a diameter of more than five feet and with tail fins spreading no more than 11.48 feet. It would have a takeoff weight of 12 tons and a liquid-fueled motor that produced 25 tons of thrust. They calculated that if the rocket entered airless space at an angle of 45° and reached a speed of 3,350 miles per hour, it would have a range of 172 miles. It could not have escaped

Dornberger's notice that a rocket with a range of 172 miles could reach the suburbs of Paris if launched from the edge of the Rhineland, which the German Army had re-militarized only weeks earlier.

Of course, there were many unknowns to define before this rough sketch could become a functioning ballistic missile. They would have to devise a pump that could handle liquid oxygen at –185°C and a motor that would not burn up during its prolonged firing time. The missile would have to withstand supersonic speeds, and its shape would have to be tested in a supersonic wind tunnel that did not yet exist. The accuracy Dornberger wanted would require the invention of a guidance system. All of the testing and developing of the new systems would be done with a purely experimental rocket that was smaller than the superweapon; the smaller rocket was designated the A-3. The behemoth that could approach Paris from the militarized German Rhineland was designated the A-4.

SPRING 1936

The engine the Kummersdorf group had developed for the Luftwaffe generated 2,200 pounds of thrust, sufficient to provide auxiliary power and acceleration to a fighter aircraft. Before it could be incorporated into an aircraft, however, they would have to demonstrate that it could stand up to some of the rigors a fighter would undergo. It would have to withstand the g-forces of acceleration and of flying tight curves. The earthbound test bed built to evaluate this new rocket motor was a gigantic centrifuge.

Wernher von Braun had experimented with a centrifuge as a means of generating g-forces. In the summer of 1931 he had taken a leave of absence from the *Raketenflugplatz* to continue his engineering studies at the Institute of Technology at Zurich. While there, he interested an American medical student named Constantine Generales in the physiological consequences of space flight. The two young students decided to conduct the first experiments in space medicine. They built a rudimentary centrifuge to give laboratory mice the experience of rapid acceleration and the high g-forces that accompany it. Not surprisingly, many of the mice expired during their trips. Generales autopsied their remains and discovered that high g-forces caused cerebral hemorrhage, which was the probable cause of death. The observation was confirmed by von Braun's landlady who discovered a ring of mouse blood that circled the room at the height of the centrifuge's rotor. The two young scientists reluctantly ended their experiments at the insistence of von Braun's landlady, who valued neatness more than scientific inquiry.

Von Braun's new centrifuge had a rotor 50 feet in diameter. One end of the steel frame held the rocket motor, its controls, a braking system, and a pilot's seat; the other end held the counterweight. Von Braun got into the pilot's seat and fired the rocket motor. The rotor began to spin on its pivot. Von Braun kept the thrust down, and kept the acceleration smooth and slow. Full power would have quickly sprayed his blood in a neat arc, much as had happened to the unfortunate mice five years earlier. Soon the rotor was whipping around a full circle in a little over two seconds. The lone rider on the rocket-propelled merry-go-round was traveling at a sedate 43 miles per hour, but in one never-ending, very tight turn. Centrifugal force was pulling on the rotor and the pilot with a force of 5g, five times the force of gravity; von Braun was being pressed into the seat of the centrifuge as if he weighed over 900 pounds. He cut off the rocket motor and threw on the brake.

Walter Dornberger watched von Braun emerge from his rocket ride a little dazed, but otherwise sound. Their motor had performed perfectly. They could now take the next logical step, attach the rocket motor to wings and make it fly.

APRIL 1936

The Luftwaffe was impressed with the rocket that the army team under Dornberger and von Braun had developed, and it wanted more. It wanted rocket motors to assist the takeoff of heavy bombers and to power fighter aircraft. Dornberger had a way the Luftwaffe could get what it wanted. He would propose a joint army-Luftwaffe rocket research establishment.

Dornberger and his team approached Lieutenant Colonel Wolfram von Richthofen, chief of the Development Division of the Air Ministry. They enthusiastically outlined their plans for a combined army-Luftwaffe enterprise, and they soon won over the man. All they needed now was to sell the idea to General Albert Kesselring, chief of aircraft construction.

A group of four made the presentation to Kesselring: Dornberger, von Braun, Lieutenant Colonel von Richthofen of the Luftwaffe, and General Becker, chief of army ordnance and Dornberger's superior. They came armed with maps, diagrams, and plans for the joint army-Luftwaffe rocket research center. It was a first draft, much like a master plan for the development of a city, Germany's future rocket city. Dornberger described it as an "Army Experimental Station" manned by an army and a Luftwaffe division under the unified administration of the army.

Kesselring listened, interested and smiling. He could not help but be amused by their enthusiastic presentation of their fantastic vision of the future. At last he gave his approval.

How much was the Luftwaffe willing to commit to the rocket base?

Five million reichsmarks.

After they left with the Luftwaffe's offer firmly in hand, General Becker reacted to the Luftwaffe's generous offer just as might be expected. "Just like that upstart," he exploded. "No sooner do we come up with a promising development than they try to pinch it! But they'll find that they're the junior partners in the rocket business!"

"Do you mean that you propose to spend more than five million on rocketry?" one of his subordinates asked.

"Exactly that," Becker answered. "I intend to appropriate six million on top of von Richthofen's five!"

Dornberger and von Braun were elated. It was a cornucopia of riches beyond their dreams, the wealth of Midas, the gold of the Incas, Christmas toys for the kids who never grew up. Kummersdorf's annual budget was never more than 80,000 reichsmarks (at the time a mark was worth about 25 cents).

That evening, before the excitement of the day had faded, Dornberger received a call from a senior official of the Air Ministry. He had been sent to the town of Wolgast, which owned the tract of land Dornberger and his team wanted for their rocket research center. The Air Ministry man had negotiated its purchase from the city fathers for the price of 750,000 marks. The rocket builders were about to take possession of Peenemünde.

*   *   *   *

The Oder River, which meanders northward through Germany, does not flow directly into the Baltic Sea, but into the Bay of Stettin, which is sheltered from the sea by two huge, sandy islands. Wollin is to the east and Usedom to the west. The bay empties into the sea by three passages around the islands, all oriented roughly north-south. The channel farthest to the east is the Dievenow; between the two islands is the Swine. The third passage, separating Usedom from the mainland, is the Peene. On the island of Usedom, near the point where the Peene meets the sea, is the small village called Peenemünde. Peenemünde means "mouth of the Peene." The seaward shore of Usedom runs roughly northwest by southeast, but at its northwesternmost extreme the shore curves gently to the north. The property acquired for the rocket research center was the peninsula at the northern tip of Usedom. It was approximately two and a half miles wide by seven miles long.

The seaward side of the island was a broad, sandy beach. Behind it were sandy hills covered with stiff grass, and beyond that was the forest, mostly pine with some oak. Scattered here and there were sand dunes and marshland. Wildlife abounded at Peenemünde. Red squirrels, rabbits, and big Pomeranian deer populated the land. The marshland inlets and small lakes were the home of swans, coots, crested grebes, and ducks.

Wernher von Braun's maternal grandfather had enjoyed duck hunting at Peenemünde, and he remembered its remote location and suitable terrain. The forest was ideal for hiding the structures of the top secret enterprise. The empty Baltic to the north and east was perfect as a secret and safe rocket-firing range. The northwestern tip of the island was broad and flat, suitable for an airfield. Von Braun had proposed Peenemünde as the site for the rocket research base, and soon thereafter construction began.

May 1936

The army's partnership with the Luftwaffe in developing rocket engines gave Wernher von Braun a welcome bonus. He had been a flying enthusiast since his first glider lesson in 1931; and, in 1933, he had received a license to pilot light single-engine aircraft. The army's growing involvement with the Luftwaffe gave von Braun the opportunity to fly the best aircraft Germany had to offer. He joined the Luftwaffe in early May of 1936, and took about three months of pilot training at Frankfurt an der Oder, 40 miles east of Berlin. Two years later, he spent an additional month on duty with the Luftwaffe at Stolp, about 140 miles east of Peenemünde. During his time with the Luftwaffe, von Braun flew the Stuka, the Messerschmitt 109 fighter, and multi-engine aircraft.

Years later, von Braun explained his enlistment as a way of avoiding being drafted into Hitler's infantry. This seems unlikely since he was already an employee of the army; and, even if conscripted, he probably would have been assigned to Dornberger's rocket development team. While the details of his enlistment and service with the Luftwaffe are elusive, it seems likely that von Braun was motivated by the opportunity to fly high-performance aircraft while he pursued his primary interest, building rockets for the army.

April 1937

The Heinkel He 112 was a single-seat fighter aircraft with a conventional forward-mounted internal combustion engine and propeller. The Kummersdorf group had mounted their 2,200-pound-thrust rocket motor in its tail, and installed fuselage tanks that would hold fuel for 90 seconds of rocket power. Flight Captain Erich Warsitz had just taken off from the small airport at Neuhardenberg, northeast of Berlin. He was conducting flight tests of the new auxiliary powerplant.

Walter Dornberger was watching from the ground as the aircraft crossed the sky, leaving behind it the distant rumble of the rocket motor. Then the rumble stopped, and Dornberger watched in horror as the airplane dipped into a crash dive. It pulled out of the dive just before impact; then, landing gear still retracted, it belly-flopped into the brush near the airfield.

The pilot, Warsitz, had noticed the smell of smoke just after he switched off the rocket power and assumed that his aircraft was on fire. He had brought it back to earth as fast as he could. There was no fire. The last puff of rocket flame had been sucked back into the fuselage around the attachment site of the rocket motor. Some cables had been charred, but no serious damage had been done by the flame. Warsitz escaped unharmed. The He 112, however, was badly damaged by its hard landing and needed massive repairs before it could fly again.

1 MAY 1937

Looking for motives in a man's soul is like trying to see what is at the bottom of a deep and dark river. There are secrets crawling through the bottom ooze, but they are slippery and inclined to wiggle away with the current.

Wernher von Braun explained how he was caught up in the current of the river of time. "In 1939 [*sic*], I was officially demanded to join the National Socialist Party. At this time I was already Technical Director of the Army Rocket Center at Peenemünde. . . . The technical work carried out there had, in the meantime, attracted more and more attention in higher levels. Thus, my refusal to join the party would have meant that I would have had to abandon the work of my life. Therefore, I decided to join. My membership in the party did not involve any political activity."

His action was, as he explained it, as innocuous as that of a college boy joining a fraternity or as civic minded as an American businessman joining the Kiwanis. It was simply an expedient for doing business in Germany at that time. Was his enlistment a simple matter of opportunism devoid of conviction as he would have us believe? Might it, instead, have been a matter of patriotism as Germany and the Nazi regime became synonymous?

One fact is clear. Von Braun was acquiring recognition and position in the established order of Nazi Germany.

In contrast, von Braun's mentor, Walter Dornberger, had a ready excuse that kept him from becoming a member of the Nazi party. As an army officer, he was legally prohibited under a law dating back to the Weimar Republic from being active in any political party. The only affiliation with a Nazi organization he allowed himself was membership in Deutsche Jaegerschaft, the German hunting organization; this he received automatically when he applied for a hunting license. Dornberger claimed, quite credibly, that he was more interested in Pomeranian deer than in politics.

CHAPTER 6

Rocket City: The Secret Base at Peenemünde

MAY 1937

The Luftwaffe crews had finished the first stage of construction at Peenemünde. The Army facilities would take up the greater portion of the land stretching in a ten-mile-long strip along the eastern shore of the island from its northern tip to the resort town of Zinnowitz in the south. The residential areas would be in the southern portion of the strip with the workshops, technical buildings, and test stands, which had yet to be built, to the north. The Luftwaffe established itself at the northwestern tip of the island where it built an airstrip. The combined operation would be under the administration of the army, and went by the name of Heersversuchstelle Peenemünde (Army Experimental Station Peenemünde), or HVP for short.

To the delight of those who would work there, the architecture was Luftwaffe modern, a functional, simple style. There was an abundance of one- and two-story buildings with steeply peaked roofs. Window shutters softened the slab walls, and rows of orderly dormers adorned the tile roofs. If the German Army had been in charge of construction, the staff could have expected lumbering fortresses that traced their style, like the army itself, back to the nineteenth century. The construction crews minimized the cutting and removal of trees, not for aesthetic reasons, but because the forest was a natural camouflage for structures, roads, and rail lines. Many more structures, including a rocket test stand that could handle a motor with 100,000 pounds of thrust were still being designed and built; and construction was expected to continue for many more years.

Most of the Kummersdorf staff, which had grown to over 90, moved to Peenemünde in the spring of 1937. Then, having room to expand, Dornberger and von Braun went about hiring more staff. It was an opportunity for von Braun to bring into the fold some of his old friends from the *Raketenflugplatz* and some talented new blood. Walter Riedel, who had worked with Max Valier, became head of the Technical Design Office. Arthur Rudolph ran the Development and Fabrications Laboratory. Klaus Riedel, who had been at the *Raketenflugplatz*, was in charge of the Test Laboratory. Dr. Walter Thiel, who had joined the group the previous year, was the head of rocket motor development. He and five assistants stayed at Kummersdorf to continue their work until the test stands at Peenemünde were completed.

Of the *Raketenflugplatz* group absent from Peenemünde were Rudolf Nebel and Willy Ley. Von Braun had no interest in hiring Nebel because he viewed his former co-worker as "a successful if unscrupulous salesman with little technical and no scientific background." Willy Ley was also absent from Peenemünde because of ethical principles. He despised the Nazis and had long since left Germany.

SPRING 1937

Unlike most of the German rocket enthusiasts, Hermann Oberth was a family man; he had a wife and four children to support. He had spent the seven years since his last sojourn in Berlin working as a high school mathematics teacher in Mediasch, Rumania. Although he was no longer engaged in rocket experimentation, he continued his theoretical analyses. His reputation as an authority on rockets was intact despite his failure in Berlin. Oberth had been approached by representatives of Russia, Japan, and Rumania to develop rockets; but he declined all three offers. His loyalties were to Germany and the Nazis. His heritage was in what was becoming known as "the greater German nation." Furthermore, the most serious rocket experimentation was being done by his former fellows from the VfR for the German Army. Oberth still dreamed about space travel and rockets, and he saw to it that Germany knew he was available.

Hermann Oberth got the call from the Reich Air Ministry to come to Berlin to talk about rockets. With Tsiolkovsky dead and Goddard in self-imposed isolation, he was the world's ranking expert on rockets. He would be a valuable asset for Germany—or so his ego would have had him believe. When he arrived, he met with representatives of the Luftwaffe and their partners in rocket research, the army. Major Walter Dornberger and Oberth's former assistant Wernher von Braun were part of the group that interviewed him. They quizzed Oberth about technical matters all day. Then they sent him back home to Rumania. Oberth's hopes were shattered, and his dream began to fade.

SUMMER 1937

A new Heinkel He 112 was in the air with the 2,200-pound-thrust rocket motor in its tail. When the pilot switched on the rocket power, the aircraft's speed jumped by 33 percent to a respectable 186 miles per hour. The aircraft made several rocket-assisted flights before it crashed, not because of any problem with the rocket, but because the pilot lost control.

Although the rocket-assisted fighter had flown successfully, it reached a technological dead end. The Luftwaffe wanted an aircraft propelled by rocket power alone. It created Projekt X to develop such an aircraft. To design the airframe, the Luftwaffe enlisted Alexander Lippisch, who, in 1928 at the request of Max Valier and Fritz von Opel, had built a rocket-assisted glider and who was then designing tail-less, delta-winged aircraft. The army declined to build the rocket motor because it wanted to focus on ballistic missiles. Furthermore, von Braun projected that he could not deliver a reliable engine until late 1939. The Luftwaffe would eventually opt to power its rocket plane with a small, hydrogen-peroxide-fueled motor which would, ironically, also be used by the Army to drive the turbine fuel pumps of its A-4 rocket.

DECEMBER 1937

After three years of planning, testing, and building and uncounted millions of marks, the army's rocket team under the leadership of Walter Dornberger and Wernher von Braun had produced the A-3. By the standards of the day, the rocket was a monster. It was a pillar of metal 2.3 feet in diameter that tapered to a point 21.3 feet above the base of its tail fins. Its aluminum skin was stuffed with oxygen and alcohol tanks, pipes, valves, batteries, wires, servomotors, instrumentation of all kinds, a camera, a parachute, and all the paraphernalia Dornberger's group thought a real rocket should have. When loaded with fuel, the rocket weighed 1,650 pounds, and it would be pushed into the sky by the reliable 3,300-pound-thrust motor, which the Kummersdorf group had developed. What really set the A-3 apart from all of the rockets that had preceded it was not its size, but that it had a guidance system. Gone were the guide rails that had pointed its predecessors along their haphazard paths. This rocket would stand on its tail fins atop a simple steel firing table and then rise straight and steady into the sky from the moment its motor flamed into life until its last drop of fuel was spent. At least, that was the plan.

Five miles north of the northernmost tip of Usedom Island and the rocket base at Peenemünde is a tiny sandy island called the Greifswalder Oie. This is the island from which Hermann Oberth was denied permission to fire his experimental rocket eight years earlier because of fear of damaging the island's lighthouse. While the test stands for large rockets were being built at Peenemünde, Dornberger and his team decided to build a launching site for the A-3 on the Greifswalder Oie. The construction team moved in during the spring and set about rebuilding the island. They dredged the small harbor, built a road, poured concrete for a launch site, built dugouts and sheds, and strung miles of wire everywhere. The lighthouse that the bureaucrats had been so anxious to protect from Oberth's tiny rocket made an ideal observation tower. On 4 December, the launch site and the first of several A-3s were ready.

From the very beginning, little things went wrong. The rocket had been painted with a water-soluble green dye that was intended to stain the Baltic at the point of impact. As the rocket was being loaded with liquid oxygen, moisture from the comparatively warmer sea air began to condense on its green skin and trickle down its tail fins, taking the dye with it. When the green "goo" hit bottom, it flowed over cable connectors, shorting out circuits and delaying the launch. Meanwhile, a boatload of dignitaries was out in the Baltic wallowing in heavy seas and waiting to view the launch. Its occupants were turning as green as the rocket and were getting desperate. Finally, all was in order, and it was time to launch.

The observers on the island, on the lighthouse, and in the boat at sea gave varying accounts of what happened. Dornberger and von Braun pieced together a scenario that, if not agreed upon by everybody, probably was not too far from the reality of the event. The rocket rose majestically; and, to all but the most perceptive observer, the flight had started successfully. To Walter Dornberger something was wrong; the A-3 made a quarter turn around its long axis and began to point into the wind. When the parachute popped out, everybody knew the rocket was in trouble. The parachute was dragged back into the exhaust flame and burned off instantly. The rocket began to tumble. After a half-dozen seconds, the rocket had fallen to an altitude of several hundred yards, then crashed into the sea.

Fog closed in on the Greifswalder Oie and gave Dornberger and von Braun several days to puzzle over the failure. They decided to remove the parachute since it was a possible cause of the tumbling. The fog cleared, and they rushed another A-3 onto the launch stand. It lifted off smoothly, then rotated along its long axis and tumbled into the Baltic as before. Perhaps the two failures had been caused by the wind. They launched their last A-3 into a windless sky, and it too began to tumble after reaching an altitude of no more than 2,500 to 3,000 feet. Like the others, it splashed into the Baltic.

At the post-mortem, Dornberger, von Braun, and the others decided that the designer of the guidance system would take the rap for the failure. The guidance system had been conceived by a man named Boykow, who was, as von Braun described him, the German Navy's number one expert on gyro control mechanisms. Well, what could one expect from somebody whose major experience was with the navy? Rockets were something far more sophisticated than anything the admirals had to deal with. With the finger successfully pointed away from the army's rocket team, they set to work planning their next project, a thoroughly redesigned version of the A-3 to be known as the A-5 (A-4 had already been reserved for the ultimate goal, the full-scale bombardment missile). It would have a completely redesigned control system that would work.

12 MARCH 1938

As the result of Nazi subversion from within and Hitler's bullying from without, the independent government of Austria collapsed, and the German Army marched in to fill the void. Great Britain, France, and Russia stood by quietly wringing their hands until there was nothing left for them to do. The Austrian people meekly submitted to the Anschluss, the annexation of their homeland. Hitler was ecstatic over his bloodless victory. His next order of business was the assimilation of the Austrian people into the Third Reich. It would be a German Reich, and the Jews of Austria would learn—as the Jews of Germany had earlier learned that there was no place for them in it.

SOMETIME 1938

The call for Hermann Oberth to return to Germany came not from the army but from the Luftwaffe. He was offered a position supported by the Luftwaffe at the Technische Hochschule (college of engineering) in Vienna. He would be able to do rocket research once again. The position paid well, and he would be in what was, since March, part of greater Germany. Oberth obtained a leave of absence from the high school in Rumania where he taught, and he took his dreams to Vienna.

The reality of the situation turned out to be less satisfying than Oberth had hoped. He was given one mechanic to assist him with his experiments and one miserable test pit. He was kept out of contact with his former colleagues and friends who were now working for the German Army. Oberth began to wonder if his appointment was not Germany's way of keeping him "on ice," out of the hands of any other nation. Wernher von Braun said later that he was unaware of Oberth's whereabouts at the time and thought that Oberth's obscure appointment was a matter of interservice rivalry: the Luftwaffe wanted to keep Oberth out of the hands of the army. Whatever the reality was, Oberth remained out of the mainstream of rocket development.

30 SEPTEMBER 1938

Prime Minister Neville Chamberlain faced the cheering crowd in front of 10 Downing Street from a second-story window. Chamberlain had just returned from Munich where he and French Premier Edouard Daladier had signed an agreement with Hitler and Benito Mussolini to cede the Sudetenland from Czechoslovakia to Germany. The Czechs neither participated in the negotiations nor signed the agreement.

"My good friends," Chamberlain said, ". . . there has come back from Germany to Downing Street peace with honor. I believe it is peace in our time."

9–10 NOVEMBER 1938

Krystalnacht, the night of the broken glass.

It began, surprisingly, in Paris, where a 17-year-old boy assassinated a counselor at the German Embassy. He was, he thought, avenging his family who had been arrested and sent to a concentration camp.

The Gestapo and Reinhard Heydrich, who ran the Security Service of the SS, the SD, choreographed the response of the Nazis to this misguided action. Official encouragement was provided by Minister of Propaganda Joseph Goebbels. Gangs of Nazi thugs, who had never heard of the dead man, took to the streets to punish the already beleaguered Jews of Germany, who also had never heard of the dead man. When the sun rose on Germany the following morning, the overwhelming image was of shattered glass that covered the streets, glass from the windows of shops owned by Jews.

The German government reacted to the night of terror by arresting 20,000 Jews, sending half of them to Buchenwald concentration camp, and demanding from the remainder collective fines of one billion marks. It confiscated factories and shops owned by Jews and expelled Jewish children from schools. The policy of the Nazi regime toward the Jews could no longer be in doubt to anybody within Germany or elsewhere.

EARLY 1939

The marriage of convenience between the Luftwaffe and the army ended, inevitably, in divorce. After supporting rocket research by Dornberger's group for four years and the joint Peenemünde establishment for three years, the Luftwaffe decided to go it alone. The rocket center at Peenemünde was just too expensive. Unforeseen construction costs had buried the original budget, and there was no end in sight. The Luftwaffe would keep possession of the airfield at Peenemünde West, but the big rockets and everything associated with them would, henceforth, be the property and the problem of the army. The shared facility that had been known as Heersversuchstelle Peenemünde (Army Research Center Peenemünde), or HVP, was no more; the Army's rocket base was given the uninformative new name Heeres-Anstalt Peenemünde (Army Establishment Peenemünde), or HAP.

While the army was willing to back Dornberger for the present, his program needed massive support for the long term. Dornberger needed a powerful patron.

II

WAR ASCENDING

CHAPTER 7

Casualties of the Blitzkrieg

23 MARCH 1939

The rain had stopped by the time Colonel Dornberger reached the entrance station of Kummersdorf West, but the sky was still overcast. Water droplets rolled off the ends of the pine needles, and a cold chill soaked the air. Dornberger was there in the roles of chief of army rocket development and tour guide to greet the VIPs from Berlin.

The cars soon pulled up to the gate, and their passengers got out. The ranking army officers were General Karl Becker, the chief of army ordnance, and Field Marshal Walter von Brauchitsch, army chief of staff. They were both outranked by the man wearing a light raincoat, Adolf Hitler. Dornberger had been in charge of rocket development for the army for nine years. Hitler had been in power for seven, and he had finally been talked into paying an inspection tour of the first home of German Army rocket development—Kummersdorf West—just seventeen miles south of the center of Berlin.

Despite the weather, the day was promising for Dornberger and his men. Hitler had a reputation for his interest in armaments. He could be counted on to ask for all the facts and figures about a new tank or new gun, and he could be expected to commit these details to memory. Dornberger was prepared to give Hitler a first-class technical tour of his rockets with all the details Hitler could handle.

Dornberger stepped forward to greet his visitors and to shake the Fuehrer's hand. His first impression was that Hitler was looking through him at something beyond, as if his thoughts were elsewhere. When Dornberger began to talk about rockets, he noticed that Hitler's eyes were now attentively upon him, but he was somewhat surprised that the Fuehrer had no questions. Visitors to Kummersdorf always asked questions.

Wernher von Braun joined Dornberger, Hitler, and the Fuehrer's entourage as the group went to the old test stand. It was a special day for von Braun; not only would he meet Hitler, but it was also his 27th birthday. When they reached the test stand, they began to stuff thick wads of cotton wool into their ears. Mounted horizontally in the test stand was a relatively small rocket motor that would generate only 650 pounds of thrust. After the group had taken shelter behind a shield, the engine was fired. It threw out a horizontal blue flame with supersonic shock waves showing as bands of varying brightness. The roar of the rocket engine thundered through the cotton wool and beat painfully against their eardrums. Hitler's expression did not change during the test firing. When the fuel was cut off and the engine died, he had no questions.

They went to a second test stand to observe the firing of a motor that would produce 2,200 pounds of thrust. It was mounted vertically and 30 feet away from the protective wall they stood behind. The rocket was fired: longer flame, louder roar. When the demonstration was over, Hitler walked beside Dornberger to the next exhibit. He stared ahead. He still had no questions, nothing to say.

At the assembly tower, Dornberger's men had put on display a cutaway model of their most sophisticated creation to date, the A-3. Related parts were painted the same color so that even an unsophisticated observer could understand how systems within the rocket worked. Von Braun explained the machine, pointing to pipes, valves, and tanks, describing the components, explaining the systems. When von Braun had finished, Hitler examined the rocket from all angles. Then he turned away, saying nothing, shaking his head.

In the final demonstration, Hitler saw an A-5 which had been stripped of its skin and fins. The purpose was to expose and demonstrate the control mechanism.

Dornberger was getting nervous. Visitors would usually have one of two reactions when they viewed at close range a rocket engine being fired: they were either terrified or thrilled. Hitler seemed unimpressed. Dornberger had to do something to retrieve the day or he would never get the support he needed. Dornberger explained to Hitler that the rockets he had just seen, the A-3 and the A-5, were research vehicles only. They were not intended to be weapons, but the Army had plans for another rocket that would be. Dornberger described the A-4 to Hitler and his intimates. Hitler appeared to be interested in the big rocket, but again he said nothing.

At lunch in the mess, Hitler, a vegetarian, ate a plate of mixed vegetables and washed it down with a glass of mineral water.

How long would it take to develop the A-4? And what will its range be? Hitler asked.

Dornberger told him he could expect a very long development time if support were continued at the peacetime level.

And, Hitler wanted to know, could it be built with steel sheeting instead of aluminum?

Dornberger did not reject the idea outright, but pointed out that doing so would lengthen the development period.

Hitler looked past Dornberger and smiled absently. Then he gave Dornberger his compliment for the day, his ration of encouragement. *"Es war doch gewaltig!"* (Well, it was grand!) In English, Hitler might have said without enthusiasm, that was swell!

Before he left, Hitler mentioned that back in Munich, in the early days of the Nazi movement, he had known the rocket pioneer Max Valier. Valier had explained the possible uses of rocket propulsion to Hitler. Hitler told Dornberger that Valier, who had been killed when a rocket motor of his design exploded, was a dreamer.

When Hitler left, Dornberger was puzzled and confused. Had his men put on an inadequate demonstration? How could a roaring rocket motor be inadequate? Did Hitler understand what he had seen and been told? Possibly. But Dornberger never understood how a man who took the delight Hitler took in the facts and figures of armaments could miss the significance of rocketry.

In later years, Dornberger and von Braun would speak of the event as a prime example of Hitler's lack of vision—at least as far as rockets were concerned. The mundane truth was, however, that they never showed Hitler a rocket that actually flew. The Third Reich had poured millions of marks into rocket development and had not seen a rocket launched successfully since the primitive A-2 twins Max and Moritz climbed to an altitude of a little over a mile in December of 1934, over four years earlier. Hitler's apparent lack of vision may have been realistic scepticism.

1 SEPTEMBER 1939

In an address from the Reichstag, Hitler announced to the German people the pivotal events of that morning: "This night for the first time Polish regular soldiers fired on our own territory. Since 5:45 A.M. we have been returning the fire, and from now on bombs will be met with bombs."

The attacks on German positions were, of course, faked by the SS; and this was no simple border skirmish. German columns had already penetrated deep into Poland with the capture of Warsaw as their goal. England and France could no longer ignore Germany's aggression. They and the other countries of Europe began to cascade, one by one, into the abyss of war.

*   *   *   *

Albert Speer had carved out his place as the most successful architect in Germany. He had completed many projects for the party and for Hitler. His most recent triumph was the new Chancellery Building, which had been completed in just one year. He had on his drawing boards grand plans for the buildings of the Reich that would last a thousand years. Speer had been honored by Hitler with the post of Generalbauinspektor (inspector general of construction).

Hitler wanted Speer to concentrate on his plans for rebuilding the cities of Germany, especially Berlin, and had forbidden his chief architect to undertake any projects for the army. But with war a reality, Speer offered his assistance to General Friedrich Fromm. Fromm accepted Speer's offer, and asked him to take over a project the Luftwaffe had abandoned earlier that year, the construction of the army's rocket testing and development center at Peenemünde.

OCTOBER 1939

Seven years after they began research on liquid-fueled rockets, five years after the seductively successful tests of the A-2s, two years after the embarrassing failure of the A-3s, the time of dreams and promises, endless spending, excuses and bluffs was over. The A-5 had been built and was ready to be fired. If it was a dud like its predecessor, the army would most likely shut down Peenemünde. They would all find themselves slogging through the mud on the Godforsaken front, with the artillery if they were lucky, with the infantry if they were not.

The previous autumn they had fired four early models of the A-5 which had reached an altitude of about five miles. That these flights appeared to be successful was as much luck as intention. The early model A-5 lacked the key feature that would make or break it, the one thing that would make the long-range rocket useful as a weapon by taking it unerringly to its target: a guidance system. Once again Dornberger's men hauled their new rockets to that overbuilt sand dune in the Baltic five miles north of Peenemünde, the Greifswalder Oie. The A-5 was the same length as its ill-fated predecessor, the A-3, 21.3 feet, but its diameter of 2.6 feet was four inches greater. It used the same reliable 3,300-pound-thrust motor as the A-3; but, after the modifications, it weighed in at nearly 2,000 pounds.

They had waited weeks for clear weather but could wait no longer. The A-5, painted bright red and yellow to stand out against the sky, was positioned on its firing stand, then fueled. It was programmed to fly a straight vertical course. The rocket thundered up from its launching platform, rising steadily, arrow straight, without a hint of rotation or the first nudge of a tumble, then it disappeared into the cloud cover 3,000 feet above. The observers on the ground could hear the rocket rumbling high above them until its fuel was spent 45 seconds after leaving the ground and five miles above. They watched the leaden underside of the clouds and waited. The rocket should be coasting to the peak of its flight by now. Von Braun gave the signal by radio control to release the braking parachute, then two seconds later he sent the signal to deploy the big supporting parachute. They waited. The A-5 should be falling back through the clouds into sight by now. And there it was, suspended under its broad canopy, gliding magnificently down till it gently touched the sea, a mere 200 yards from shore.

A launch left the island to retrieve the brightly painted rocket from where it bobbed in the Baltic. A little more than half an hour after liftoff, the A-5 was out of the water. It was in near-perfect condition. They could have refueled it and relaunched it immediately if it had not been soaked with sea water.

The following day the army team launched a second A-5 on a vertical flight path. It performed exactly as the first rocket had and landed in the sea only a few hundred yards from the point where the first rocket had landed.

The true test of the guidance system was to fly the rocket along a curved trajectory, like an artillery shell. The third A-5 flew vertically for four seconds; then, according to plan, it slowly tilted over to the east. After its fuel was spent, the rocket coasted to a maximum altitude of two and a half miles at a distance of four miles from the launching site. The parachute deployed and lowered the A-5 to the dark waters of the Baltic. The rocket was retrieved intact.

All three flights of the A-5 had been brilliantly successful. A little over a month after Germany began World War II, Dornberger and von Braun presented the Fatherland with its first successful guided missile. Now Hitler could not refuse them anything they wanted. It seemed as if once again anything was possible.

FEBRUARY 1940

Adolf Hitler had spent most of World War I as an infantry corporal in the trenches. This experience had given him what many army officers described as his "trench perspective." He understood the armaments of the earlier war: rifles and howitzers and tanks. He did not understand and had little insight into the value of potential military innovations such as radar, jet fighters, the atomic bomb, and rockets.

The war was going in Germany's favor. Poland had been crushed. Denmark and Norway were soon to fall. France and England had shown themselves to be impotent. Nevertheless, before they could be counted out, they would have to be dealt with; and that would require armaments, not innovations.

Hitler ordered the termination of all development projects that would not reach the production stage within a year. Projekt X, the Air Ministry's rocket plane, was grounded. Army rocket development under Dornberger and von Braun at Peenemünde was struck from the priority list. Rocket research in Germany was, like Poland, Denmark, and Norway, a victim of the blitzkrieg.

Hitler's decree was not going to stop the rocket builders. The Luftwaffe and its aircraft designer, Alexander Lippisch, improvised. Lippisch began to adapt one of his airframes originally intended for propeller drive to accept the rocket motor. He planned to dazzle the powers of the Air Ministry by demonstrating the feasibility of a rocket plane well within the year of Hitler's attention span.

Colonel Walter Dornberger, head of the army rocket development team, was not as lucky. He did not have the hardware needed for a flashy demonstration of feasibility, and he needed the enormous manufacturing and testing facilities at Peenemünde to continue development. The Army's financial support was ended and skilled workers were called up for active military duty. Dornberger went on "begging missions" to Berlin, pleading for continued support through official channels. With the aid of Field Marshal Walter von Brauchitch, he found a way to staunch the hemorrhage of skilled workers from Peenemünde. While he could not countermand the Fuehrer's order, von Brauchitch ordered 4,000 skilled workers in uniform to Peenemünde, where they were classified as being on front line duty. Since von Brauchitch was army commander in chief, only the commander in chief of the armed forces, Hitler himself, or his chief of staff of the armed forces, Field Marshal Wilhelm Keitel, could countermand his order. If his superiors knew about von Brauchitch's subterfuge, they benignly allowed it to continue. This bureaucratic sleight of hand assured that the army's rocket program was not only top secret, but also invisible to the state.

SOMETIME 1940

After two years of fruitless research in Vienna, Hermann Oberth took on another assignment at the Technical College in Dresden. There he was assigned the job of developing a fuel pump system suitable for a large rocket. After beginning the project, he learned that the problem had already been solved by the group at Peenemünde for their A-4. Oberth had had his fill of being given pointless jobs and of being wasted. He informed his superior, Dr. Georg Beck, that he was going back home to Rumania.

"You are still a Rumanian citizen," Beck told him, "and you have seen too much of German Military matters to be permitted to leave. Once in a foreign country we could not prevent you from talking. The only thing for you to do is to acquire German citizenship; then you'll get a job commensurate with your abilities. If you continue the way you have and refuse to become a German citizen you'll have to expect concentration camp."

Oberth applied for German citizenship. Since his stay in Germany had become permanent, his wife and four children left Rumania to join him in Dresden.

1 MAY 1940

The SS was the muscle behind the mind of the Nazi party. It was at first the elite guard of Hitler and then the guardian of Nazi Germany. The SS had flexed its muscle publicly and regularly against dissenters, rivals, and Jews. It had done so since it eclipsed the influence of the SA, the brown-shirted Storm Troopers, in 1934. It was populated by zealots, true believers in the Nazi cause. The Army was for conscripts. The SS was for volunteers and for the honored leaders of the Third Reich.

"In spring, 1940," said Wernher von Braun, "one SS-Standartenfuehrer (SS Colonel) Mueller from Greifswald, a bigger town in the vicinity of Peenemünde, looked me up in my office at Peenemünde and told me, that Reichsfuehrer SS Himmler had sent him with the order to join the SS. I told him that I was so busy with my rocket work that I had no time to spare for any political activity. He then told me, that my being in the SS would cost me no time at all. I would be awarded the rank of a 'Untersturmfuehrer' (lieutenant) and it was a very definite desire of Himmler that I attend his invitation and join.

"I asked Mueller to give me some time for reflection. He agreed.

"Realizing that the matter was of highly political significance for the relation between the SS and the Army, I called immediately on my military superior for many years in the Kriegsministerium (War Department), Major General Dr. Dornberger. He informed me that the SS had for a long time been trying to get their 'fingers in the pie' of the rocket work. I asked him what to do. He replied on the spot that if I wanted to continue our mutual work, I had no alternative but to join. He added that he hoped that our old cordial relation of confidence would avoid any future difficulties that could arise.

"After having received two letters of exhortation from Mueller, I finally wrote him my consent. Two weeks later, I received a letter reading that Reichsfuehrer SS Himmler had approved my request for joining the SS and had appointed me Untersturmfuehrer (lieutenant) in the staff of Obergruppenfuehrer Mazow, Stettin (Whom I did not even know).

"From then on I received a written promotion every year. At the war's end I had the rank of 'Sturmbannfuehrer' (Major). But nobody ever requested me to report to anyone or to do anything within the SS."

Von Braun's acceptance of his SS commission may have been less passive than he claimed. While he generally favored civilian attire, he was seen wearing his SS officer's uniform—not the uniform of his employer, the army, or the uniform of the Luftwaffe in which he had served—on occasions when high-ranking Nazi officials visited Peenemünde.

Heinrich Himmler had maneuvered to infiltrate his control into all aspects of German life by conferring honorary commissions in the SS on government officials and other influential men. He had offered Albert Speer the particularly prestigious rank of SS Oberstgruppenfuehrer, an SS rank above general and just below Himmler's own rank of Reichsfuehrer. Speer politely declined the offer, noting that he had already declined similar offers from the army and SA. Of course, Speer, unlike von Braun, could rely on his direct relationship and allegiance to Hitler to protect him from any unpleasant consequences of his refusal.

As significant as von Braun's recruitment by the SS is the fact that he and the army's rocket development activities had drawn the attention of Heinrich Himmler—if von Braun's account is to be believed. Not long after Hitler had given his order to terminate long-term weapons projects, including the army's rockets, and long before the A-4 would fly, Himmler had taken his first step to infiltrate the rocket program. He would watch it closely.

APRIL–DECEMBER 1940

With Poland conquered and divided with Russia, the Nazi juggernaut turned its attention back to the west. In April 1940, Germany moved on Norway and defenseless Denmark. German forces invaded Belgium and the Netherlands on 10 May, which was—not entirely coincidentally—the day that Winston Churchill replaced Neville Chamberlain as prime minister of Britain. By the end of the month, British troops were making their desperate departure from Dunkirk. On 22 June, France surrendered.

To secure its domination of Europe, Germany required the defeat of Britain. By August, the Luftwaffe, under the command of Reichs marshal Hermann Goering, took on the job of softening up England from the air. German bombing took a murderous toll on many English cities—especially London—where large areas were turned to rubble; but British resolve and German strategic blunders tilted the balance in England's favor. The Battle of Britain did not end with a single climactic encounter but faded away with the lethal attrition of the Luftwaffe by RAF fighters.

With the defeat of the Luftwaffe, London would be relatively safe from air attacks until Hitler deployed his "wonder weapons."

SOMETIME 1941

With his German citizenship papers in hand, Hermann Oberth finally arrived at the Mecca of German rocketry, Peenemünde. What he saw there at first astonished, then disappointed, him. He was amazed to see the German Army's enormous complex devoted solely to the development of rockets and to see the giant A-4 missile, which was being prepared for its first test firing. After the initial thrill of stepping into this technological wonderland wore off, however, he began to question what he saw. The design of the A-4 was not very different in concept from the Model B, which he had described in his book *Die Rakete zu den Planetenraumen*, published 18 years earlier. He began to propose improvements in the design, but he was too late. Changes—even for improvements—would cause delays, and any delay was unacceptable. The field he had founded had passed him by —like a rocket. He may have been the father of German rocketry, but his sons were not going to turn the rocket around to let him climb aboard.

SUMMER AND FALL 1941

At 3:30 A.M. on 22 June 1941, 127 years to the day after Napoleon's army crossed onto Russian soil, Hitler's forces did the same. Operation Bar-

barossa, as it was called by the German High Command, advanced along a 2,000-mile front that extended from the Black Sea in the south to the Arctic Ocean in the north. The Blitzkrieg was projected to bring the Soviet Union to its knees within four months.

The German advance quickly gobbled up 500,000 square miles of land and 40 percent of the Soviet Union's population. By October, the invaders had reached within 30 miles of Moscow but were beaten back by fierce Soviet counterattacks. Then Hitler and the German forces learned what Napoleon had learned painfully 127 years earlier: the enemy was not only Russia, but also the Russian winter.

CHAPTER 8

The Architects of Destruction: The Men Who Built Armaments and Auschwitz

7 FEBRUARY 1942

Albert Speer exuded confidence, resolution, and authority. His appearance made him a presence. He was an athletically built six-foot-three, with a large handsome head. He had strong, aristocratic features, and his dark hair and receding hairline gave him the appearance of maturity. He was one of the few truly handsome men among the gnomes who ran the Third Reich. His critics have described him as aloof, proud, stubborn, vain, and opportunistic. In the years following the war, he put forward the image of being intelligent, introspective, compassionate, and repentant. There is probably a lot of truth in both views.

Speer had found his first real successes as an architect working for the Nazi party in the early years after it took power. He gained his first international recognition for the design of the 1934 Nazi Party Rally in Nuremberg. Hitler, who had once aspired to be an artist and architect, found Speer a willing collaborator in drawing up his monumental plans for the rebuilding of Berlin. To Speer's chagrin, however, the outbreak of World War II and its demands on resources postponed and then ended these ambitious projects. But fate and Adolf Hitler had other projects for him. At the age of 36, Albert Speer became one of the most powerful officials of the Third Reich.

As Speer was returning from occupied Russia, where he had been on an inspection tour of the repair of railroad construction that he was supervising, he stopped in at Rastenburg, the location of Hitler's East Prussian headquarters, in hopes of seeing the Fuehrer. It was his first visit to the Rastenburg headquarters, which Hitler had named pretentiously "Wolfsschanze" (Wolf's Lair).

When Speer arrived, he had dinner in the dining barracks where Hitler and his generals normally ate; then he met briefly with Dr. Fritz Todt, the incumbent minister of armaments and munitions. Todt had been entrusted with overseeing the major technical tasks of the Reich which included production of armaments and munitions, all road and other major construction in Germany and the occupied territories, and supervision of the operations of power plants and all navigable waterways. Not surprisingly, Todt appeared tired and depressed, having just emerged from a lengthy discussion with Hitler. He was to return to Berlin the following morning and offered Speer an empty seat in his private airplane. Speer accepted, and moments later he was summoned to report to Hitler. Hitler was, like Todt, tired, but he was also in a bad mood. Nevertheless, he kept Speer occupied until three in the morning. By then Speer only wanted a good night's sleep, and sent word to Todt that he would not be joining him on the flight back to Berlin.

The following morning, 8 February, Speer was awakened from a sound sleep by a telephone call informing him that Todt's plane had crashed and that Todt had been killed. At about one in the afternoon, Speer was summoned as Hitler's first caller of the day. Hitler and Speer exchanged appropriate condolences about the loss of Todt to the Reich.

Then, without further formalities, Hitler said, "Herr Speer, I appoint you the successor to Minister Todt in all his capacities."

Speer, who had expected to be given responsibility for construction in the Reich, said he would try his best to replace Todt in his construction duties. Hitler answered that he wanted Speer to replace Todt in all of his capacities, including minister of armaments. Speer started to protest that he knew nothing about armaments, but Hitler did not let him finish. He told Speer to contact the ministry and take over immediately.

Before Speer could leave, Hitler's chief adjutant announced the arrival of Reich Marshal Hermann Goering. Hitler appeared annoyed, but he asked that Goering be shown in and that Speer remain. The corpulent Reich Marshal entered, and after the requisite formalities got to the point. He offered to assume Todt's duties. Hitler seemed pleased to tell Goering that Speer had agreed to take over all of Todt's responsibilities to the Reich immediately.

By his expeditious appointment of Speer, Hitler had cut Goering's power grab off at the wrists. It was Hitler's policy to keep power diffuse and his ministers subordinate to him by fostering competition among them.

An inquiry into the accident that claimed Todt's life revealed that the plane had been returning to the airport shortly after takeoff when it exploded at low altitude, short of the runway. The formal report written by a commission headed by a Luftwaffe lieutenant general concluded that the accident was not the result of sabotage. Nevertheless, Speer was never completely convinced that Todt's death was accidental or that Goering's offer to take over the dead man's responsibilities was unrelated and based only on spontaneous opportunism.

Speer did not have much time to ponder the circumstances and implications of Todt's death. He assumed Todt's responsibilities and was soon involved in the operation of the war machinery, a job for which he was largely unprepared. He was a fast learner and an able administrator. He soon had control of over 80 percent of German industrial production, including all of Germany's armaments and its rockets.

13 JUNE 1942

Albert Speer dressed the part of minister of armaments and war production. He wore a military uniform, double-breasted topcoat with brass buttons, and a high-peaked officer's cap encrusted with gold. At six-foot-three he towered over his entourage, and there was no doubt that he was the most important official present. He was accompanied by General Fromm, Admiral Witzell, and Field Marshal Milch, the armaments chiefs of the army, navy, and Luftwaffe, respectively. He had come with them to Peenemünde to learn about rockets.

The visiting VIPs mingled with resident officers and civilian engineers on the Air Ministry's sod airstrip at Peenemünde West. A tall, young man wearing a dark leather raincoat and white hat had come over from the army's facility on the eastern side of the island. Wernher von Braun was interested in all rocket testing, and the Air Ministry's projects were almost as interesting as his own. They exchanged greetings all around, and then it was show time at Peenemünde.

The task of the Luftwaffe's Projekt X team was simple: if it wanted increased or even continued funding from the government, it would have to dazzle Speer. The Luftwaffe was prepared to show off the result of years of effort, the prototype of what it hoped would become a combat interceptor, the Messerschmitt Me 163A.

Three identical rocket planes were parked on the flight line. They were tiny aircraft with sweptback wings; they lacked conventional tails but had vertical stabilizers with rudders. Three pilots squirmed into the cramped cockpits of identical aircraft and bolted down the canopies. In rapid succession the rocket engines cracked to life; and the three rocket planes began to scream down the sod, trailing behind three billowing plumes of exhaust. Within seconds, they roared across the airstrip; then they rotated in unison, lifted off, dropped their wheel undercarriages, and climbed at a dizzying rate. Still in tight formation, they disappeared into the overcast that covered the Baltic like a soggy blanket. When the aircraft returned, their fuel spent, they glided to their landings, not on wheels, but on skids mounted to their bellies that slid along the sod.

The flight of the Me 163A rocket planes was perfect. It showed the top man, Speer, that the Luftwaffe's rocket plane could be launched from the ground on demand. The aircraft could be flown in tight formation, and it would outperform all aircraft Speer or anybody else had seen before. How could the government resist pouring money into Projekt X for the development of an advanced rocket-powered interceptor?

$$* \quad * \quad * \quad *$$

It was the army's turn to dazzle Speer at its rocket center two miles across the island at Peenemünde East.

The A-4 was a creature very unlike the Me 163A. The tiny rocket plane was like a hunting falcon, a fast, graceful killer, but domesticated nonetheless. By contrast, the A-4 was a hulking monolith, as big as a whale and as hard to tame. It stood almost 47 feet tall, as tall as a four-story building; and it was five feet five inches in diameter with tail fins that spread 11 feet eight inches. When filled with alcohol and liquid oxygen, it weighed 14 tons. When its engine would fire, it would produce 25 tons of thrust, 30 times the power generated by the toy fireworks that pushed the rocket plane.

The missile was dangerous. It stood over a concrete pad in the center of an elliptical arena surrounded by an earthen wall. The technicians who controlled the missile at Test Stand VII were hunkered down in a concrete bunker astride the dirt wall. They observed the untamed leviathan through periscopes. All was still around the missile; the only movement to be seen was the lazy billowing of condensation caused by cold oxygen vapor escaping from the open vent valve at the rocket's stern. The valve closed, and even the motion at the vent stopped.

The rocket was a 14-ton bomb ready to go off in a 58-second explosion that would throw the burnt-out metal skin 50 miles into the sky and 120 miles to the east across the Baltic.

Sparks and flame shot down from the engine and against the conical blast deflector under it. Smoke churned in a symmetrical storm around the missile. The random fire drew itself into a reddish-yellow blade thrusting down, stabbing into the heart of gravity, pushing the ground away. The flame roared and hot exhaust billowed over the launching pad and around the rocket for three seconds until . . .

At 11:52 A.M. the first A-4 rocket to win out over gravity lifted, slowly at first, but then more quickly in a drunken wobble toward the sky. The missile was already on its way when the rolling thunder of its engine crossed the 1,500 yards to the VIP's observation position. Cheers rang out but went unheard; they were small human background squeaks against the supernatural roar that thundered through the testing range. The rocket had taken off. After nearly ten years of false starts, blunders, and hard work, it had actually gotten off the ground. Fourteen tons of dreams and labor were being carried into the overcast sky above the Baltic on the backs of 650,000 flaming horses.

The A-4's creator, Wernher von Braun, was beaming as the rocket rose. Albert Speer watched in thunderstruck awe as the giant missile pushed its shaky way into the sky and disappeared into the colorless clouds over Peenemünde. Then, as the technicians began to explain step by step the progress the rocket was making in its flight downrange, something changed. The fading roar of the rocket engine turned into an approaching, swelling howl. The rocket was falling. Somewhere above the cloud cover something had gone wrong, and the rocket's planned flight changed direction. Everyone froze, their eyes on the clouds, waiting, watching for the out-of-control monster to come tumbling down into sight, back into the air over Peenemünde. The wait was shorter than it seemed. The missile tumbled into view, its tail fins torn away. The errant monster crashed into the sea and exploded barely a mile from the visiting dignitaries.

What went wrong during the first test flight of the A-4 was a matter for conjecture. Possibly the guidance system had malfunctioned, possibly the fuel delivery system had failed, possibly both. The evidence had been smashed and scattered over the water when the missile exploded, and the pieces had been lost forever beneath the waves of the blue-gray Baltic.

Ten days later, Reichsminister Speer gave Hitler a discouraging report on the A-4 launch, and in reply Hitler stated that he had the "gravest doubts" that the missile could be guided to a target. They would both change their minds as the performance of the A-4s improved and the pressure of the Allies on the flanks of Germany increased.

When he wrote his memoirs 28 years later, Speer vividly recalled the unsuccessful launch of the A-4, but he did not mention the brilliantly successful flight of the Me 163A rocket planes. Somehow the uncontrolled power of the errant missile overwhelmed his memory of the three rocket pilots who bravely strapped themselves to three tons of fuel and let it blast them into the sky. Speer was more impressed by power than by courage.

17–18 JULY 1942

It has become a cliché. His biographers and historians have routinely said that Reichsfuehrer of the SS Heinrich Himmler gave the impression of being a schoolmaster. Certainly he looked like a schoolmaster. He was a slender man of average height who looked unremarkable in his black uniform with silver trim. He had a weak jaw, a small, closely trimmed mustache tucked under his straight nose, and gray-blue eyes that squinted through no-nonsense spectacles. He appeared to be a quiet, unemotional man with exquisitely courteous manners; but underlying this cool exterior was an implicit hint of swift and terrible retribution for misbehavior.

Himmler was in the conquered eastern territories on an inspection tour. His entourage included Fritz Bracht, the *Gauleiter* of Silesia, SS Obergruppenfuehrer (general) Ernst Schmauser, and SS Brigadefuehrer (major general) Dr. Hans Kammler. Upon their arrival at Auschwitz, Himmler with his entourage went to the SS officers' mess for an introduction by the commandant of the camp, Rudolf Hoess. Hoess went through his recitation like a conscientious schoolboy.

Hoess pointed at a map. This is the overall layout of the camp. Here are the agricultural areas, the stock-breeding areas, the tree nurseries. Here are the factories, over here the living quarters, the kitchens, the hospital. Yes, it is a big camp with many enterprises critical to the Reich.

When Hoess finished, the group moved to the architect's office where one of Himmler's group, Major General Dr. Hans Kammler, took the floor. Kammler was chief of the construction division, Amstgruppe C, of the SS Economic-Administrative Main Office. He held a doctorate degree in engineering, and he was a brilliantly resourceful architect.

Hans Kammler was a man on the fast track to the top of the SS, and he looked the part. A photo of him in his Nazi party record showed that he had clean-cut features and a narrow, hooked beak of a nose. His full head of dark hair was brushed almost straight back; and, at the age of 41, it showed an occasional thread of gray. His most striking feature was his eyes. They were purposeful, focused, and intense, only hinting at the Machiavellian mind behind them.

Kammler was of average height with broad shoulders and narrow hips. Walter Dornberger later described him as having the slim figure of a cavalryman. Indeed, he was known in pre-war Berlin for his horsemanship, and during the war he was fond of wearing a SS uniform with jodhpurs and knee-high boots. His overall appearance exuded confidence and authority. In background, position, and ambition, Hans Kammler was the SS counterpart to Albert Speer. Because of their positions, the lives of the two men would inevitably intersect, much to the displeasure of Speer.

The camp had a problem of insufficient facilities, and Kammler had developed an ingenious solution. In his presentation to Himmler and Camp Commandant Hoess, he said the new installations would be larger than the makeshift units now in use. They were designed to have an efficient traffic flow by having operational areas in adjacent locations.

Kammler produced blueprints and scale models to explain the construction. This anteroom is where the inmates will undress. They will then walk into the adjacent room. Signs above the doorways will indicate that they lead to showers—in order to prevent panic. Some of the interior support columns will be perforated. Guards on the roof will drop pellets of Zyklon B into these columns, then place caps over their tops to prevent leakage of the cyanide gas.

Himmler was attentive, occasionally asking about technical details.

In 20 to 25 minutes, when the gas has finished its job, exhaust fans will vent the chamber. *Sonderkommandos* (prisoners), will then hose down the bodies and scavenge for hidden jewelry and gold teeth. Then they will load the bodies onto trolleys and carry them to the crematoriums.

Of course, Herr Reichsfuehrer, Kammler concluded, all of this is being done in the face of great difficulties. Supplies are totally inadequate, and all of the construction is being done by unreliable prisoner labor. These difficulties may even prevent the realization of these plans.

Himmler did not immediately answer Kammler's complaints; but, as Camp Commandant Hoess noted later, Himmler always found it more pleasant and interesting to hear positive reports rather than negative ones.

After the introductory presentations, Hoess led Himmler and his entourage on a tour of the camp. Himmler saw the agricultural areas, the factories, the Russian camp, the Gypsy camp, and the Jewish sector. Hoess made certain that Himmler saw the overcrowding, the grossly inadequate sanitary conditions, and the disease.

By now the Reichsfuehrer had had a bellyful of the complaints and excuses. "I want to hear no more about these difficulties!" he lectured Commandant Hoess. "An SS officer does not recognize difficulties; when they arise, his task is to remove them at once by his own efforts! *How* this is to be done is *your* worry and not mine!" Not only that, Himmler warned, transport of prisoners would not be limited, as Hoess would have liked. The number of prisoners being shipped to the camp was likely to be increased.

Himmler then continued his inspection by watching the processing of a trainload of Jews that had just arrived. He observed without comment the selection of able-bodied individuals who would go to the work camp. He watched impassively as the remainder were processed through the gas chambers.

When Himmler completed his inspection tour the following day, he could not have been too dissatisfied with Hoess. He promoted Hoess to the rank of SS Obersturmbannfuehrer (lieutenant colonel) as a reward for his past services to the Reich.

Himmler also gave his schoolmaster's reprimand for complaints and excuses to Hans Kammler, the man responsible for new construction at the camp. Unlike Hoess, Kammler did not get a promotion; but he soon learned his lesson. He would see to it that in the future Himmler received satisfactory, even optimistic reports, even in the face of doom. Nothing and nobody would prevent him from completing his assignments. Kammler was an ambitious man who was not going to spend the rest of his career doing the Reichsfuehrer's dirty work in the eastern wilderness. His rightful place was in Berlin, the Reich's center of prestige and power. He would finish his job and leave Auschwitz-Birkenau to third-rate bureaucrats like Hoess.

16 AUGUST 1942

The rocket builders put their hopes and dreams onto a *Meillerwagen* and hauled it out to Test Stand VII. They jacked it upright over the blast shield, and prepared it for launch. They tested every system, then tested them again. With Speer and Hitler doubting that the A-4 could ever become a truly guided missile, their credibility and dream were in jeopardy. They would have to launch the missile successfully.

The rocket engine roared to life, and the A-4 lifted from the test stand. It began to climb, rock stable—unlike the missile launched on 13 June in front of Speer and his entourage of VIPs from Berlin. As it rose, the hopes of the rocket builders rose with it. This could be it, the culmination of a ten-year dream. Then, four seconds into the flight, the internal electrical system failed. The ground-controlled guidance system was dead, and the missile continued into the sky on a ragged dead-reckoning flight, leaving behind it a jagged trail of exhaust condensation. Some 20 seconds later the A-4 did what no other self-propelled object—including the Me 163 rocket plane— had ever done before: it slammed through the sound barrier and kept increasing its speed. Forty-five seconds into the flight at more than twice the speed of sound and at an altitude of 35,000 feet, the rocket motor cut off prematurely, and the missile exploded.

Many in von Braun's team were discouraged by the failure. Some questioned his ability to lead the development project. He was too young and too inexperienced to be directing a project of this scope, they said. Wernher von Braun had been involved with the army's rocket development project for ten years, longer than any of them. He had been Walter Dornberger's first recruit. He was not one to be discouraged by failure or to let criticism by his subordinates shake his self-confidence. He continued to press his demands for perfection.

Many years later, von Braun explained his attitude toward failures: "To the average citizen who hears how much depends upon the successful outcome of a particular launching, it must seem that with all this money and time—how can we still have 'failures'? What most people do not realize is that in rocket engineering there is no such thing as a complete failure, that data is [*sic*] data—and each bit of data makes the next step more certain of success."

15 SEPTEMBER 1942

The journey to hell is made by many small steps and some big ones. If one's soul is numb, it may not be obvious that the steps are big or little or are steps at all. Albert Speer took a giant step this day, breaking the laws of both God and man. He would ultimately be held accountable for his actions; but at the time, his conscience anesthetized by success and power in the Nazi regime, it seemed to him that he was simply taking care of business.

Speer had a problem. The primary purpose of his existence had become the production of the armaments needed by Germany to conduct its war. With its enemies pressing in on all fronts and the Allies routinely bombing Germany's factories, Speer faced a shortfall. There were not enough factories and workers to supply Germany's needs for armaments.

Heinrich Himmler had a problem too, as his subordinates had pointed out to him during his visit to Auschwitz two months earlier. The SS needed construction materials so that they could expand the concentration camps being built to hold Jews swept up by the "eastern migration." Among his powers as minister of armaments, Speer had control of materials of all kinds in the Third Reich. Himmler was prepared to trade the assets he controlled for those Speer controlled.

Albert Speer chaired the meeting of representatives of the Ministry of Armaments and the SS who worked out the trade. In addition to Speer, the Armaments Ministry was represented by two of its department heads, Walter Scheiber and Karl Saur, and by two men from the construction sector named Steffens and Briese. Himmler sent SS Obergruppenfuehrer (general) Oswald Pohl, chief of the SS Economic-Administrative Main Office, and Hans Kammler, the chief of the construction division under Pohl. At the time, Speer had no reason to question the loyalty of his deputy Scheiber, who was an honorary SS Brigadefuehrer (major general); and he would not know until 25 years later that Scheiber was Himmler's confidential agent in the ministry.

The conference, which was weighted in favor of the SS, quickly agreed on two points. Speer would approve the acquisition of building materials valued at 13.7 million reichsmarks for the construction of 300 barracks to house 132,000 inmates at Auschwitz. Some of the materials would be used, no doubt, in the construction of Hans Kammler's gas chambers and crematoriums, although Speer would not know about that. In return, the SS agreed to supply concentration camp inmates as slave laborers for armaments plants; 50,000 Jews would be made available in the very near future. In essence, Speer's factories would become concentration camps.

Speer soon had second thoughts about the deal. He began to question and restrict the allocation of materials requested by the SS for construction of factories at the concentration camps. But Speer had made his pact with the devil; the precedent was set. The SS would increase its involvement in armaments production through concentration camp labor. Its slaves would build weapons of long-range destruction and terror that Himmler, the prisoners, and the Allies had never imagined.

CHAPTER 9

The First Spaceship and the Fuehrer's Dream

3 OCTOBER 1942

Colonel Walter Dornberger watched the missile on the primitive television set. The body of the rocket had been painted black and white; the four fins on which the missile stood had been painted four different colors to make it easier to see and photograph against the cloudless blue sky. Barely visible on the aft of the rocket, between two of its fins, someone had painted a logo. It showed the A-4 crossing behind a crescent moon. Perched in the curve of the crescent and in front of the rocket was a pinup girl in black stockings. The rocket builders had not forgotten the dream of space travel and its symbol "Frau im Mond," the girl in the moon.

"X minus three." The voice over the loudspeaker began the countdown.

Dornberger's only companion on the roof of the Measurement House was his friend and subordinate, Colonel Leo Zassen, the military commander of the army base at Peenemünde. Zassen leaned against the brick rampart that surrounded the roof of the building, saying nothing, looking through his Zeiss binoculars toward Test Stand VII, which was hidden in the pine forest 1,500 yards to the north. Wernher von Braun and some of his senior staff were also watching Test Stand VII from the roof of the assembly workshop of the Development Works. It was almost four in the afternoon.

"X minus one."

After two unsuccessful firings of the A-4—the first of them in front of Reichsminister Speer and his entourage of armaments chiefs—the army's rocket builders were trying again. They would not be allowed too many more failures before their funds would be diverted to bomber and tank production, and they would find themselves carrying rifles at the front.

The steering gyroscopes were running now. The oxygen-venting valve had closed. The motion picture cameras were rolling. It was white knuckle time again at Peenemünde.

"Ignition!"

Dornberger watched the rocket on the television monitor. Billows of smoke poured out of the engine nozzle and were followed rapidly by a shower of sparks.

"Preliminary stage!"

The shower of sparks clumped into a flame that stretched into eight tons of incandescent thrust. The two umbilical cables linking the missile's instruments and controls to the ground fell away, and the rocket was on internal power. It crouched on the firing stand, power building for three painfully long seconds till it was pumping out 25 tons of savage power and . . .

"Rocket has lifted!"

Now everybody was watching through their binoculars as the gleaming body of the A-4 popped up through the dust cloud kicked up by its exhaust, then rose above the pine trees. The missile climbed into the cloudless sky. The roar of its engine took its time crossing the pines and hit them with all the surprise of yesterday's newspaper. The rocket rose smoothly, steadily; then, according to its flight plan, it began to gently incline itself toward the east-northeast.

"Twenty-one . . . twenty-two . . ." The voice from the loudspeaker counted the seconds since liftoff. "Speed of sound."

The rocket slipped through the sound barrier and kept going. It had tipped over to 50 degrees from the vertical and was still tracking a smooth arc, still accelerating.

"Thirty-nine . . . forty . . ."

Suddenly a thick, white cloud following the rocket appeared. There was surprise and shock on the ground. Had the missile exploded? No. The rocket's exhaust, which was mostly water vapor, was condensing into a thick, snow-white exhaust plume. The rocket kept climbing until it was just a speck at the end of the white fluff. Soon, only radar was accurately tracking the missile's distance and speed.

"Fifty-two . . . fifty-three . . . fifty-four . . ."

The A-4 was still on course and was nearing the end of its fuel supply.

"*Brennschluss!*" (End of burning!) The command had been given from the ground by radio to close the fuel valves; and, after 58 seconds of flight, the rocket engine flickered out. The missile was traveling at a speed of almost 3,500 miles per hour. The streak of white condensation against the crisp, blue sky trailed off into a thin, misty thread. The crosscurrents of winds at higher altitudes pushed the vapor trail back and forth in the sky till it resembled, as the local residents described it, frozen lightning.

"Ninety . . . ninety-one . . . ninety-two . . ."

All of them had left their roof observation posts and were in the street shaking hands and congratulating each other on their success. Dornberger hustled von Braun into a car, and they sped to Test Stand VII. There they congratulated Dr. Thiel and his crew who operated the test area. Among those at the test stand was Hermann Oberth, the middle-aged man who had started it all with his slim book describing the dream.

"That is something only the Germans could have achieved," he is reported to have said as he shook Dornberger's hand. "*I would never have been able to do it.*"

Dornberger returned the compliment, congratulating Oberth for showing the rest of them the way.

The missile, its rocket motor silent, was still following a ballistic trajectory, guided only by its inertia and the law of gravity. It coasted to an altitude of 52 miles then . . .

"Two-ninety-one . . . two-ninety-two . . . two-ninety-three . . ."

The missile was falling, re-entering the earth's atmosphere at over 3,000 miles per hour. The friction of the air on the missile slowed its speed to 2,000 miles per hour and raised the temperature of its skin to 1,250°F. Then, 296 seconds after liftoff, the Doppler radar lost contact with the missile.

The A-4's trajectory, speed, and time of flight placed its point of impact about 120 miles across the Baltic to the east of Peenemünde. The nose cone of the rocket had been filled with bags of a bright green dye to mark its point of impact in the sea. Dr. Ernst Steinhoff took off in a Messerschmitt Me 111 to reconnoiter the predicted area of impact. Less than an hour later he spotted the bright green stain on the blue-gray water of the Baltic. It was only two and a half miles from the target. After Steinhoff directed a motor launch to the spot to chart its coordinates, he returned to Peenemünde to rejoin the celebration.

That evening, Dornberger hosted a celebration for von Braun, Steinhoff, and the other senior men of his team. Availing himself of one of the privileges of rank, Dornberger redundantly told his associates of the significance of their achievement that day. "We have invaded space with our rocket," he said, "and for the first time . . . have used space as a bridge between two points on earth; we have proved rocket propulsion practicable for space travel. To land, to sea, and [to] air may now be added infinite empty space as an area of future intercontinental traffic." Then he brought them all back down to earth. "So long as the war lasts, our most urgent task can only be the rapid perfecting of the rocket as a weapon."

Dornberger went to bed that night believing that the test flight had been a total, dazzling success, and that Hitler would supply him with the men and materials to put the A-4 into mass production. He would learn to his dismay that he was wrong on both counts.

As a result of what appeared to be the successful development and flight of the A-4, von Braun added to his collection of awards from his country. He received the Kriegsverdienstkreuz I Klasse mit Schwertern (War Merit Cross, First Class, with Swords), while his teacher Hermann Oberth, the man most responsible for developing and promoting the concept of the liquid-fueled rocket in Germany was, as usual, forgotten.

MID-DECEMBER 1942

The first member of Hitler's inner circle to take an active interest in the German Army's A-4 rocket after its first successful flight was Reichsfuehrer of the SS, chief of the Gestapo, keeper of concentration camps, and quintessential political opportunist Heinrich Himmler. Himmler emerged from his airplane wearing a white silk scarf around his neck, a long, double-breasted leather coat, a peaked officer's hat, and the SS air of superiority. He had just landed at the Peenemünde West airfield. Although Himmler's visit was—according to Walter Dornberger—unexpected, the chief of the rocket program, nevertheless, met his guest when his plane landed at the Peenemünde West airfield. Dornberger was accompanied by General Fromm and the head of the Army Weapons Department, General Leeb, who felt obliged to be present.

How to deal with Himmler was a problem. Dornberger chose to present a respectful, though low-key, tour. No rockets were scheduled to be fired that day. Himmler would learn the basics of rocketry from lectures and from static firings of rocket engines. It was as if Dornberger wanted Himmler to go away unimpressed.

After the lectures and demonstrations were over, Dornberger and his colleagues brought Himmler to the Hearth Room of the officers' mess, a room frequently used to entertain visitors to Peenemünde. The room was paneled with wood, and a stylized map of the area dominated the wall over the fireplace. Festive brass chandeliers hung from the high ceiling. As they sat in plush chairs, Dornberger explained to Himmler the work his team was doing and their plans for the future. Himmler listened attentively and politely. Himmler was always polite. Then Himmler began to give a reason for his surprise visit to Peenemünde.

There had been much discussion of rocketry in Hitler's inner circle, he said. The army's rocket development team was in the limelight. Himmler wanted to learn all he could about this new weapon that would be so valuable to the Reich; and, of course, he wanted to find out how he could use his powers to support Dornberger and his group. Then Himmler got to the point of his visit. Invoking the Fuehrer's authority, he said that the rocket development program was no longer just the concern of the army, but of the German people as well. He was there to protect them from treason and sabotage.

Dornberger stiffened at the suggestions that rocket development was no longer the army's or his domain and that an army base needed to be protected by a bunch of amateur opportunists wearing uniforms. But before he could respond, Colonel General Fromm, the ranking army officer present, attempted to put Himmler back in his place. Fromm courteously reminded Himmler that Peenemünde was an army establishment and that the army was responsible for security. He did, however, suggest to Himmler that his SS could take responsibility for tightened security in the areas surrounding Peenemünde.

Himmler paused for a moment before replying, then took what he could get for the time being. He delegated the task of security to the police commissioner of Stettin, SS General Mazow, who was conveniently present.

Their meeting over, Dornberger accompanied Himmler back to his airplane. Before getting on board, Himmler told Dornberger of his great interest in the rocket development work. He promised to return.

*   *   *   *

Himmler's visit was followed up by a communication to Himmler's headquarters from Lieutenant Colonel Gerhard Stegmaier, military commander of the Pre-Production Works at Peenemünde and Walter Dornberger's subordinate. Although Dornberger, in his account of Himmler's first visit to Peenemünde, makes no mention of subsequent communication with Himmler, it seems unlikely that Stegmaier would have sent the communication without his commanding officer's knowledge or approval.

Himmler's chief of headquarters, Gottlob Berger, summarized Stegmaier's communication in a memo to Himmler dated 16 December 1942. Stegmaier had obsequiously stated that Dornberger's group at Peenemünde had been greatly impressed by Himmler's visit. Furthermore, Stegmaier proposed that the Reichsfuehrer, who had said that he might be able to help Dornberger with his work, should use his influence to organize a meeting with Hitler where Dornberger and Wernher von Braun could present for discussion the status of the A-4 rocket program. Though Himmler noted the request, he did not act upon it immediately.

In this attempt to gain an influential ally outside the army hierarchy, Stegmaier—and presumably his commanding officer, Walter Dornberger—recklessly neglected to realize that Himmler had an agenda of his own.

8 JANUARY 1943

Walter Dornberger was in Berlin again on another one of his begging trips. He had brought Wernher von Braun along to present a broader front in dealing with Albert Speer and the Ministry of Armaments. Dornberger wanted, as always, higher priority status for his A-4 project. Speer told Dornberger that he could not have higher priority until the Fuehrer was convinced that the rocket would succeed, and the Fuehrer was not convinced. What Speer offered Dornberger instead was an ally in the Ministry of Armaments. Speer had asked a man named Gerhard Degenkolb to set up an A-4 production committee.

"He has shown such drive and ruthlessness," Speer said of his appointee, "that he can manage the seemingly impossible without any high priorities, purely on the power of his name and personality." To pacify the disappointed Dornberger, Speer added, "You can trust Degenkolb. He has a reputation to lose."

Gerhard Degenkolb had made his reputation by building locomotives. He had been chairman of the Locomotives Special Committee within Speer's ministry, and had delivered on the seemingly impossible production quota of 2,000 locomotives a month. If he could produce 2,000 locomotives each month, then production of a rockets at a similar rate just might be possible.

Speer abruptly left the meeting with Dornberger and von Braun and sent in Degenkolb to meet his new partners. Gerhard Degenkolb was a middle-aged man of average height. His torso was shaped like a barrel, and perched atop it on a bull-neck was a bald, round head. His fleshy features were complemented by keen blue eyes that moved restlessly, taking in everything. His hands and body moved restlessly too, giving him the aura of a man of action. He gave the impression of a heavier, more animated Mussolini.

Dornberger began this first meeting with Degenkolb by outlining the plans and organization of the A-4 program. He asked Degenkolb for his help in getting what was needed to produce and use the A-4 operationally: materials. In response, Degenkolb set forth his plans for the A-4 Special Committee. It would be organized along the lines of the Locomotive Special Committee, which he had headed; and it would have subcommittees devoted to development, materials, subassemblies, construction projects, management, labor, and so forth. Degenkolb assured Dornberger that some of his senior subordinates would be needed to head these subcommittees.

Dornberger was not interested in another layer of bureaucracy, certainly not one that would compete with his own authority. He wanted Degenkolb's help—in lieu of a higher priority rating conferred by Hitler—in obtaining materials. He invited Degenkolb to visit Peenemünde to see the A-4 and to meet Dornberger's technical department heads. Dornberger concluded on a cordial note by saying, "I put my trust in your drive as chairman of a committee in the Ministry of Munitions, in your reputation, and in your great industrial experience."

Degenkolb then began to lecture Dornberger and von Braun on his practical experience and success in building locomotives. As Degenkolb talked, Dornberger's new collaborator's name kept running through his mind. Where had he heard the name before?

Then Dornberger remembered a chilling incident of several years earlier. Degenkolb's name had been linked—at least in Dornberger's mind—with the untimely death of the former head of the Army Weapons Department, General Karl Becker. Becker had been Dornberger's superior officer and loyal supporter from the beginning. He had given Dornberger his start at Kummersdorf, and he had arranged for Wernher von Braun's rocket research there to be accepted as a doctoral thesis at the University of Berlin. Becker's seemingly secure position turned sour, however, when Hitler set up the Ministry of Armaments on an equal basis with the Army Weapons Department, then staffed it with men from the Technical Office of the Nazi party. Control of the armaments industry by Becker's department was challenged by the new ministry, and Degenkolb had been one of the most outspoken of the new regime. He had, as Dornberger recalled, spoken contemptuously to representatives of the army and industry of industrial work initiated and directed by the army and of the organization Becker headed. General Becker succumbed to the pressures and insanities of leadership in the Third Reich, and became one of the first in the parade of high-ranking officers who found their escape by suicide. Rightly or wrongly, Walter Dornberger held Gerhard Degenkolb responsible for the death of his idol and mentor.

Wernher von Braun was more open to cooperating with Degenkolb than was Dornberger. Perhaps he saw no connection between Degenkolb and Becker's suicide. Perhaps he was less challenged by Degenkolb's forceful—some would have said abrasive—personality. Perhaps von Braun saw Degenkolb as the only man who could help him mass produce his giant rockets.

*   *   *   *

In the weeks that followed the unsatisfactory meeting with Speer's representative, Degenkolb, Dornberger gained support from his secret patron. On 23 January 1943, Heinrich Himmler followed through on Lieutenant Colonel Gerhard Stegmaier's communication of the previous month and asked Hitler to meet with Colonel Dornberger and Wernher von Braun.

On 26 January 1943, Lieutenant Colonel Stegmaier wrote a second letter to Gottlob Berger at Himmler's headquarters. In it, he specifically requested that Himmler use his influence with Hitler to give the A-4's electrical components priority over the radar program of the German electronics industry. Stegmaier's communications to Himmler's headquarters were obvious attempts to circumvent the German Army's chain of command and to effect a significant change in war policy. While Himmler did not take Stegmaier's specific request to Hitler, on 10 February, he again asked the Fuehrer to meet with Dornberger and von Braun.

29 January 1943

His subordinates at the scene reported to Dr. Hans Kammler, head of construction of the SS, on the progress at Auschwitz-Birkenau.

"By making use of all available labor, work on Crematorium II has been completed, save for a few construction details—and this in spite of every sort of difficulty, and temperatures below freezing day and night. The ovens were fired by the chief engineer of the firm that did the work—Topf & Sons of Erfurt—during his tour of inspection, and they functioned perfectly. Due to the frost it has not been possible to complete the reinforced concrete roof of the mortuary cellars, but this is of minor importance as we can use the gas cellars instead.

"Topf & Sons have not been able to deliver the ventilation plant on the date specified by the central works department. As soon as it is delivered, it will, of course, be installed, and we anticipate that everything will be in full working order by 20.2.43."

Despite the promises, Kammler's crematoriums at Auschwitz were not brought into use until the spring. Even in the Third Reich, building an extermination camp was not easy.

31 JANUARY 1943

Armageddon began at Stalingrad.

The German armies, which had stalled at the gates of Leningrad in the north and Moscow in the center, plunged deep into the south of Russia. By November of 1942 they had occupied a protrusion of land that reached as far east as Stalingrad.

The Soviet counterattack came amidst a blizzard on 19 November 1942. Neither Hitler nor the German High Command thought it a serious threat until Soviet pincers closing from the north and south had cut off some 330,000 German troops. As winter and the Russian Army tightened their grips, all attempts to break through to Stalingrad failed. On 31 January 1943, seeing the cause lost and wishing to save lives, Field Marshal Friedrich von Paulus surrendered his surviving army, which had dwindled to little more than 100,000 men. Those who survived Stalingrad were marched off to prisoner-of-war camps in Siberia. At the end of the war, only about 5,000 men lived to return to Germany.

Back home in the Fatherland, the debacle became known because of the silence. Letters that had come from the front telling of the bitter winter and the desperate siege came no longer. Albert Speer's family no longer received desperate airmail letters from his brother, who was in the artillery at Stalingrad. Hermann Oberth's son Julius disappeared. The silence was repeated in hundreds of thousands of families throughout Germany. The German Sixth Army, which had once numbered 330,000, simply vanished; it was swallowed in one bloody gulp by the Russian bear. All that was left was an emptiness that had once been sons and brothers and husbands.

MARCH 1943

Albert Speer had just returned to Berlin from Hitler's headquarters, where he had spent the days from 5 March through early 10 March. He had bad news for Colonel Walter Dornberger when they met. The Fuehrer was not going to approve the top priority rating Dornberger wanted for his rocket program.

"The Fuehrer has dreamed that no A-4 will ever reach England," Speer said.

How could Hitler rationally formulate policy based on a dream? How could Dornberger, whose own cause traced its origin to another dream, rationally argue against it? It is not known if Hitler ever had the dream or if the story was just a convenient way for Speer to give the bad news to Dornberger, but the message was clear. Hitler wanted the rocket research and its expenses to end.

CHAPTER 10

The Missile Arsenal: Demonstrations for Leaders of the Reich

29 MARCH 1943

Albert Speer had no reason to distrust Heinrich Himmler, although he found Himmler to be aloof, enigmatic, and annoying in his insistence that others, including Speer, defer to his rank as Reichsfuehrer of the SS. Speer was loyal to Hitler and to the Reich, and he would do his job.

Speer was at Hitler's Obersalzberg retreat, and his job this day was to have a rare interview with Himmler. The meeting took three hours; and, by the end of it, Speer had told Himmler in detail about the German Army's rocket development program. At the time, Speer was unaware that Himmler had already proposed to Hitler that Dornberger and von Braun brief the Fuehrer on the status of the A-4 project.

The following day, Himmler had a four-hour meeting with Hitler. Although it is not known with certainty, it is likely that Himmler again brought up the subject of the A-4.

26 APRIL 1943

Walter Dornberger directed all of the German Army's rocket research from his office in Berlin. Since 1940, he had controlled the HAP, the Army Establishment at Peenemünde, through its military commander Colonel Leo Zassen. Zassen was, all seem to agree, an able administrator who saw to it that the secret rocket development got done without interference from anybody. He was Dornberger's subordinate and friend.

It was nearly 6 o'clock in the evening when Dornberger received a curt order from the Army Weapons Department. He was to relieve Colonel Zassen of his command immediately; Zassen was to depart from Peenemünde before the day was over. Dornberger pressed for an explanation, and all he could learn was that "there seemed to be some dispute with the SS." In the days that followed, Dornberger learned that the order to dismiss Zassen was precipitated by a letter to the Personnel Office at Hitler's headquarters characterizing him as a poor security risk. Zassen was allegedly a devout Catholic, which was viewed as being incompatible with loyalty to the Third Reich. The accusatory letter was signed by Heinrich Himmler, and it was supposedly backed up by incriminating letters signed by Zassen. Dornberger asked the SS to see the evidence against Zassen, but his request was denied.

To comply with his order to remove Zassen from Peenemünde and at the same time not give in to Himmler's meddling, Dornberger assigned Zassen to Berlin where he would be in charge of the A-4 program. Dornberger himself would take over as commander of Peenemünde and would then, paradoxically, report to his own subordinate. The arrangement was convoluted enough to keep Himmler at bay for the time being.

While Dornberger won the first round, the meaning behind the accusations against Zassen was clear: Himmler was making his first overt move to take over the rocket program. Himmler would strike again at Dornberger and the Army's control of the rocket program.

26 MAY 1943

As Albert Speer explained years later, "The German Air Force was disturbed that the Army alone would be bombing London." The Luftwaffe's own attempts to turn London to rubble had been decisively stopped by the RAF during the Battle of Britain in 1940. Now, three years later, the Luftwaffe was losing the airspace over Germany. To make matters worse, its development teams at Peenemünde West watched enviously as the army's wizards on the other side of Usedom Island fired their giant rockets and, worse still, hit their targets 160 miles down range across the Baltic. Something had to be done about it. The Luftwaffe had to develop a "wonder weapon" of its own if for no other reason than to salvage its tarnished honor.

The Luftwaffe's response to the A-4 project began in early 1942, and by June of that year the basic design of its weapon had been settled. The weapon, designated as the Fieseler Fi 103, was a pilotless flying bomb. The Fieseler company designed its airframe, and the Argus firm produced its unique "pulse-jet" engine. The flying bomb would be the aerial equivalent of the naval torpedo, and, not surprisingly, looked like a torpedo with stubby wings. The fuselage of the aircraft was 25.4 feet long with 1,874 pounds of high explosives in its nose. Aft of the warhead was a 150-gallon fuel tank, and behind that was the weapon's simple guidance system. Midway along the fuselage were stubby wings with a span of 17.7 feet.

The missile was propelled by the Argus As 014 pulse-jet engine mounted above the rear of the fuselage. The engine resembled a cannon pointed to the rear. The forward end of the pulse-jet had spring-mounted horizontal flaps that alternately opened to let air into the combustion chamber and closed as fuel was ignited within the body of the engine. The explosion was vented out the rear, and the recoil, like a cannon firing in rapid succession, propelled the aircraft forward. Photographs of the Fi 103 flying in the night sky showed the exhaust from the pulse-jet as a string of fiery beads.

To get the cycle of air-intake and fuel-ignition started, the aircraft was thrown into the air from a fixed catapult at a speed of 150 miles per hour. The flying bomb then cruised along on its dead-reckoning course at nearly 400 miles per hour. When an internal timing mechanism determined that it should be over its target, it stopped the engine and moved the control surfaces to put the flying bomb into a dive. The unstated irony of the Luftwaffe's Fi 103 was that Walter Dornberger's army department had financed development of its pulse-jet engine by Dr. Paul Schmidt of Munich from 1933 until 1940 when Dornberger decided to focus his limited resources on the A-4.

Albert Speer had recommended to Hitler that a committee be formed to review the development status of the army's and Luftwaffe's new weapons. The Long-Range Bombardment Commission was made up of the ranking officers of the armed services with a sprinkling of civilian bureaucrats: Colonel General Fromm of the army, Field Marshal Milch of the Luftwaffe, Grand Admiral Doenitz, Minister of Armaments Speer, and his deputy Karl Saur, among others. The commission convened at Peenemünde on 26 May 1943 to review the Luftwaffe's Fi 103 program and the army's A-4 program and to decide which had the greater probability of success.

The day's activities began in the mess where both development teams presented the characteristics of their weapons and the status of their projects. It turned into a compare and contrast exercise, not unlike a high school final exam. Both weapons had similar explosive payloads, about a ton, and ranges, about 200 miles. The Fi 103 was a "cruising missile" that flew like an airplane to its target, while the A-4 was a "ballistic missile" that followed a trajectory like an artillery shell. The Fi 103 could be detected on radar and shot down by anti-aircraft guns or by interceptor aircraft. The A-4 dropped terror from the sky unannounced, faster than the speed of sound; there was no defense against it. The flying bomb was launched from a catapult in a fixed position that was vulnerable to enemy attack; the A-4 could be launched from easily concealed mobile platforms. The pulse-jet engine of the Fi 103 used about 150 gallons of 80 octane gasoline; the A-4 burned ethyl alcohol and liquid oxygen, both commodities of questionable availability. The cost of each A-4, according to the best guess at the time, would be several times as much as for the simpler Fi 103.

During the discussion, Walter Dornberger took the position that it would be a mistake to make a choice between the two weapons. They were complementary; the deficiencies of one were made up by the other. Furthermore, if Germany was to have a hope of turning back the Allied offensives, there could be no limit to the numbers of flying bombs and giant rockets deployed.

The bureaucrats and brass of the Long-Range Bombardment Commission considered the matter and decided. They would recommend to Hitler that both programs be supported with the highest possible priority. This outcome should not have surprised anybody. Who would have had the courage to stand up and advocate killing a project—regardless of its expense or imperfections—that might save Germany? The leaders of the Third Reich were not noted for their bravery. Then, with the hard choice avoided, they went outside to see the demonstrations.

With the members of the Long-Range Bombardment Commission watching, an A-4 lifted off its firing platform with its normal, spectacular display and vanished into the low cumulus clouds. Radar tracked the missile throughout its flight. It rose to a height of 64 miles; then, 348 seconds after liftoff, it fell into the Baltic 175 miles to the east, about three miles from its target. The demonstration was the first completely successful flight of an A-4. Five and a half hours later a second A-4 lifted off from Peenemünde East, just as spectacularly as the first. Its rocket motor shut down prematurely 40 seconds later, and it fell into the Baltic having covered a distance of 17 miles. The first rocket had been such a spectacular success that the minor failure of the second was overlooked.

The long catapult that would launch the Fi 103 into the air stood at the very northern tip of Usedom Island, at the northeast corner of the Luftwaffe's airfield. A slotted tube ran along the length of the ramp. Inside the tube was a piston with a projection that attached itself to the underside of the flying bomb. The decomposition of hydrogen peroxide behind the piston would push it and the Fi 103 along the ramp and into the air. The flying bomb would leave the end of the ramp at 150 miles per hour, at which point its pulse-jet engine would take over. That afternoon the catapult snapped two flying bombs into the air. They both drifted lazily out over the Baltic and crashed. No one, not even the Luftwaffe's Field Marshal Milch, was very disappointed. After all, it was a temperamental instrument, still being developed.

After the spectacular success of the A-4 that day and with the backing of the Long-Range Bombardment Commission, Speer finally felt that he could present Walter Dornberger and Wernher von Braun to Hitler. He still did not know that Heinrich Himmler had been maneuvering for such a meeting for months.

28 MAY 1943

The successful flight of an A-4 during the visit of the Long-Range Bombardment Commission to Peenemünde brought its first tangible dividend. Albert Speer called Walter Dornberger from headquarters. He told Dornberger that he, Dornberger, had been promoted to the rank of major general.

23 JUNE 1943

Just after noon, an RAF Mosquito set down on the runway at Leuchars Airfield. It had returned from a flight over northern Germany with a full cargo of exposed photographic film. Before the day was over, the Photographic Reconnaissance Unit had printed the photographs, and had in its hands chilling proof of their worst fears.

Suspicions had been growing for years based on rumors and random bits of fact—a flood of intelligence with trickles of truth. The first hints that something of concern was taking place were contained in the "Oslo letters," so called because they were sent by an anonymous source to the British naval attache in Oslo. The documents described in detail secret German weapons development, and told of experiments with long-range rockets taking place from an island off the Baltic coast. They were great reading, but they could not be verified independently.

Over the preceding six months, intelligence sources on the ground and water began to report strange happenings in the Baltic area. Danish fishermen had reported seeing strange objects with "flaming tails" racing across the night sky. They seemed to come from Peenemünde on the island of Usedom.

The Polish Underground reported that two of its members had been conscripted to work with other Poles at an installation on Usedom Island. The men found a way to leak out word that they had seen a winged torpedolike object in a shed at the research installation.

Two German Army generals who had the misfortune—or good fortune, depending on one's point of view—to become prisoners of war revealed to their interrogators that they had seen the big rockets under development. Neither could give any useful details.

Something very dangerous for England was happening at Peenemünde, and the RAF Mosquito had been sent to take a close look. The photographs it brought back showed the long shadows of early morning on a cloudless day. Photos of the airfield at the northeastern end of the island revealed four small tailless aircraft that left behind dark streaks as they took off from the airfield. Photos of the far north end of the island showed two long objects pointing out over the water. They were written off as lengths of pipe related to an offshore dredging operation. Only later when similar structures were seen near the English Channel and pointed toward London was it realized that they were catapults for launching the flying bomb.

The aerial photos also revealed a large construction east of the airfield. Its perimeter was an earthen embankment about the size and shape of a football stadium. Within it were a few structures of unknown purpose. Nestled within the embankment and at its entrance were what appeared to be a trailers carrying torpedo-shaped objects about 40 feet long. The blunt ends of the objects broadened into what appeared to be fins.

These photographs held evidence of several major secret weapons under development at Peenemünde. While the Photographic Reconnaissance Unit did not interpret all the evidence in their hands correctly, they had the evidence that let British intelligence draw one critically important conclusion: the Germans were developing a rocket with a range of between 90 and 130 miles. They also projected that the missile would weigh in at 40 to 80 tons and carry an explosive warhead of from two to eight tons—significant errors on the high side.

Prime Minister Winston Churchill soon learned about this danger to England, and England began planning its response to the threat.

28 JUNE 1943

Heinrich Himmler, at the wheel of his own small armored car, came back to Peenemünde just as he had promised. This time there was no private airplane, no entourage of drones wearing black and silver uniforms and jack boots. Forget about his rank of SS Reichsfuehrer, his reputation for ruthlessness. He was just a man who wanted to learn about rockets. He was a loyal and sincere officer of the Reich. His demeanor said, trust me.

According to Walter Dornberger's account of the event, the only version that is available, his reception for Himmler was similarly reserved. After Himmler's arrival, Dornberger, Himmler, some local Nazi dignitaries, and a few of Dornberger's closest colleagues ate a modest dinner in the officers' mess. After dinner, the local dignitaries departed, and those remaining adjourned to the Hearth Room for an informal—such as it could be—after dinner conversation.

The Hearth Room was a cozy room with wood paneling and brass chandeliers. It was furnished with comfortable furniture and a low, circular, glass-topped table as a center for social activities. Besides Dornberger and Himmler, those present included: Lieutenant Colonel Gerhard Stegmaier, military commander of the Pre-Production Works and the man who had twice communicated with Himmler's headquarters requesting that the Reichsfuehrer involve himself in the A-4 program; Ministerial Councilor Godomar Schubert; Eberhard Rees, director of the experimental workshop; Dr. Ernst Steinhoff, head of the Department of Instruments, Guidance, and Measurement; and Wernher von Braun, who wore his black SS dress uniform that day.

In his account of the event, Dornberger said the conversation began awkwardly. He was tempted to confront Himmler about his involvement in the dismissal of his subordinate, Colonel Leo Zassen, but decided to postpone doing so until he could speak to Himmler alone.

The discussion eventually reached the safe ground of politically neutral technology: rockets. Wernher von Braun took the lead. He told the history of rocket development, beginning with the primitive facilities at Kummersdorf. The research group had grown and moved to Peenemünde, and it was now a unified team dedicated to reaching its goal, the development of the long-range rocket as a weapon. Of course, there were still problems. Despite their successes, Hitler had not yet favored the team by including it in the top priority group.

Others began to contribute to the conversation, talking about their areas of expertise and responsibility. In the relaxed mood that developed, they even told Himmler of their dream of using rockets for space travel and the steps to be taken in its realization.

Himmler sat back with his legs comfortably crossed, his elbows resting easily on the arms of the chair, taking it all in. He was a man of calm, a man without nerves. When he spoke, his only gesture was to tap his fingertips together for emphasis. He asked enough of the right questions to convince his hosts that he understood what they told him about rocketry. The hours ticked by; and gradually, imperceptibly, the topic being discussed changed from the dream of space travel to the reality of war.

Dornberger, according to his account, got to the crux of the matter and began a verbal duel with Himmler.

"Reichsfuehrer, what are we really fighting for?"

Himmler took several hours to answer this simple question. In his discourse, he hit most of the themes that propelled the Third Reich: the master race, the conquest of the eastern territories, German expansion into the conquered lands, the enslavement of the inferior races. The only significant Nazi policy he neglected to mention was the annihilation of the Jews. Of course, nothing Himmler said was new. He was only explaining German national policy and what had been hammered into their heads by the press and radio for years.

The marathon discussion broke up at about 4 A.M. Himmler had been traveling since the 26th of June and was tired, and Dornberger wanted everybody to get some rest before the big event scheduled for the morning, the firing of an A-4 rocket.

Dornberger said of this discussion, dominated by Himmler, that he and his engineers were not politically sophisticated and had difficulty under-standing the ideas Himmler presented. One did not have to be as bright as a rocket scientist to figure out that Himmler, like Hitler, was a murderous sociopath with a lust for power and without a trace of conscience, and that by building rockets they would become accomplices to mass murder. But somehow the rocket scientists could not figure it out.

*   *   *   *

Several facts suggest that Walter Dornberger's account of Himmler's visit to Peenemünde was deficient in candor. Despite his claim that he argued with Himmler against the use of slave labor, Peenemünde operations were supported by hundreds of conscripted Polish laborers and Russian prisoners of war. They had first arrived in 1940 and were currently there as servants to Speer's construction group. They did construction and menial work during the day, and at night they returned to the barbed wire enclave of Trassenheide. Presumably, they worked on the base with the approval of the army and Walter Dornberger.

Slave laborers not only worked at Peenemünde, they were requisitioned from the SS by the army's rocket development group. In a note dated 16 April 1943, Arthur Rudolph, who headed the Development and Fabrication Laboratory, reported on his observations of the exploitation of prisoners at the Heinkel aircraft works in Oranienburg. He wrote, "The employment of detainees [*haeftlinge*] in general has had considerable advantages over the earlier employment of foreigners, especially because all-non-work-related tasks are taken over by the SS and the detainees offer greater protection for security." Rudolph concluded, "Production in the F-1 [the main assembly building in Peenemünde] can be carried out by detainees." On 2 June 1943, Rudolph formally requested 1,400 slave laborers from the SS. The first 200 members of this group arrived on 17 June. It is inconceivable that Rudolph would have made such a request without the knowledge and approval of his boss, Wernher von Braun, and of the chief of the Army rocket program, Army General Walter Dornberger.

Furthermore, according to Nazi records, Wernher von Braun was promoted by the SS to the rank of Sturmbannfuehrer (major) on 28 June, the day Himmler arrived at Peenemünde. Since von Braun had been promoted to Hauptsturmfuehrer (Captain) less than eight months earlier, it is likely that his promotion to SS major was timed to coincide with Himmler's arrival at Peenemünde. Himmler may have personally announced the promotion and pinned the symbols of new rank on von Braun's SS uniform as an act of apparent conciliation and to enhance the visibility of the SS within Dornberger's organization. Since von Braun's involvement with the SS would later become an embarrassment to himself and his mentor, Dornberger may have consciously avoided recording or commenting on the incident.

While Dornberger and von Braun may have been uneasy about the growing involvement of the SS in the activities of Peenemünde, they were not above requesting its assistance or participating in its ranks.

29 JUNE 1943

The morning broke with low, thick clouds hanging over the test stand. At 9:15 A.M. the A-4 prototype was fired for the benefit of Heinrich Himmler.

The missile lifted smoothly from its launching stand, but from the very beginning something was wrong. It began to tip away from its intended flight path over the sea, and leaned toward the west. It did not respond to steering commands from the ground, and it became a "reluctant virgin," as the rocket men called missiles that failed to follow the flight program. Within seconds, it was nearly horizontal and flying out of control several hundred feet over the pine forest toward the Luftwaffe airfield. Dornberger and his men watched in shock, helpless, as their rocket collapsed under the strain 15 seconds after liftoff, then fell to earth. The rocket crashed onto the runway, and nearly eight tons of high-energy fuel exploded in a fiery black mushroom cloud. The concussion of the explosion rattled windows two miles away at Peenemünde East.

A few minutes later, Dornberger arrived at Peenemünde West with Himmler at his side to survey the damage caused by the errant missile. Luftwaffe personnel were running about, apparently in chaos. Dornberger and Himmler drove to the site of the A-4's impact a few hundred yards from the nearest hangar. The fuel-laden rocket had blown a hole in the runway 100 feet in diameter, and muddy water was rapidly rising in the bottom of the crater. The green grassy area around the hole was peppered with clods of the dark subsoil and sprinkled with white sand. Nearby were the smashed wrecks of three aircraft. Miraculously, the disaster had caused no injuries.

After viewing the damage, Himmler commented, "Now I can return to Berlin and order the production of close-combat weapons with an easy conscience."

Dornberger did not think Himmler's quip was funny, and he was not going to see the day end in humiliation if he could avoid it. A second firing of an A-4 was scheduled for the afternoon.

The morning overcast was clearing, and Dornberger and Himmler took the opportunity to cross by motor launch to the Greifswalder Oie for lunch. They were standing on the foredeck as the boat left the mouth of the Peene River and entered the open Baltic. At last Dornberger was alone with Himmler, and he took the opportunity to confront the Reichsfuehrer with the issue that had been on his mind since Himmler's arrival. He asked to hear the reason for Colonel Zassen's dismissal.

Himmler said that he did not remember the case. Dornberger persisted, reminding Himmler that an injustice had been done to Zassen. Himmler finally advised Dornberger to be satisfied that Colonel General Fromm was reinstating Colonel Zassen. As far as Himmler was concerned, the matter was closed.

*   *   *   *

The second rocket of the day lifted off straight and true. It punched through the high alto-stratus clouds and was lost from view, but its thunderous roar continued until the engines cut off 63.6 seconds after ignition. The missile covered a range of 147 miles over the Baltic and presumably came down near its target far out in the Baltic, although no one observed its impact.

Himmler was apparently impressed. Before he left, he promised to take the cause of the rocket men and their request for top priority status to Hitler. Of course, Himmler pointed out, he could do nothing unless Hitler himself reached a favorable decision.

CHAPTER 11

A Command Performance for the Fuehrer

7 JULY 1943

Whether Heinrich Himmler discussed the army's A-4 rocket program with Hitler after his visit to Peenemünde is not known. Nevertheless, one week after Himmler watched the flawless flight of the A-4 and Walter Dornberger asked for his support with the Fuehrer, Dornberger got the action he wanted. Hitler instructed Albert Speer to invite Dornberger and Wernher von Braun to report on the status of the A-4 project. Speer, unaware that Himmler had requested such a meeting at the urging of Dornberger's subordinate, Lieutenant Colonel Stegmaier, believed that the Fuehrer was honoring his own request.

At 11:30 A.M. Dornberger received the order from Speer to report to headquarters. By early afternoon, Dornberger, von Braun, and Ernst Steinhoff had gathered together their props and film, and taken off through a thick fog in a Heinkel He 111 for the Wolf's Lair at Rastenburg in East Prussia. They flew across eastern Germany and across occupied Poland; and, as their airplane crossed the Vistula River, which formed part of the boundary of Poland with East Prussia, the clouds cleared to reveal below idyllic dark forests, sparkling lakes, and fertile meadows. They were soon on the ground and being driven with all of their exhibits to Hitler's headquarters.

When Dornberger, von Braun, and Steinhoff arrived at the Army Guest House, they received passes that would allow them into Hitler's innermost restricted area. They learned that they were scheduled to make their presentation to Hitler at 5 P.M.; and they left for Hitler's inner enclave an hour early so they could set up their displays, diagrams, and models. The Fuehrer's headquarters was a collection of barracks and concrete shelters set in a clearing among the old oaks. They were ushered to a projection room where they set up their display. It was well past the scheduled five o'clock, and it got later and later.

Suddenly the door opened.

"The Fuehrer!" somebody announced.

The rocket builders came to attention.

Hitler entered the projection theater accompanied by Field Marshal Wilhelm Keitel, chief of staff of the armed forces, General Alfred Jodl, chief of the armed forces operations staff, General Walter Buhle, chief of armaments for the army, Albert Speer, and their personal aides. Hitler seemed to have aged greatly since Dornberger and von Braun had met him last, a little more than three years earlier when he inspected their facility at Kummersdorf. He wore a field-gray tunic and black trousers, and he walked hunched over under an enormous black cape. He appeared tired.

After the greetings and introductions, Hitler sat down between Speer and Keitel in the front row of the theater. The others took seats behind them in the tiers that rose to the back of the room.

Dornberger and von Braun had had plenty of practice since their first disappointing meeting with Hitler at Kummersdorf in 1939. There is also a report based on notes left behind by Dornberger that he and his group had a second meeting with Hitler at Rastenburg on 20 August 1941; the second meeting went much like the first with the Fuehrer being unimpressed by the potential of rockets. Not surprisingly, neither Dornberger nor von Braun mention this inconclusive meeting in their memoirs. This was probably their last chance to sell the rocket program to Hitler and they knew it. If they could not get his support, they could—and probably would have to—turn off the lights, lock the doors, pick up their rifles, and go to the front. This time von Braun was prepared. His presentation was polished, if not slick.

The lights dimmed, the film—in brilliant color—began, and Wernher von Braun started his commentary. The 100-foot high doors of the assembly building at Test Stand VII opened, and the mobile test frame carrying the 46-foot-long rocket rolled out and over the water-cooled blast shield. The men attending the missile were dwarfed by its massive size. Held tightly in the test frame, the engine was fired, and close-ups showed the graphite vanes below the engine directing the rocket's blast.

Von Braun then described the mobile launching system Dornberger's group had devised for use in the field. The rocket was loaded onto a *Meillerwagen*, then hauled along straight and curved roads. At its destination, soldiers used the hydraulic "erector" to put the weapon into vertical position on the launching table; and they loaded it with fuel. The message was simple: an army crew could transport the weapon to the front along existing roads, then fire it under field conditions at a target over 160 miles away.

Then came the actual triumph, the first successful firing of the A-4, which had taken place nine months earlier on 3 October 1942. Hitler and his cronies watched in awe as the image of the rocket lifted over the pines of Peenemünde and into the cloudless blue sky. Their eyes tracked it as it shrank into the sky, then left behind a bloom of a vapor trail in the upper atmosphere. After the rocket faded from sight on the projection screen, an animated cartoon took over, showing the rocket's trajectory, speed, altitude, and range. Then in case Hitler missed the message, the key events shown in the presentation were repeated, from the arrival of the rocket at the test stand to its dramatic launching.

As the film ended, the screen filled with the words,

"We made it after all!"

Fritz Lang could not have done it better.

Nobody said a word. Hitler leaned back in his chair, apparently lost in gloomy thought.

Dornberger took the stage and gave the hard facts. He summed up the current status of development. He described the launching options from motorized batteries and from bunkers. He explained the realities of manufacture, giving production figures and delivery dates.

After Dornberger finished his statement, Hitler came to him, shook his hand, and thanked him. The Fuehrer spoke in a confidential whisper to the general about the importance of the rocket to Germany and how the rest of the world would not be able to resist it.

Hitler then turned to the model of the rocket-launching bunker. He wanted to know more about the firing of the A-4 from the permanent, hardened site. The rocket builders showed how all prelaunch activities could be done under the protective concrete cover and how the rocket would be pushed out of doors fully fueled, with internal guidance gyroscopes spinning, moments before being fired. Hitler was impressed.

Dornberger told Hitler of his preference for the mobile batteries over the bunker. The mobile weapons could be taken almost anywhere, set up quickly, and fired before the enemy could take countermeasures. The bunker was a sitting duck for air attacks. Nevertheless, Hitler, the frustrated artist and architect, loved construction; and he wanted an excuse to build the bunkers.

Hitler asked Speer, his personal architect and now his minister of armaments, if this bunker was anything like the U-boat shelters built along the coast.

They were essentially similar, Speer agreed.

Then Hitler would have his bunker. He would have two, or even three, rocket-firing bunkers built. Their roofs would be 23 feet thick to make them impregnable to the heaviest of bombing attacks. Hitler observed that these massive structures would be irresistible targets for enemy bombers. They would divert the enemy's destructive force from other German targets; and if they worked as launch sites for the A-4, so much the better.

Dornberger showed Hitler photographs of craters made by the impact of the rockets with their one-ton warheads. Hitler examined the photographs in silence. Then he asked if Dornberger could increase the cargo of explosives to ten tons.

Dornberger patiently explained that increasing the load of explosives could be done only at the expense of range. If the Fuehrer wanted a rocket to hurl ten tons of explosives, his team would have to develop a much larger rocket. With the current resources, that would take at least another four or five years.

How many A-4 rockets could be built? Hitler wanted 2,000 rockets each month.

Dornberger explained that he could not possibly supply that many weapons. Germany could not produce enough alcohol for fuel. A change to an alternative fuel would require engineering changes that would delay production for years.

Hitler did not like to hear that something could not be done. His eyes flared with a fanatical light. "But what I want is annihilation—annihilating effect!"

Hitler wanted more than the army's rocket program was designed to give. Dornberger tried to explain this to him. He pointed out that the original aim was to increase the range and accuracy of heavy artillery. They had gone beyond that and produced a weapon for which there was no defense. Yet, as Dornberger talked, he realized that after the years of neglect of the rocket program, Hitler now expected the A-4 to produce a dramatic reversal of the dismal direction of the war. Dornberger knew that even if Hitler's senseless demand could be met, the new wonder weapon was not enough. "When we started our development work," Dornberger explained lamely, "we were not thinking of an annihilating effect. We . . ."

Hitler turned to him in a rage and shouted, "You! No, *you* didn't think of it, I know. But *I* did!"

Dornberger did not reply; Hitler had beaten him down. Hitler was the Fuehrer; he was in command. He alone had seen how rockets could reverse the course of the war. After ignoring the rocket program since its inception, Hitler was now its champion. He would give Peenemünde the top priority rank that Dornberger had been asking for for years.

Wernher von Braun was putting a polish on his successful day by explaining to Hitler some technical details of rocketry, when Dornberger drifted away to talk to Albert Speer. Dornberger reminded Speer that he had promised earlier at Peenemünde to propose that a titular professorship be given to von Braun. A titular professorship was a civilian honor granted only by the head of state.

Speer acted immediately on Dornberger's reminder by making the proposal to Hitler. The Fuehrer agreed enthusiastically. Speer later had Dr. Otto von Meissner, state secretary in the Chancellery, prepare the diploma which Hitler would sign. Speer would then make the formal presentation to von Braun.

Hitler had already turned and was about to leave when he returned for a final word with Dornberger.

"I have had to apologize to only two men in my life," Hitler said. "The first is Field Marshal von Brauchitsch. I did not listen to him when he told me again and again how important your research was. The second man is yourself. I never believed that your work would be successful."

Dornberger was always proud of the fact that he had been worthy enough to receive an apology from Hitler.

Von Braun—at least after the war—did not have much to say about the titular professorship he had received from Hitler.

*   *   *   *

After Dornberger and his group had left for Peenemünde and Hitler had returned to his bunker, the Fuehrer spoke with Speer.

"The A-4 is a measure that can decide the war." Hitler's enthusiasm was burning as fiercely as a rocket's exhaust flame. "And what encouragement to the home front when we attack the English with it!"

Hitler ordered Speer to drive production of the A-4 rocket as hard as he could. He assured Speer that he would get all the resources he needed. "But in this project," Hitler added cautiously, "we can use only Germans. God help us if the enemy finds out about the business."

Hitler then spoke of von Braun. Hitler was amazed that the 31-year-old German could have created that technical marvel, the A-4. He would later compare von Braun with Alexander the Great, who had conquered his empire by the age of 23, and Napoleon, who had won his most brilliant military victories when he was 30. Hitler overlooked Napoleon's most devastating defeat when he sent his armies into the Russian winter, a tactical error the Fuehrer himself had repeated.

Summer 1943

Major General Hans Kammler, chief of the construction division, Amstgruppe C, of the SS Economic-Administrative Main Office had another job to do. He was back in the eastern territories walking through the rubble of a half-destroyed city, and his charge was to complete the job of destruction.

In April of 1943 the Jews of the Warsaw ghetto who had until then escaped relocation to concentration camps rose up in a final futile resistance to their German tormentors. When the battle ended on 16 May, their number had been reduced to 56,065 from 380,000. The survivors were sent to labor camps, shipped to their deaths at Treblinka and Lublin, or immediately shot. When these troublesome Jews had been disposed of, Heinrich Himmler decreed that the site of the Warsaw ghetto would be turned into a park.

Hans Kammler had an enormous project on his hands. The ghetto had originally covered 445 acres. The Jewish resistance had built barricades and several hundred dugouts, some of which connected with the sewer system. Kammler's job was to tear down every wall, plug every dugout and sewer, and haul away the rubble. He enlisted nearly 3,000 Poles under the supervision of 34 loyal Germans to obliterate the ghetto. They took more than a year to complete the job. When it was done, not one stone of the Warsaw ghetto was left standing upon another.

Early July 1943

Even before Hitler gave the A-4 its official top priority rating, the bureaucrats seized power. Karl Saur, Speer's head of the Central Office at the Ministry of Armaments and Munitions, invited key representatives of the Peenemünde group, manufacturers, and the chairmen of the German Labor Commissions to a conference at the ministry in Berlin. The 250 attendees convened—appropriately, as it turned out—in a barracks at the zoo.

Dornberger and von Braun sat with Saur and Gerhard Degenkolb at a long table at the front of the room. Even before the conference was convened, the men from Peenemünde were hearing bad news: the plan of the Ministry of Armaments and Munitions as presented by Saur was now to produce 2,000 missiles each month. Dornberger and von Braun wondered in astonished disbelief where this number had come from. They soon figured it out.

Six months earlier, Dornberger had given the Army Weapons Office a proposal for a total production run of 6,000 missiles to be built at the pilot factory at Peenemünde, by Henschel's Rax Works at Wiener Neustadt, and by the Zeppelin airship factory at Friedrichshafen. Production at these three plants was to be done largely by concentration camp prisoners, a plan to which Dornberger had expressed no objections. Although there is no way of knowing, it is likely that Dornberger, who had been repeatedly disappointed by the support given to his program, presented an overly ambitious proposal in the hope of getting at least part of it approved.

Ironically, Degenkolb's incredible production plans were based on Dornberger's original proposal to produce 300 missiles per month at each of the three factories. To this was added an additional 900 missiles from a new underground factory to be built in the Harz Mountains near Nordhausen. The sum of production at all of these factories was rounded off to a neat 2,000 impossible units per month.

The meeting began with Degenkolb in the chair. There were preliminaries with Saur praising Dornberger and his team and then giving the sales pitch to those present on the need to build the weapon. Dornberger addressed the assemblage and called for reason. "Better fewer rockets of first-rate quality," he said, "than masses of inferior ones that cannot be used except as scrap." Dornberger felt as if he had been speaking in a vacuum. Nobody heard what he had said.

Degenkolb began working his way through the industrialists, asking them, one by one, to sign on to the program, to pledge themselves and their companies to the Reich. The industrialists were reluctant, claiming that they could not make promises unless they were assured of materials and equipment. Degenkolb was not interested in their problems. He pushed on like one of the locomotives he had built in his previous job. Locomotives, rockets, what's the difference? It's just a matter of getting these people to agree to a schedule, then making them live up to their commitment.

Degenkolb and Saur took turns bullying the industrialists until their objections faded away. Eventually they all fell into line promising what they knew they could not deliver, hoping their failures would not stand out in the collective disaster-in-the-making.

As the mad plan was being laid out, Dornberger and von Braun fell deeper into depression and despair. They had given Hitler the good news about the A-4, but they had held back on a few awkward details. Of the 29 prototypes that had been fired by the date of the meeting with Hitler, no more than a half-dozen had landed anywhere near their target. The norm was for the missile to misfire or go astray. Furthermore, despite the evidence of radar tracking and a few green dye stains at points of impact in the Baltic, the Peenemünde group had yet to demonstrate that the A-4 could deliver and explode a ton of explosives on target. Dornberger and von Braun had oversold their case; and now they, like the manufacturers, would be expected to deliver.

25 JULY 1943

"You can only smash terror with counter-terror!" Hitler held center stage at the War Conference held at his Wolf's Lair headquarters. "You have got to counter-attack! Anything else is rubbish."

Hitler was justifiably upset. The day before, the British had begun a nine-day bombing attack on Hamburg, Germany's second largest city. Before the assault was over, 40,000 civilians would die, a million would be evacuated, and Hamburg would be pounded to rubble.

"You can only smash terror with counter-terror!" Hitler pounded his new axiom into his subordinates. "If they bomb my airfields, I don't bat an eyelash. But if they wipe out my Ruhr cities . . . ! You can only force them to give up by getting at their people. . . . The only thing that will have any effect is a systematic attack on their villages and towns."

Later that afternoon, Albert Speer presented to Hitler the draft of the edict that would make counterterror national policy. It required peak output of the A-4 missile as quickly as possible; it allocated to the manufacturing plants skilled German workers, materials, machinery, and power; it gave Speer authority to draw upon the resources of the military; and it specifically charged him with direction of the A-4 program. Hitler greedily signed the edict that gave sweeping powers to Albert Speer.

As expert as Hitler was in aggression and mass murder, he did not understand the simple arithmetic of terror. Speer himself had been so enraptured by the visual display of power the A-4 gave when launched that he did not do the simple calculations until years later. The original plan was to manufacture 900 missiles per month to be launched at targets in England. This worked out to 30 metric tons of high explosives crashing down on English civilians daily. This number seems impressive until one realizes that by the time the A-4 was actually in operation in 1944, Allied bombers were dropping an average of 3,000 tons of bombs a day on Germany. Thus, in response to Hitler's cry for "counterterror," Germany committed its dwindling resources to an experiment in technology.

III

TERROR AND COUNTERTERROR

CHAPTER 12

The Flames of Peenemünde

17 AUGUST 1943

General Walter Dornberger had had a bad day. It was about to get much worse.

The summer sun had been baking Usedom Island for several days, and the sultry weather gave no sign of breaking. The heat, piled on top of the demands to get the job done, began to take its toll on Dornberger's team. At a meeting in his office that afternoon, the development and production departments had gone for each other's throats; they were holding each other responsible for delays in producing an operational missile. Before the shouting was over, several key men in Dornberger's group, including von Braun, had offered their resignations. Von Braun, for heaven's sake. He had been the first man to join the team. Dornberger did some fast and fancy talking, making liberal use of the word "duty"; and finally he got them all to calm down and sign back onto the team.

The top priority status conferred on the A-4 program by Hitler not only gave Dornberger's group materiel and men, but it also put the whole team under tremendous pressure to succeed. They had agreed to mass produce an operational weapon, but they were beginning to have doubts that they could keep their promise.

*　　*　　*　　*

After the sun went down, the air and tempers cooled. The rocket builders and one woman sat in the Hearth Room of the mess at Peenemünde East, the same room where less than two months earlier Heinrich Himmler had held court. They had just finished dinner and were relaxing, talking about their projects and plans for the future. The men who gathered around the low, glass-topped table were Walter Dornberger, Wernher von Braun, Ernst Steinhoff, Kurt Debus and Werner Gengelbach, both missile launch experts, and von Braun's younger brother Magnus, a chemist who had come to Peenemünde to work on rocket fuels.

The lone woman, curled up in a deep arm chair, was Hanna Reitsch, who had been Wernher von Braun's friend since they met while taking glider flying lessons in 1932. Hanna Reitsch had given up her goal to become a missionary doctor in favor of a career of flying. Through skill, daring, and personal charm, she had achieved a position as a Luftwaffe test pilot, and in that position she had received honors from the Luftwaffe and the Fuehrer. She wore on her dark blue uniform the Iron Cross, First Class, and the Luftwaffe Gold Medal for Military Flying. Ten months earlier, she had been seriously injured in a crash landing of the Messerschmitt Me 163B Komet, the rocket-powered interceptor that was the culmination of the Luftwaffe's Projekt X; yet, she showed no obvious signs of her near-fatal crash. She was at Peenemünde to reacquaint herself with the rocket plane and was scheduled to fly it the following morning.

Dornberger, at almost 48, was the old man of the group. Wernher von Braun and Reitsch were 31; Steinhoff was about their age. The company of this happy group of young, energetic people, made Dornberger less concerned with the worries he had faced that afternoon. Perhaps the worst was over.

*   *   *   *

Operation Whitebait was a small but critical maneuver. Eight RAF Mosquitoes flew south across Denmark dropping masses of metal foil "window" to announce their presence. They were to the west of Peenemünde following a clear course to Berlin. German radar could not miss the activity, and within moments the first Messerschmitts were in the air. Forty minutes later, the air raid sirens were screaming over the German capital, and civilians were running for cover. Berlin was ready when the Mosquitoes arrived. Searchlights bathed the sky, and anti-aircraft guns began to bang away. The Mosquitoes filled the sky with flares and dropped their token loads of bombs. German radar detected hundreds more aircraft massing over the Baltic, and it was clear that a massive attack on Berlin was in the offing. Hundreds of German interceptors scrambled into the air from bases reaching across occupied Europe and were committed to defend Berlin from the invaders. Better than that, they would be waiting to deliver the British a humiliating defeat.

*   *   *   *

When the group at the Hearth Room at Peenemünde East broke up, Steinhoff went home to his wife and three children at the *Siedlung*, the "Settlement" to the south of the rocket development and production areas. Wernher von Braun escorted his old friend Hanna Reitsch to the car that would take her back to the visitors' quarters of the Luftwaffe Experimental Station three miles to the west. He wished her good luck with her flight in the rocket plane the following day, then he went to his own room in the bachelor quarters.

At about 11:30, Walter Dornberger went to the guest house he used when he came to Peenemünde from his office in Berlin. The air raid siren began to wail the "early warning." It was no cause for alarm, he thought; they had heard it many times before. The British bombers usually rendezvoused over the central Baltic before crossing over Usedom Island on their way south to attack Berlin. They were prepared. The entire base was blacked out, but Dornberger was nonetheless uneasy. The British had regularly flown reconnaissance aircraft over the island when the weather was clear, and several days earlier the Air Ministry had warned Dornberger that Peenemünde might be a target for an air raid. As he walked to his quarters that night, Walter Dornberger noticed that all of Peenemünde glowed in the reflected light of the full moon.

18 August 1943

The first red marker flare blossomed to life over Peenemünde nine and a half minutes after midnight. One minute later 16 more flares hanging from parachutes like multicandle chandeliers filled the sky with cold white light. Peenemünde lay under the full moon and the flares like a sleeping patient on an operating table prepared for major surgery.

The 497 Stirling, Halifax, and Lancaster bombers of "Operation Hydra" were flying south over the Baltic toward their brightly illuminated target. They carried 4,000 men, 1,593 tons of high explosives, and 281 tons of incendiary bombs. The men were risking their lives to destroy what they had been told was a "research station"; and if their attack that night failed to destroy it, they would return again and again until they succeeded.

The RAF had identified three target areas on the eastern side of Peenemünde that were aligned on a north-south axis. They were to bomb the southernmost first, then the middle target, and then the northernmost area. The first target was the scientists' housing estate, the Settlement. The action was to unapologetically kill the essential technical personnel; without rocket scientists there could be no rockets. A mile north of the Settlement was the Pre-Production Works, which contained the massive new concrete building of the pilot rocket factory that was planned to produce 300 missiles per month. It was to be the target of the second wave of the attack. A mile north of the rocket factory was the cluster of buildings of the Development Works, the target of the final wave of the air raid.

The attack began with miscalculation. The sky on the approach from the north had been cluttered with patches of strato-cumulus clouds, and the radar on the lead planes, intended to find ground markings, did not work. Furthermore, a fog was beginning to roll in over the beaches of Peenemünde, obscuring the topography. Some of the lead aircraft had dropped their marker flares two miles south of the initial target. Others dropped their flares out to sea.

Fifteen minutes after midnight, the first bombers were 7,000 feet above Peenemünde. Below them, the RAF crews could see the first evidence of the enemy's defenses: generators were belching out smoke that drifted west over the target, obscured the landscape, and hid the buildings. The bomber crews would have to drop their bombs through the smoke screen and ground fog and hope that their targets were beneath them. Seventeen minutes after midnight, they began to release their deadly loads on the Settlement.

High over Berlin the Luftwaffe had its main force of over 200 fighters chasing phantom attackers. The pilots could see the glow of the flares over Peenemünde 120 miles to the north. Was the RAF attacking a lightly populated coastal area? It did not make any sense. The German pilots did not know about the secret rocket base. Finally, the Luftwaffe ordered its fighters into battle over Peenemünde, and the handful that had enough fuel rushed north to attack.

The bomber crews went about their business expecting the defenses to strike back at any moment. The lethal reflex was not there. The Luftwaffe fighters did not attack. Only a few searchlights raked the sky, and the flak was light. Fire and more smoke erupted from the ground as the bombs began to take their toll. For ten agonizingly long minutes the bombers lined up over the southern targets raining fiery death and destruction, but still the Luftwaffe's fighters did not appear.

The second wave of bombers swept in over its target, the centrally located Pre-Production Works with its pilot rocket factory. Smoke and fire now covered the ground below; huge patches of the tinder-dry pine forest that concealed the rocket base were in flames. The bombers released their loads. Then the Luftwaffe fighters attacked, and all hell broke loose. Bombers began to explode and fall in dizzying spirals from the night sky.

When the Pre-Production Works had been dealt with, the Development Works, the northernmost and final target, became the focus of the British raid. The last of the RAF bombers that had lined up north of Peenemünde took their turn at running the gauntlet of Luftwaffe fighters. Below them was a sea of flame and smoke; the target was no longer visible from the air. The attackers were flying along predetermined coordinates and finding their way to the target by dead reckoning. By now, 30 Luftwaffe fighters had broken away from the charade over Berlin and were taking a heavy toll on the bombers. Still more bombers came to drop their incendiary burdens, having been delayed by blunders and the chaos of war in the night sky.

The whole operation was to take 45 minutes. It lasted at least 15 minutes longer, and the last bombers over the target paid the heaviest toll in casualties. As they scrambled back toward England, they left Peenemünde behind them in flames from end to end, and more Luftwaffe fighters took to the air and pursued them. Additional bombers were lost on the way back home.

When the air forces of Britain and Germany tallied up their losses, both had reason for grief. The RAF had lost 40 bombers on the raid over Peenemünde and one Mosquito in the sham attack on Berlin. The Luftwaffe had lost nine fighters in the air battle, but its total losses were far greater. The fighters that had chased the phantom attackers over Berlin blundered catastrophically on their return to the ground. In the chaos of the moment, and lacking clear orders to do otherwise, the majority of the force opted to land at the Brandenburg-Briest airport. Fighters came in for landings faster than those on the ground could clear the runway. Over 100 fighters glided into a massive pileup of twisted aircraft; more than 30 were not salvageable.

As details of the disasters at Peenemünde and Berlin drifted in, the chief of the German air staff, Colonel General Hans Jeschonnek, decided not to deal with the aftermath of the Luftwaffe's embarrassing performance. He secluded himself in his room, and, revolver in hand, ended his own life.

*   *   *   *

S-s-s-st BANG. Walter Dornberger awoke with a start.

S-s-s-st BANG. S-s-s-st BANG. The windowpanes around him rattled with the detonations.

He groggily tried to make sense of all the noise. It must be Captain Stoelzel, he surmised. Dornberger had authorized the man to fire an experimental solid-fueled anti–dive bomber rocket. S-s-s-st BANG. But why was he firing them off in rapid succession? That was no way to get decent data. S-s-s-st BANG. And why at night? S-s-s-st BANG. Dornberger counted the explosions. Nineteen. Twenty. Twenty-one. Twenty-one? Dornberger was wide awake, and he had the answer: anti-aircraft guns. Then he heard the full symphony of light and heavy anti-aircraft artillery banging and popping away.

He switched on his bedside light and picked up the telephone to call the command shelter. The line was busy. No matter. He had to act. He jumped into his breeches, pulled on his socks, and slipped into his jacket.

S-s-s-st BANG. The windowpanes began to shatter from the shock of the blast.

Dornberger attended to the trappings of a commanding officer: overcoat, cap, gloves, and cigar case. He was ready to move; but, he wondered with chagrin, where the hell were his riding boots? He put on his slippers.

Two miles to the south, the first wave of the RAF began to drop its bombs. They fell on the Settlement and on the foreign laborers housing adjacent to its south side, Karlshagen camp. When the first bombs blasted him awake, Ernst Steinhoff hustled his wife and three children into the cellar of their duplex. Moments later a high-explosive bomb struck the house and brought down everything above the cellar. Dr. Walter Thiel ushered his wife and four children out of their house and into a slit trench cut into the soft sand. When a high-explosive bomb exploded nearby, they were buried.

When the first wave of RAF bombers began their attack on the Settlement, some of the planes followed a misplaced marker flare and dumped their loads of high explosives and incendiaries over Trassenheide, three miles farther south. The residents of Trassenheide did not have the option of leaving the area. They were euphemistically called foreign laborers, but were in reality slaves. They were mostly Poles and Russian prisoners of war conscripted to do construction and maintenance work. Trassenheide was basic housing, orderly rows of barracks surrounded by chain-link fence, barbed wire, and SS guards equipped with machine guns and Doberman pinschers.

The barracks were shattered and set ablaze. Men ran in panic, looking for a way out. Frantically, they tried to climb over and through the chain-link fence and barbed wire. Accounts differ as to whether the gate to the camp was opened to let the workers escape, or the SS guards with their Dobermans kept the prisoners from escaping. In the chaos of war, both could have happened.

S-s-s-st BANG. Every remaining windowpane shattered, and tiles clattered down the peaked roof and rained into piles of shards around the guest house. The door had been jammed by the blast, and Dornberger had to push it to get to the hallway. The inner vestibule door had been blown off its hinges, and the outer door had been thrown out onto the steps leading to the garden.

Outside everything was covered with a sprinkling of white sand, like sifted sugar. The fog and smoke rolled by in malevolent red waves winding around and alternately hiding and revealing the buildings of the Development Works. Red? There must be enormous fires somewhere, maybe not far away, filling the air with their rose-red glow. The sky above was criss-crossed with searchlights and raked with anti-aircraft fire. The peace of night was shattered by the barking of the anti-aircraft guns, the thunder of heavy bombs, and the unending drone of the RAF bombers 7,000 feet above.

Dornberger saw von Braun standing with another man in front of the concrete air raid bunker no more than a few yards away. He asked what reports had been received, and he was told that the lines to the Pre-Production Works, the Settlement, and Karlshagen were out. Before it was cut off, the Settlement had reported that it had been hit by seven bombs.

The exchange was interrupted by the sound of objects rushing through the air, rapidly growing louder. They scrambled through the door of the air raid shelter just in time to hear the muffled sound of the bombs burying themselves in the soft sand and exploding in muffled plops.

Inside the crowded shelter, Dornberger found a telephone and called the command post again. He did not like what he heard. The Measurement House, the assembly workshop, the components shop, the repair shop, and the scrap dump of the Development Works were on fire. The fire brigade was trying to save the components shop. The lines to the Pre-Production Works and the Settlement were out. It was obviously a concerted raid on all of Peenemünde.

Dornberger ordered the chief warden on duty to send runners to the Pre-Production Works, the Settlement, and Karlshagen to get status reports. Then he said he was on his way. Somebody handed Dornberger his boots; somebody had risked his life to retrieve them. Dornberger put them on. It was 12:35 A.M., and the focus of the raid was about to shift to Dornberger's destination, the Development Works. Dornberger left the shelter with Wernher von Braun. The ground around them was littered with hissing incendiary bombs bathing the night in a dazzling white light.

Dornberger ordered von Braun to get all the men from the shelter and from the air force construction labor gang, and with them defend the Construction Bureau. They were to check the fire and to get the safes, cabinets, records, and drawings out of the burning building.

The salvage efforts were already underway. Hermann Oberth had organized groups of workers. It was Oberth, the father of German rocketry, who was rallying the men, leading them into burning buildings to save documents and equipment from destruction. He had started it all with his theories and his blundering attempts to build rockets over a decade earlier. Once again he was the leader, this time in the efforts to save the treasures that had been created at Peenemünde.

Dornberger took off for the command shelter, passing barracks engulfed in flames, dodging bomb craters in his path. He ran along the main avenue of the Development Works till he arrived at the command post. There he picked up two wardens and led them to the most valuable building in the complex, which had been reported to be in flames, the Measurement House. They were in luck. Three barracks near the building and the assembly workshop behind it were masses of wild flame, but the flames were just beginning to take hold of the Measurement House. Using the fire extinguishers in the building, they put out the fires within 15 minutes.

Dornberger checked on the progress of the fire brigade at the component workshop, then ran back through the falling bombs and burning buildings to the Construction Bureau. Von Braun's recruits had filled the forecourt with files, safes, and furniture. They were busy putting out the last of the flames.

Dornberger wondered what was keeping the reinforcements from the Settlement and the army camp. Where was the labor service crew, which should have arrived immediately in trucks? Why wasn't the emergency plan being followed? Dornberger would learn that the emergency plan was one of the first casualties of the bombardment. His rocket base was burning to the ground, and there was nothing he could do about it. Then Dornberger saw the guest house where he had been peacefully asleep less than an hour earlier. Its top floor was on fire. The entire house would soon be gone, including his family papers, stamp collection, shotguns, and hunting gear, which he had brought from Berlin for safe keeping. He rushed into the burning building.

Flames were already rising from the floor of the hall as Dornberger entered the guest house. He started to grab suitcases; and, as fast as he could, he dragged them out the main door. When he ran to the door for the third time, he was pushed back by a wall of flame. He broke in through the bathroom window and threw out everything he could. Then he went into the bedroom after his shotguns. A huge flame blew open the door and set fire to the curtains and furniture. Dornberger was trapped. He had to get out somehow. He dropped his precious shotguns, tore a blanket from the bed, and wrapped it around himself. He lurched through the burning room; and just before he leapt through the window to safety, he grabbed for something, anything, that he might still save. He crawled on hands and knees away from the flames and the heat. When he finally stood up and threw off the blanket, he found he was holding an ashtray. He threw it back.

The time was 1:45 A.M. The anti-aircraft fire had stopped. The constant droning of the bombers was fading into the distance. The dominant sound now was the crackling and crashing of the fires all around. The air raid had ended.

*   *   *   *

The losses of life were almost exclusively at the Settlement, as the RAF intended, and at Trassenheide. When the sound of the last RAF bomber had faded in the night sky, 735 people lay dead. Of the approximately 4,000 inhabitants of the Settlement, 178 men, women, and children were killed. The most significant loss to the rocket program was Dr. Walter Thiel, who, together with his wife and four children, died in a slit trench cut into the soft sand near their house. Some army personnel also died, but most of the remaining fatalities were slave laborers who were trapped in the Trassenheide camp. Among those presumed dead were the two members of the Polish Underground who had leaked word of German rocket development at Peenemünde to the English. They were never heard from after the air raid they helped to inspire.

When the dust had settled and the dead had been buried, Germany handed out honors to put the best face on the disaster. Hermann Oberth received the Kriegsverdienstkreuz I Klasse mit Schwertern (the War Merit Cross First Class, with Swords), the same award his student Wernher von Braun had received the previous year for successfully developing the A-4. Oberth was not recognized for his pioneering work in rocketry, but for leadership and bravery in responding to the air raid.

*   *   *   *

Just after 10:00 A.M. a Mosquito reconnaissance plane flew high over Peenemünde and photographed the damage. When the photographs were developed and analyzed, the RAF leadership was elated. Operation Hydra had caught the Germans flat-footed, pants-down unprepared. The operation had destroyed Hitler's "wonder weapon" factory. They would not have to go back for a second attack.

Soon after the Mosquito left, the minister of munitions and armaments, Albert Speer, was approaching Peenemünde in his personal airplane. He could see from the air the extent of the disaster: the damaged and destroyed buildings, the craters that had been churned in the earth by heavy bombs, the scorched ground that had once been pine forest, the smoke and the fires that were still burning. The enemy had left a north-south band of destruction through Peenemünde East. At the Trassenheide foreign laborers camp at the south, 18 of the 30 crude barracks had been destroyed. At the Settlement two miles to the north, every one of the 100 structures nestled in the pine forest had been destroyed. To the north of the Settlement at the Pre-Production Works, the damage was surprisingly light. One of the large assembly buildings had sustained minor damage; the other was untouched by the raid. Farther north at the Development Works, 50 of 80 buildings had been completely destroyed or severely damaged. At the far north end of the establishment, the test stands appeared from the air to have been hit hard; however, the essential equipment had escaped significant damage.

The Luftwaffe test facility at Peenemünde West was ignored by the attacking force. The enemy had somehow overlooked the main testing facility for the Messerschmitt Me 262 jet aircraft, the Fieseler Fi 103, the unmanned flying bomb, which would later be renamed the V-1, and the Messerschmitt Me 163B Komet rocket interceptor.

After his plane landed at Peenemünde West, Speer met with Major General Walter Dornberger. Dornberger, tired from lack of sleep and covered with the dust and ash of the previous night, delivered his report. They discussed relief measures for the shattered base. Then Speer returned to his airplane to continue his survey of damage caused by air raids the previous night.

19 August 1943

Albert Speer, accompanied by his department head Karl Saur and Saur's staff, arrived at the Wolf's Lair in the evening. They were there to brief Hitler on the damage to Peenemünde, and also on damage caused by the Allied bombing of Schweinfurt, Nuremberg, and Regensberg. They illustrated their report with photographs of shattered and burned buildings. The conference delved into the impact of Allied bombings and on everything from crankshafts to anti-aircraft and antitank guns.

Hitler turned their attention to the A-4. The manufacture of the weapon must be kept top secret. The attack on Peenemünde had proven that. The attack crippled the pilot factory, and another air raid could destroy it entirely. Furthermore, the two other factories where the rocket was to be built had also been bombed, the Zeppelin factory at Friedrichschafen on 21 June and the Rex factory at Wiener-Neustadt on 13 August. The sites of production of the wonder weapon must be kept secret in the future.

Then Speer and his group were caught as totally unprepared by what Hitler had to say as the base at Peenemünde had been by the RAF attack. Himmler has made a proposal, Hitler said, that could ensure the essential secrecy: build the rocket with concentration camp labor. There would be no contact between the work force and the outside world. Concentration camp inmates were not even allowed to receive or send mail. Himmler had guaranteed that all of the skilled technicians could be found in the camps. They would work under the supervision of knowledgeable Germans. Yes, Hitler said, Himmler had given a lot of thought to the proposal. "He has asked a young, energetic construction expert, who has already proved his outstanding ability to take charge of the enterprise."

Speer was far from enthusiastic about the proposal; however, his reservations were not on ethical grounds. He had had previous experience with the SS in attempting to produce armaments at the Buchenwald and Neuengamme concentration camps. The programs were dismal failures. Speer and his ministry had taken the blame because they were, after all, in charge of armaments production.

Hitler summed it up as an order. Reichsminister Speer would work with SS Reichsfuehrer Himmler to exploit the manpower available from the concentration camps to build A-4 factories and also to build the A-4 rockets. Hitler abandoned his decree of just six weeks earlier that for security reasons "in this project we can only use Germans."

CHAPTER 13

Rockets Rising from the Ashes

20 AUGUST 1943

On Hitler's orders, Speer and his deputy Saur went to Himmler's headquarters at Hochwald near the Wolf's Lair to work out the details of A-4 production. When they arrived at three in the afternoon, Himmler dropped a bombshell on them—their second major surprise in two days. Hitler had just appointed Himmler minister of the interior. While he had wielded considerable power within the Third Reich as Reichsfuehrer of the SS, Himmler's only legal position within the German state had been as head of the Gestapo, a position theoretically subordinate to then Minister of the Interior Wilhelm Frick. Now, with Frick unceremoniously pushed aside, Himmler was prepared to deal with Speer as more than his equal.

Himmler got down to business: plans for the manufacture of the A-4. "I require a first-class staff of your engineers, who will have to be responsible to both of us for the strict execution of the Fuehrer's orders. On my side, I have assigned Kammler, one of my most capable SS commanders."

Speer recognized the name and remembered the man. He had known Hans Kammler years earlier when Kammler was, according to Speer, "running the construction division" of the Air Ministry. Speer remembered Kammler as a very hard-working bureaucrat, sociable and inconspicuous.

It may have been significant that Kammler, who had been with the Air Ministry, was now Himmler's point man in infiltrating the A-4 program. The Air Ministry, which had given birth to the Luftwaffe, had picked up half of the expense for the initial construction of the facilities at Peenemünde. The

Luftwaffe had, in fact, been in charge of construction. While Kammler may not have involved himself with the day-to-day details of construction, as head of the construction division he undoubtedly knew about the rocket development facility; and, although there is no evidence to prove it, he may have participated in its design. Curiously, Walter Dornberger and Wernher von Braun claimed they first met Kammler when he became involved in the rocket program as Himmler's representative.

While Kammler may have had the prestige of a doctorate in engineering and a high position in the Air Ministry, he was, like all technical people in the Air Ministry, a civilian; and civilians in the Air Ministry were second-class citizens. Field Marshal Erhard Milch, state secretary of the Air Ministry and armaments chief of the Luftwaffe, phrased it succinctly: "After all, engineers are only plumbers of a kind, in white shirts. Plumbing is useful and unavoidable. But all the same no officer would dream of having social intercourse with a plumber, or would he?"

Kammler left behind his status as a civilian and as an employee of the Air Ministry on 9 November 1938. He joined the SS as an Untersturmfuehrer (lieutenant) on the staff of Rasse und Siedlungshauptamt (the SS Central Office of Race and Settlement), the RuSHA. Kammler had gotten his officer's uniform just in time to participate in the carnage of *Krystalnacht*, which took place the night of the day he entered the SS. By 1941 he was chief of Amstgruppe C, the SS Construction Department, and before long he was directing the building of the Third Reich's extermination camps. It is unlikely that Speer knew the details of Kammler's achievements with the SS, his gas chambers and ovens, and his leveling of the Warsaw ghetto, which now qualified him to manage the manufacture of the A-4.

Himmler told Speer that coordination between the SS and the technical groups under Speer's control was critical to success. Such cooperation, he pointedly informed Speer, was Hitler's expressed desire. He then told Speer that Hitler wanted them both to join him at the Wolf's Lair to continue the discussions.

Back at his headquarters, Hitler expounded enthusiastically about using the A-4 against London. He saw the missiles raining down death and terror, forcing the capitulation that the Battle of Britain had failed to achieve three years earlier. Hitler's enthusiasm turned to fantasy as he demanded an absolute minimum of 5,000 rockets in the very near future.

Speer was aghast. He tried to get Hitler to moderate his demands. To put the A-4 into mass production, he said, was like putting a new racing car into mass production. There was no telling what technical problems would come up which would turn the immoderate production schedule into an expensive failure. Furthermore, although he did not say so to Hitler, there was the SS's dismal record on armaments production. If the SS could not successfully use concentration camp labor to manufacture rifles and ammunition, its chances of mass producing this most complex of weapons were slim indeed. Nevertheless, as the meeting ground on into the early evening, Hitler's order to immediately produce thousands of rockets became more entrenched.

"This will be retribution against England," Hitler said. "With this, we will force England to her knees. The use of this new weapon will make any enemy invasion impossible. For the south and southeast of England can now be dominated by us."

21 August 1943

Just in case Speer had not gotten the message at the meeting with Hitler, Himmler put the gist of it in icy clear writing. Himmler informed Speer in a letter that he was formally taking charge of the manufacture of the A-4, that he intended to produce 5,000 rockets in a short time frame, and that he had assigned the project to SS Obergruppenfuehrer (general) Pohl with the SS brigade commander as the responsible project director. He asked Speer to meet personally with Kammler to facilitate the SS's involvement in the rocket's production.

Himmler took more than Speer remembered Hitler giving him at their meeting the day before; but, with Himmler's power growing, there was little that could be done about it. Four months after Himmler first saw the A-4, he had taken control of its production. Speer tried to console himself over his loss of control with the belief that Himmler, by "taking charge," would be taking the responsibility for failure when it inevitably came. He told himself that the responsibilities of managing rocket production would also keep Hans Kammler's ambition in check. Speer was naively unaware that within the SS, Kammler was viewed as his successor.

23 August 1943

The Harz Mountains lie in central Germany southwest of Berlin between the Elbe River to the east and the Wesser River to the west. It is a relatively low mountain range covered with abundant forests and pastures. Its wealth has been found below the ground as well as on its surface. Since the tenth century, its people have burrowed into the earth to extract silver, gold, copper, lead, iron, sulfur, arsenic, and alum; they have quarried marble, granite, and alabaster.

Just three miles northwest of the town of Nordhausen at a village named Niedersachswerfen was a large cavern, a tunnel carved into the heart of the mountain. Sodium sulfate had been mined there for centuries. In 1938 a government-owned company had used the cavern as a motor fuel depot in anticipation of the needs of war. It was secluded, centrally located, and immune to enemy bombing attacks. It would have been exactly what Himmler and his SS needed for their rocket factory, except for the fact that it was too small.

The first train from Buchenwald arrived with 100 prisoners under the malevolent control of the SS. The prisoners were mostly deportees from occupied countries. They were there because they actively opposed the German occupation, or spoke imprudently about their conquerors, or because somebody found it convenient for them to be removed. The prisoners marched into the cavern, which was bare except for a few tents and a sentry box for the SS guards. The tunnel would be the prisoners' home, labor, and life. Their job was to widen the tunnel and drive it through the mountain to a second entrance two miles away. Tools were few. The prisoners dug with their hands for 12-hour shifts, then slept in the subterranean world till their next shift began. The SS guards and the *Kapos* pushed them to their limit in this sunless world.

In the days that followed, more trains arrived from Buchenwald with a flood of slave laborers. A community of misery was formed. The concentration camp under the mountain was given the name "Dora," a woman's name, soft and beautiful. Dora: diminutive of Dorothy, from the Greek meaning "gift of God." The obscene irony of the name given to the hell under the mountain was, no doubt, lost on the SS masters.

27 AUGUST 1943

As the A-4 was entering the final stages of its development and factories were being prepared to manufacture the missile on a large scale, a primary launching site was being built for the inevitable attack on England. The site at Watten near Calais was chosen because it commanded a field of fire from England's southern coast to its eastern coast with London near its center. In addition, the site had excellent access to transportation and electric power. The bunker would be enormous. Its interior was to hold up to 108 missiles and rocket fuel sufficient for three days of operation. The facility was to be cast from a mind-boggling 120,000 cubic meters of concrete. The bunker would be impregnable; the missiles' vulnerability to enemy attack would be minimal. When the bunker went into operation, the rockets would be prepared within its shelter, then rolled out under the open sky moments before being fired.

The English and Americans patiently watched as the Watten bunker was under construction, as the site was excavated, as the forms were put in place, and as the concrete was being poured. Before the concrete work could be finished, the United States Eighth Air Force attacked. On 27 August, 185 Flying Fortresses flew low over the bunker in four waves, dropping 370 tons of bombs. The bunker collapsed like a cake falling in an oven. It was reduced to a useless mass of shattered lumber, twisted steel, and hardening concrete.

Hitler refused to give up the idea of a bunker launching site for the V-2s. The concept was too delicious, too seductive, not to carry through. Plans were soon underway for the construction of a second bunker at a nearby site, in a chalk quarry at Wizernes. The Germans would use a novel construction method to protect the bunker from bombing during its construction. First, they would pour a 20-foot-thick concrete dome on the edge of the 100-foot-deep quarry. Then they would excavate the soft chalk from underneath it to form a maze of tunnels and rooms where the rockets would be prepared for firing. When readied, the rockets would be moved outside to the launching pad through two concrete-lined tunnels and past five-foot-thick bomb-proof steel doors. There would be no way to stop the rockets, no defense against missiles launched from the new bunker.

Once again the Allies watched patiently as the Germans poured enormous effort and materiel into the new bunker at Wizernes.

6 SEPTEMBER 1943

General Walter Dornberger claimed to have first met SS Brigade Commander Hans Kammler on one of his periodic trips to Berlin. From the outset Dornberger was not enthusiastic about having the SS involved in the A-4 project. He had spent ten years developing rockets with the support of the army and a brief involvement of the Luftwaffe. Now that the A-4 could realistically be viewed as a weapon, the other bureaucracies were cutting themselves in for a piece of the action. First, the Ministry of Armaments and Munitions had brought in Degenkolb to direct the manufacture of the weapon the way he had driven the manufacture of locomotives. Now, Himmler's SS was contributing Kammler to supervise construction of the factories that Degenkolb would use. Dornberger could see his control of the rocket program slowly eroding, and he resented the participation of what he considered to be amateurs.

Dornberger's initial favorable impression of Kammler turned sour within minutes. Kammler seemed to be a handsome, virile, captivating personality. Dornberger compared his appearance to that of a romantic hero of the Renaissance. Then Kammler opened his mouth and would not stop talking. Dornberger, who had a forceful personality of his own, could not break through Kammler's monologue. The man told Dornberger how he could be counted on to speak his mind, how much influence he had, what a wonderful human being he was. He was, as Dornberger pointed out, simply incapable of listening. He did not have the time to take in information or to think. His only objective was to command. Don't bother him with the facts, forget the details, just do what you are told.

At the time, Dornberger was thankful that Kammler's authority covered only the construction of factories. He was unaware of Kammler's previous construction achievements for the SS or the agenda that had been laid out for him by Himmler. It did not occur to Dornberger that Kammler was dangerous.

Kammler was already thinking beyond construction to the division of functions that had been under Dornberger's direction at Peenemünde. As a result of the bombing raid by the RAF 19 days earlier, it became prudent, if not imperative, to move the entire rocket operation to sites beyond the range of Allied bombers or to hardened sites within Germany. The Development Works would move to Traunsee in Austria where a cavern would be cut into a mountain. Von Braun's group would have to make do with the vulnerable facilities at Peenemünde for the present, but the Austrian cavern would be big enough for all their future needs. The A-4 manufacturing facility would be placed in a complex of tunnels being cut at that moment under the Harz Mountains in central Germany. Test firings would be conducted over land in an area beyond the range of Allied bombers. The firing range would be located at the SS *Heidelager*, or "health camp," at Blizna in Poland.

According to Kammler's plan, he would build the facilities, and before Dornberger knew it, the SS in the person of Hans Kammler would be in command of Germany's rocket program.

10 SEPTEMBER 1943

By the spring of 1943 when Allied bombers were releasing their loads at will over German armaments factories, Adolph Hitler had developed what Albert Speer described as the "cave fantasy." The only certain way to defend factories from destruction was to put them beyond reach under bomb-proof concrete. Since building the concrete-sheltered factories would take much time—something the Third Reich did not have—Hitler's attention turned to building factories in cellars, nonoperating mines, and large caves.

Hitler's "cave fantasy" obtained a tangible reality at a meeting held at the Wolf's Lair, his East Prussian headquarters. In attendance was his most senior staff including, Goebbels, Goering, Himmler, General Jodl, Armed Forces Chief of Staff Field Marshal Keitel, and Grand Admiral Doenitz. Hitler announced that the first major armaments factory to be placed underground would produce the long-range rocket, the A-4. The factory would be located in a former mine under the Harz Mountains of central Germany. The facility would be known by the uninformative name of the Mittelwerk G.m.b.H., or Central Works, Limited. The Mittelwerk became a formal reality two weeks later as a government-owned company with headquarters in Berlin; it was financed through Speer's ministry with substantial control in the hands of the SS.

SEPTEMBER 1943

Peenemünde's injuries from the air raid were far from fatal, but it began to die nonetheless. To begin with, the housing project, which had sustained extensive damage during the raid, was completely evacuated. Residents were dispersed to the small villages and resort communities that surrounded Peenemünde. There would be no reconstruction of the facilities that had been bombed, at least none that could be seen from the air. Nothing would be done that would alter the aerial photogenicity of the area. The Allies would be allowed to believe that the RAF raid had been a complete and devastating success. Then word came down to Dornberger through official army channels of Kammler's plans for test firing of the A-4. Henceforth, all test firing, especially that by future combat units such as the 444 Experimental Battery, would be done overland from the secure SS *Heidelager* camp at Blizna, Poland. With diminishing responsibilities and opportunities at Peenemünde, key personnel began to slowly drain away.

One of the first to leave was Arthur Rudolph, the 36-year-old engineer who had worked with Max Valier and had been one of the first men hired by Walter Dornberger at Kummersdorf. When the decision was made and presented to Dornberger that rocket production would go underground at the Mittelwerk, he said to Rudolph, "You go with Sawatzki." Sawatzki was Alwin Sawatzki (more common spelling), an engineer who had been enormously successful in directing production of the "Tiger" tank and who had been sent by Degenkolb to Peenemünde to learn all he could about rocket production. Sawatzki would direct all manufacturing in the Mittelwerk, and Rudolph would be his subordinate in charge of A-4 production. Rudolph and his staff dismantled the pilot production plant and shipped it to the underground factory. Many years later, after the underground plant had been assembled, the rockets built, the war lost, and the ghosts of the past had returned to haunt him, Rudolph would observe that he "knew [he] was in a trap" as soon as he arrived at the Mittelwerk. Others were brought into the trap at Rudolph's request. He requisitioned slave laborers from the Dora concentration camp, which was run by the SS, just as he had requested workers for Peenemünde from the SS the preceding June.

Many of Peenemünde's staff went to the test range at Blizna, some followed Rudolph to the Mittelwerk, and others chose voluntarily to find new projects. Having played no significant role in the development of the A-4 and seeing no opportunity to be involved with anything significant, Hermann Oberth requested to be transferred. He had earlier written a proposal for a gunpowder rocket for anti-aircraft defense, and the proposal had been accepted. Oberth moved to the Westfalisch-Anhaltische Springstoff A.G. (Westphalian-Anhaltain Explosives Company), or WASAG, at Reinsdorf in central Germany, where he worked in anonymity with the diminishing resources of the Third Reich on a weapon that would never be completed.

5 NOVEMBER 1943

In the south of Poland the San River flowing northwest meets the Vistula River flowing northeast to form at their confluence a triangle of land. On this triangle was the village of Blizna where the SS located its *Heidelager*, or "health camp," which was to become Hans Kammler's overland rocket-firing range.

Within a forest of pine, fir, and oak was a clearing that covered half a square mile; it was surrounded by two barbed wire fences. A decomposing stone house and thatched stable were the only evidence that, in more peaceful days, the clearing had been someone's home. Now a concrete road and a railroad siding entered the clearing; and barracks, sheds, and a large magazine revealed the presence of the military. Rockets were arriving by rail. The 444 Battery of the army artillery led by Major Weber had arrived from Koeslin near the Baltic. It had test fired a few rockets, but it was still relatively inexperienced. Its charge was to test fire the A-4 under a variety of field conditions.

Winter was making an early appearance. The temperature persisted at 14°F, and the ground was stiff with frost. The men of the 444 Battery placed the firing table on the frozen ground. It was a simple steel frame with four upright supports, one for each fin of the rocket, and a pyramid-shaped blast deflection shield under the rocket motor. The men of the 444 Battery then positioned the A-4 on the table, filled it with fuel, and prepared to launch it.

As fuel poured into the engine chamber, the rocket burst to life. Flames gushed downward out of the motor as thrust increased. They were deflected by the pyramid-shaped shield toward the surrounding ground. The frozen earth melted. One second passed. A leg of the firing table began to sink into the soft underlying soil, but not enough thrust had yet developed to lift the rocket.

Two seconds passed. The firing table continued to subside, and the rocket began to tilt.

Three seconds. The full 59,500 pounds of thrust finally lifted the rocket from the misaligned firing table. The missile rose at a wacky angle, moving faster and faster, drifting out of control farther and farther off course. It disappeared beyond the trees and crashed two miles from the launch site.

General Heinemann of the army, who had been placed in command of field operations of the A-4, was on the scene to watch his first firing of the rocket. The cause of the blundered launch and the means of its correction were perfectly clear to him. Henceforth, all firings of the missile, including those at the frontlines, would be done from concrete platforms even though a jury-rigged foundation of lumber would work just as well.

*   *   *   *

It was bad enough that the initial firings of the A-4 from the Heidelager at Blizna were failures. What made it worse was the presence of an uninvited and unwanted observer, Hans Kammler. As far as Walter Dornberger was concerned, Kammler's only connection with the A-4 project was to build the factory where the rockets would be assembled. Anything else Kammler did was unwarranted interference. Regrettably, the training of field units was not under Dornberger's command, and the test firings were being done at an SS installation. There was no way of escaping Heinrich Himmler's obnoxious protégé. He sat in on conferences and ingratiated himself with the army personnel who were responsible for the test firings. Kammler was following the SS's standard policy of infiltrating any promising enterprise. Today he was learning the basics of rocketry. Tomorrow, who could say?

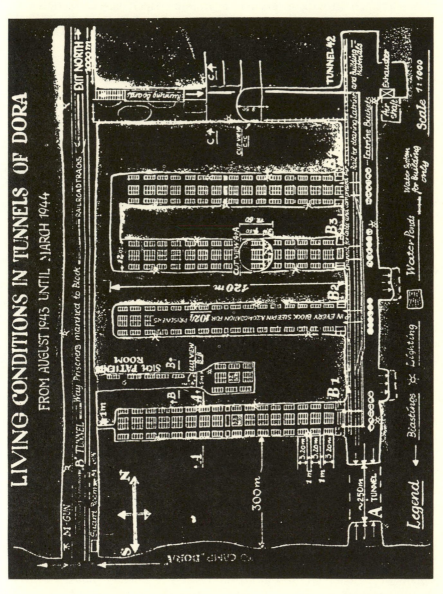

Illustration of the tunnel system of the Mittelwerk rocket factory. (Prosecution Exhibit 23, *United States of America vs. Kurt Andrae et al.*)

CHAPTER 14

The Nazi "Metropolis": A Subterranean Rocket Factory

FALL 1943

They had seen it before on the silent silver screen, and now they were part of it: *Metropolis*.

Two years before Fritz Lang directed and produced *Frau im Mond*, he gave the world a darker view of the future with *Metropolis*. There were two worlds in *Metropolis*. In the brilliant modern city on the surface where all was ruled by the Master, the leisure class lived in luxury. Below them, deep within the bowels of the earth, the city was powered by an army of slaves. The workers, clothed in drab shapeless uniforms with heads bowed and shoulders bent, marched with shuffling feet to their dehumanizing jobs. They fed their lives to the insatiable machines, exhausting shift after exhausting shift. Fritz Lang's perverse utopian vision had become real, but as prophetic as *Metropolis* was, it lacked the inhuman horror that had become incarnate in the subterranean Mittelwerk under the Harz Mountains. If anyone looked beyond the details of the inhumanity and the suffering, the real difference between *Metropolis* and the Mittelwerk was hope. The Master of *Metropolis* ultimately understood his crime and freed his slaves. For the slaves of Dora and the Mittelwerk there was no way out except as smoke.

The underground Mittelwerk factory had expanded rapidly since the arrival of the first 100 workers in late August. Camp Dora, which supplied it with slaves, was still within the complex of tunnels, and it now housed thousands of men. It was no longer a subsidiary camp of Buchenwald, but an independent camp with more inmates arriving daily by rail in what the prisoners called "traveling coffins." The slaves were inventoried and labeled with stereotypical German efficiency. They wore on their twill jackets their identification numbers, and below them colored triangles identifying their offenses to the Reich. The color code was as follows:

red: political prisoners (resisters and Communists)

black: social misfits

green: convicted common criminals

blue: the stateless

violet: conscientious objectors

pink: homosexuals

white: deserters from the Wehrmacht

A letter within the colored triangle gave the prisoner's nationality: A, American; B, Belgian; E, English; F, French, R, Russian; and so forth. Jews wore a yellow star of David inscribed with the word "Jude," though it is unlikely many were sent to Dora while the extermination camps were in operation. The concentration camps were run by the Totenkopfverbande of the SS (the Death's Heads units), with the collaboration of *Kapos* who were drawn from the ranks of the inmates. They wore armbands on the left sleeves of their jackets inscribed with their function. At the Dora concentration camp and the Mittelwerk, the *Kapos* also wore the green triangles of common criminals.

In the tunnels of the Mittelwerk, the conditions which were initially intolerable got worse. Two shifts alternated sleeping in bunks, which were stacked four deep. There were no heat, no ventilation, no sinks, no tubs to bathe in. The food was often soup, usually vile and always insufficient. There was no water. The prisoners found themselves drinking the water that oozed from the rock walls and condensed from the cold, damp air; it collected in muddy puddles on the tunnel floor. The latrines were half barrels with planks laid across their open tops. Not surprisingly, disease ran rampant amid the inescapable filth. Scabies, ulcers, abscesses, gangrene, anemia, and dysentery were the common lot.

Besides the endemic diseases, there was the fear of sudden death. The slaves soon learned that they risked being beaten or murdered by the sadistic SS guards and the *Kapos* for not working fast enough, failing to follow an order, or failing to comply with an order spoken in a language they did not understand. The bodies of those who died of disease or were murdered were stacked like cord wood until they could be loaded onto trains for transport to Buchenwald. Dora did not yet have its own crematorium.

The slaves worked most of their conscious hours. They continued to expand the system of tunnels, and they hauled building materials, railroad tracks, and equipment. They unloaded machinery from a railroad train that entered the far end of the tunnel. They soon learned that the equipment was from some place called Peenemünde and that it was to be used to build secret weapons.

The entire construction operation at the Mittelwerk was under the command of Hans Kammler, and his attitude toward the barbarous conditions in the underground factory was stated concisely in a comment he is reported to have made to one of his subordinates: "No matter the number of human victims, the work must be executed and finished in the shortest possible time."

Dr. A. Poschmann, medical supervisor of the Armaments Ministry, visited the Mittelwerk at this time. A few years later at the Nuremberg war crimes trials, he would describe what he had seen, confirming the reports of inmates who had survived. The slaves, Dr. Poschmann said, "worked a minimum of 72 hours a week, they were fed 1,100 calories a day. Lung and heart disease were epidemic because of the dampness and intense air pressure. Deaths averaged 160 a day. When a deputation of prisoners petitioned for improved conditions, SS Brigadefuehrer Hans Kammler responded by turning machine guns on them, killing 80."

10 December 1943

Even though Albert Speer had joined the Nazi party in early 1931, he viewed himself as being apolitical. He was a technocrat. His job was to run the industry that produced the armaments Germany needed to defend itself. He kept aloof from Hitler's inner circle, and, in later years, he professed his distrust of and contempt for the lot of them. In his own mind, he was not involved in or responsible for the deportation of the Jews. He claimed he carefully avoided learning about their fate: when in 1943 his friend Karl Hanke warned him to stay away from the Polish town of Oswiecim (Auschwitz in German), Speer took the advice. Despite his protest to the contrary, he could not avoid seeing the overwhelming evil.

In early December 1943, Dr. Poschmann reported to Speer that he had seen Dante's Inferno. Poschmann told him about the appallingly unhealthy conditions at the Mittelwerk for which the Ministry of Armaments was partly responsible. Speer was compelled to arrange a tour of the underground rocket factory several days later.

On 10 December the workers of the Mittelwerk knew that something big was about to happen. Inspections were scrupulous and beatings from the SS guards and *Kapos* seemed to double. Rumors spread as fast as the latest disease, but truth, like a cure, was elusive. Amid this great commotion, limousines arrived at the entrance to the cavern and unloaded a group of VIPs. It would be a long time before any of them knew who was inspecting their living hell.

Speer was guided through the subterranean labyrinth alternately by Director Gerhard Degenkolb and Brigadefuehrer Hans Kammler who represented the two parties of the unholy marriage that gave life to the Mittelwerk, the Ministry of Armaments and the SS. Speer recalled seeing "expressionless faces, dull eyes, in which not even hatred was discernible, exhausted bodies in dirty gray-blue trousers. At the approach of our group, they stood at attention upon hearing a cutting command and held their pale blue caps in their hands. They seemed incapable of any reaction. . . . The prisoners were undernourished and overtired; the air in the cave was cool, damp, and stale and stank of excrement. The lack of oxygen made me dizzy; I felt numb."

The tour lasted about one hour. Speer claimed that he ordered the construction of a respectable concentration camp above ground and that he allocated the materials necessary to build a barrack city to house 10,000 workers. Furthermore, he demanded of the SS camp command that they immediately improve the sanitary conditions and the quality of the prisoners' food. The SS officers promised to do so. Speer accepted their word of honor.

The impact of witnessing the conditions of the Mittelwerk for just one hour had a severe impact on several members of Speer's staff who had accompanied him on the site visit. After returning from the concentration camp and factory, they were so severely shaken that they were ordered to take vacations to restore their nerves.

17 DECEMBER 1943

Perhaps Albert Speer had exaggerated his moral outrage at what he had seen at the Mittelwerk, its impact on his staff, or the remedial actions he claims to have set into motion. Perhaps he had a lapse of moral attention. Shortly after his tour of the Mittelwerk, he wrote a letter of commendation to Kammler stating that what had been accomplished under his direction at the cavern under the Harz Mountains was nothing less than sensational. He observed, "In an almost impossible short period of two months, he [transformed] the underground facilities [in the Harz Mountains] from a raw state into a factory." Somehow Speer neglected the contribution of the thousands of slave laborers who worked and died under Kammler's direction. Furthermore, Speer wrote to Kammler that his achievement "does not have an even remotely similar example anywhere in Europe and is unsurpassable even by American standards." Speer meant it as high praise since he greatly admired American methods of production.

31 December 1943–1 January 1944

Alwin Sawatzki had promised the Ministry of Armaments that the Mittelwerk would be producing A-4s by the end of 1943. He told Arthur Rudolph that he wanted 50 missiles in December. Rudolph told Sawatzki that if the underground factory produced five, he would be lucky. Sawatzki told Rudolph that if missiles were not rolling off the assembly line by the end of the year, he could find himself a worker in the underground factory rather than its manager.

Rudolph drove the workers, and estimated that they could finish assembling four A-4s before the tireless clock clicked over into the new year. He was relaxing at a New Year's Eve party with a few close friends when he received a call from the factory. There was a problem. The rockets were essentially completed, but the crew at the plant was having a problem loading them onto camouflaged railway cars. Arthur Rudolph was caught between a demanding boss and slaves who were not doing their jobs. He went out into the snow to make sure he met his deadline.

"It was very cold," he complained when he described the event later, "and I cursed at having to leave the party just to get those missiles out before the end of the year so that their timely delivery could be officially reported."

Rudolph may have been doubly upset at having been torn away from the New Year's Eve party because he knew that the four rockets were junk; there was no point in attempting to make them fly. Quality control had taken second place to getting them out by the end of the year. After the missiles had been logged onto the production list and the Ministry of Armaments had been satisfied that the Mittelwerk was in fact producing A-4s, they were returned to the factory and scrapped.

When the job was done, Arthur Rudolph could go back to his party or to his warm bed with the satisfaction of knowing that the job had been completed, if not done well. The slaves of the Mittelwerk, who actually did the work, who built and loaded the rockets onto the railway cars, did not have the same options. They shuffled back to the cold, filthy bunks of their subterranean world where they could take satisfaction—if they wished—in the fact that they had survived to see another year in hell.

18 JANUARY 1944

Two years as Hitler's minister of armaments, dealing with internal intrigues and constant stress, had taken their toll on Albert Speer. He needed an escape, and he thought he found it in the most remote corner of the dwindling Nazi empire, northern Lapland. He had gone there with his wife to conduct an inspection tour and to fit in a little recreation. He got to see the reality of war, the equipment shortages at the front, and the brutality of winter above the Arctic Circle. After a nocturnal ski tour and a night in a reindeer skin sleeping bag with the outside air at −22°F, he awoke with a sharp pain in his left knee. The pain stayed with him constantly for weeks, and he finally went to a hospital with what he described as a bloody effusion in his knee joint.

On 18 January, Speer enter the Red Cross hospital at Hohenlychen about 60 miles north of Berlin. The hospital was under the direction of Dr. Karl Gebhardt, a noted orthopedist, who had treated many athletes and celebrities. Speer intended to continue working during his hospital stay, and he had a direct telephone line to his ministry in Berlin installed with secretaries quartered in nearby rooms.

At the time Speer entered the hospital, he was unaware that Dr. Gebhardt was a close personal friend of Heinrich Himmler, that Gebhardt held the rank of SS Gruppenfuehrer (lieutenant general), and that the hospital was in reality an SS institution. Speer did not know that his telephone line would be tapped. He did not suspect that Dr. Gebhardt was conducting surgical experiments on prisoners in concentration camps and that, after the war, Gebhardt would be tried at Nuremberg and sentenced to death for his crimes. Speer was unaware that his treatment by Dr. Gebhardt would fall far outside of what was then viewed as standard medical practice and that his condition would get much worse.

25 JANUARY 1944

The A-4, which had appeared to be such a success when built at and fired from Peenemünde, had turned into a disaster when built at the Mittelwerk and fired at Blizna in Poland. Barely 20 percent of the rockets were coming anywhere near hitting their targets.

Walter Dornberger put his analytical mind to the problem and identified three types of failures. Some A-4s would make an apparently normal start and rise 60 feet above the firing table when the rocket engine would prematurely shut off. The rocket with its nearly full load of fuel would fall back to destroy the launch table and all support equipment within a broad radius. Other missiles would rise to between 3,000 and 6,000 feet, then inexplicably explode. Many of those that survived launch and full flight under power detonated on re-entry, showering burnt and twisted scraps of metal over the target area.

Categorizing the types of failures and then identifying and correcting their causes were two different matters. It was a good bet that many of the failures could be laid at the door of the new underground manufacturing plant. Dornberger sent Wernher von Braun on an inspection tour of the Mittelwerk to see what could be done to improve the quality of its product.

What information survives about von Braun's visit is a brief documentary record and the vivid memory of a prisoner. A Frenchman who survived the Mittelwerk, Jean Michel, would record his recollection of the fuss caused by the arrival of a man he would many years later recognize as Wernher von Braun.

Von Braun had first visited the Mittelwerk site in September or October 1943 when it was still being used as an oil storage site. By late January 1944 most of the machinery and equipment was in place, and 10,000 slaves were at work in the subterranean "Metropolis." One can reasonably assume that, on 24 January 1944, von Braun observed the assembly line in operation, that he recommended some actions that would improve the quality of the Mittelwerk's major product, his A-4 rocket, and that he witnessed the same horrors Albert Speer had seen six weeks earlier.

One can only speculate on von Braun's internal reaction. After joining the Nazi party and the SS, after accepting honors and perks from the Nazi regime, after conspiring to subvert his own dream of space exploration to the building of a weapon of mass destruction and terror, after accepting the forced labor of foreign slaves at Peenemünde from the Trassenheide camp, he now faced the atrocities of the Mittelwerk. Granted, if he made too big a fuss about the brutal treatment of the workers, he would run the risk of being sent to join them in building the rocket he had designed. Nevertheless, von Braun chose the course of discretion, silence, and complicity.

Nearly three decades later, Wernher von Braun let his guard down and commented on the underground factory. "I saw Mittelwerk several times," he said, "once while these prisoners were blasting tunnels in there, and it was really a pretty hellish environment. The conditions there were absolutely horrible." This public statement contrasts with one made in a deposition for a 1947 war crimes trial in which he stated that he had been in the underground factory approximately 15 to 20 times. The conditions in the tunnels, he said, were initially extremely primitive; but they were continually improving. Von Braun even listed the improvements, which included adequate lighting and air conditioning.

Von Braun remembered the Mittelwerk as a detached observer. He did not view himself as a participant in its management, and he never even hinted that he felt in any way responsible for the horrors that were committed there.

30 January 1944

Brigadefuehrer Hans Kammler's diligence and success in managing SS construction projects, particularly the construction of the subterranean rocket factory of the Mittelwerk, were rewarded. He was promoted to the rank of SS Gruppenfuehrer (lieutenant general).

February 1944

Wernher von Braun was back at the SS *Heidelager* firing range at Blizna to watch more launches of the A-4. He stood behind a brick wall about 300 yards from the rocket, watching as the engine was fired and the missile lifted from the firing table. A few feet into its flight, the missile exploded into a ball of orange flame. Von Braun fell to the earth and buried his face in the snow behind his crude shelter as torn and twisted pieces of hot metal fell around him like hail.

Once again Walter Dornberger and Wernher von Braun went over the possible causes of the continuing failures, but it did not take a rocket scientist to figure out the cause of the problem. The A-4 was the most technically sophisticated instrument of war that had ever been developed. Expecting it to work perfectly under the pressures of war and under varied field conditions was simply not realistic. Furthermore, although nobody wanted to make an issue of the point, the rockets were being built in a filthy cave by slaves living under barbarous conditions. Not only could the workers be expected to lack interest in producing defect-free rockets, they could be expected to sabotage the weapons every chance they got.

Dornberger sent von Braun back to Peenemünde where he could do some real engineering and, possibly, work out some solutions to the problem of the high failure rate. There was little they could do about getting the slaves at the Mittelwerk to produce better quality rockets. Their motivations and fate were under the control of the SS.

10 FEBRUARY 1944

Albert Speer was in critical condition.

When he had arrived at the Red Cross hospital at Hohenlychen, Dr. Karl Gebhardt immediately prescribed that Speer's ailing left knee be immobilized in a cast. The knee and Speer were further immobilized by confining him to bed. He was allowed to stand again after 20 days on his back; but, within a few hours, he felt intense pain in his chest and back. He was soon coughing up bloody sputum. Ignoring the blood, Dr. Gebhardt diagnosed Speer's attack as muscular rheumatism, and he treated his patient accordingly. Two days later Speer had a second, more severe attack, and Gebhardt stuck to his diagnosis of and treatment for muscular rheumatism.

Speer's wife, Margarete, realizing the seriousness of the situation, went to Dr. Karl Brandt, who was plenipotentiary for hygiene and health and one of Hitler's personal physicians. Brandt immediately dispatched Dr. Friedrich Koch, an internist from Berlin University, to take over Speer's care. When Dr. Koch arrived at Hohenlychen on the night of 10 February, he found Speer's condition to be "distinctly critical: extreme respiratory difficulty, intense blue coloration, considerable acceleration of the pulse, high temperatures, painful cough, muscular pain, and bloody sputum. The development of the symptoms could be interpreted only as the result of embolism." Thrombosis and pulmonary embolism were, as Speer was to learn later, hazards of long periods of bed rest such as he had endured.

While the doctors were preparing his wife for the worst, Speer himself was euphoric. He was free of the systematic mistreatment of Dr. Gebhardt, and he hallucinated that his depressing room had been transformed into a magnificent hall. Speer lingered near death for three days, then he returned to the living and to his anxieties. He desperately wanted to leave the oppressive hospital at Hohenlychen.

With the backing of Hitler's personal physician, Dr. Karl Brandt, Dr. Koch was able to hold Gebhardt at bay until Speer's crisis passed. Dr. Koch then began looking for a way to get his patient out of the SS clinic and away from Dr. Gebhardt, who had nearly killed him.

OFFICE OF MILITARY GOVERNMENT FOR GERMANY (U. S.)
APO 742

FILE NO: DC/20779/158 T
SUBJECT: NSDAP Records Check

NO.	TO	FROM	DATE	(Has this been coordinated with all concerned?)
1	S-2 BC	7771 Doc. Ctr.	23 Apr 47	Att'n.: Capt Hirsch

1. Reference telephone conversation this date.

2. The following information is certified as being a true extract from original Nazi party records in the custody of this Center:

Dr. phil. Wernher von BRAUN
Born: 23 Mar 1912 at Wirsitz
Occupation: Technischer Leiter & Professor
      d. Heeresversuchsanstalt Peene-
      muende
Party-No.: 5738692
Entered Party: 1 May 1937
SS-No.: 185068 ("Wiederaufnahme"1 May 1940)
Untersturmfuehrer 1 May 1940
Obersturmfuehrer 9 Nov 1941
Hptsturmf.   9 Nov 1942
Sturmbannf.   28 Jun 1943
Assigned: Stab Oberabschnitt Ostsee
8 Semesters Technische Hochschule & University
majored in Techn. Physik (studied in Switzer-
land: March/Sept 1931).
Military Service (Luftwaffe) 1.5.36 – 15.6.38
Flugzeugfuehrerschule Frankfurt/Oder & Stolp.

FOR THE COMMANDING OFFICER:

KURT ROSENOW
US- Civilian
Chief of Branch

Tel.: 44 344

168

(Page No.)

Wernher von Braun's membership in the Nazi party, ranks held in the SS, and service in the Luftwaffe are summarized in a document from the Office of Military Government for Germany (U.S.) (from U.S. Army von Braun FOI file, p. 168).

CHAPTER 15

Dangerous Occupations: Rockets and Politics in the Third Reich

21 FEBRUARY 1944

Heinrich Himmler summoned Wehrner von Braun by telephone to meet with him at his headquarters at Hochwald in East Prussia. Von Braun's boss, Army General Walter Dornberger, was not invited. In his account of the meeting, von Braun claimed to have entered Himmler's office with considerable trepidation. Despite his benign appearance, Himmler was, in von Braun's words, "as mild-mannered a villain as ever cut a throat."

Himmler got right to the point. "I hope you realize that your A-4 rocket has ceased to be a toy, and that the whole German people eagerly await the mystery weapon. As for you, I can imagine that you've been immensely handicapped by Army red tape. Why not join my staff? Surely you know that no one has such ready access to the Fuehrer, and I promise you vastly more effective support than can those hidebound generals."

Himmler had reason to believe that his guest would be receptive to his offer. He was, no doubt, familiar with the contents of von Braun's dossier, which listed the following:

SS No.: 185068
Untersturmfuehrer (SS second lieutenant) 1 May 1940
Obersturmfuehrer (SS lieutenant) 9 November 1941
Hauptsturmfuehrer (SS captain) 9 November 1942
Sturmbannfuehrer (SS major) 28 June 1943

Von Braun's dossier may have even recorded that his association with the SS dated back to 1933, when he had enrolled in the SS riding school in Berlin. His record was one of rapid advancement and continued honor. It had reached a peak eight months earlier when von Braun was promoted to SS major on the day of Himmler's most recent inspection tour of Peenemünde and, although not documented, it is probable that Himmler personally conferred on von Braun his new rank.

Von Braun also knew that Himmler's offer of support to build the A-4 rocket was not an idle promise; his SS was driving its production at the Mittelwerk in a way the army never could.

While von Braun claimed a greater obligation to the German Army than to the SS, he could also see that Himmler's offer was one without a future. Himmler had made a crude attempt to divide and conquer the German Army's rocket development team. Himmler's next moves, if von Braun joined his staff, were obvious. Dornberger would be forced out; and von Braun would be shoved into a secondary position, probably subordinate to SS construction chief Hans Kammler. If von Braun then objected to serving Himmler through Kammler, he would be fired.

"Herr Reichsfuehrer," von Braun answered Himmler, "I couldn't ask for a better chief than General Dornberger. Such delays as we're still experiencing are due to technical troubles and not to red tape. You know, the A-4 is rather like a little flower. In order to flourish, it needs sunshine, a well-proportioned quantity of fertilizer, and a gentle gardener. What I fear you're planning is a big jet of liquid manure! You know, that might kill our little flower."

Himmler answered von Braun's crude rejection of his offer with a sardonic smile. Then he changed the subject. After a few minutes, Himmler dismissed von Braun with what the rocket engineer described as entirely feigned politeness. Von Braun naively thought the issue had been closed, that Himmler had accepted his "no" as an answer.

15 MARCH 1944

Three weeks after his meeting with Himmler, Wernher von Braun was awakened at three o'clock in the morning by three men who introduced themselves as agents of Himmler's Gestapo. They arrested him and took him to the Gestapo prison in Stettin, the major city nearest Peenemünde. They did not tell him the charges that would be brought against him but, as the Jews and dissidents of Germany had learned, charges were an irrelevant formality. If Gestapo justice took its usual clandestine course, von Braun's destination would be a concentration camp, possibly Dora, where slaves were building his A-4 missiles.

Von Braun was not alone. The Gestapo had also arrested two of Peenemünde's senior engineers, Klaus Riedel and Helmut Groettrup, as well as von Braun's younger brother Magnus. They also arrested Hannes Luehrsen, chief architect of Peenemünde, and Luehrsen's wife and mother, who were all friends of the rocket scientists.

*   *   *   *

The ringing of the telephone on Walter Dornberger's bedside table woke him in the early morning hours. At the other end of the line was General Buhle, the army's representative to the Oberkommando der Wehrmacht (High Command of the Armed Forces), the OKW, at Hitler's headquarters in Berchtesgaden. Dornberger was ordered to come to Berchtesgaden immediately for a meeting with Field Marshal Keitel.

Dornberger was at his quarters in Schwedt, 50 miles northeast of Berlin. Berchtesgaden was over 400 miles to the south. Dornberger's driver guided his Opel through late winter snowstorms, over icy roads, and around the previous night's air raid damage in Munich. He arrived late in the afternoon, and went to the accommodations arranged for him at the Berchtesgadener Hof. He immediately called General Buhle to announce his arrival. General Buhle came to Dornberger's room to speak to him.

Buhle told Dornberger that Wernher von Braun, Klaus Riedel, and Helmut Groettrup had been arrested for sabotage of the A-4 project. They were in jail in Stettin. Dornberger was stunned. He wanted details. Buhle said that he would have to wait until the following morning when Field Marshal Keitel would give him more information.

The news of the arrests churned through Dornberger's mind like worms in a compost heap. Von Braun, Riedel, and Groettrup were in very serious trouble, and the future of the A-4 project was tied to their fate. How could the missile ever become operational without von Braun, the chief engineer who brought it into being? The program could not handle the loss of Klaus Riedel, who had worked out the entire ground support system for firing the missile, or Helmut Groettrup, Steinhoff's deputy in the telemetry department. The very importance of the men to the project argued against the charges of sabotage. Dornberger had worked with von Braun for ten years and never doubted his energy and devotion to the A-4. The rocket was von Braun's dream. It made no sense that he or the other engineers would sabotage their creation. Dornberger would have to wait through a nearly sleepless night before he could hear an explanation of who had made the accusations and why.

16 MARCH 1944

Dornberger met with Field Marshal Keitel at 9 A.M. Wernher von Braun, Klaus Riedel, and Helmut Groettrup had been under arrest for over 30 hours.

Keitel repeated to Dornberger what he already knew, that the engineers had been arrested by the Gestapo. The charges against them, in Keitel's estimation, were so serious that arrests were inevitable; it was likely that they would pay for the allegations with their lives.

Dornberger protested. He conceded that he did not know the specific charges, but he vouched for von Braun and Riedel. He knew Groettrup less well, and was not as willing to back the man.

Keitel went on to tell Dornberger that his engineers had been overheard to say when they were in Zinnowitz, just south of Peenemünde, that they had no intention of making their rockets into weapons for war. They were working for the army only because it supported the development of rockets, which they wanted as vehicles for space travel. Sabotage was seen in the fact that the engineers were giving their hearts and souls to space travel and, consequently, were not giving their full attention and energy to the development of the weapon Germany desperately needed.

So there it was in all its ridiculous, stupid malevolence. Von Braun and many of his engineers had fantasized about space travel since they were teenagers shooting off toys at the *Raketenflugplatz* on the outskirts of Berlin. Now the Gestapo had converted this fascination into a justification for the arrests.

Dornberger protested to Keitel that the arrests would do irreparable harm to the project, especially in view of the technical problems it still needed to solve. Keitel answered that there was nothing he could do about it. Himmler was in charge of the situation.

Himmler had been actively pursuing control of the rocket program ever since he had first seen the A-4 at Peenemünde nearly a year earlier. If he succeeded in prosecuting von Braun and the engineers, he could run the army's program by intimidation, if not by actual authority. Dornberger had to confront Himmler, who commanded both the SS and the Gestapo.

Dornberger challenged Keitel, reminding him that civilians working at Peenemünde were subject to military law; the Gestapo had no authority at a military base. Keitel stood firm, refusing to interfere in the Gestapo's activities.

Dornberger then asked permission to take his demand for the release of his men to the authority in charge: Himmler. Keitel called Himmler's office to arrange an appointment for Dornberger to present his case. Himmler refused to see Dornberger, and Dornberger was referred to the chief of the Gestapo, SS Obergruppenfuehrer (general) Kaltenbrunner, at his office in Berlin.

Before Dornberger left Berchtesgaden, Field Marshal Keitel asked him to treat what had been said between them in the strictest confidence. After all, said the chief of the armed forces High Command, the highest ranking military officer in Germany, people were watching him, waiting for him to make a mistake.

17 MARCH 1944

It was 11:00 A.M. Wernher von Braun and the others had been in the Gestapo jail in Stettin for over two days. General Walter Dornberger had traveled almost a thousand miles by automobile over ice-glazed roads, through snowstorms and the destruction of war, and he had accomplished nothing.

Dornberger was now accompanied by his chief of staff, Lieutenant Colonel Thom. When dealing with the Gestapo or the SS it was wise to have an entourage or at least a witness. They walked into the SS Security head office on Prinz Albrecht Strasse in Berlin. The building had taken a beating from Allied bombs. Some areas were boarded up, others had shattered windows and crumbled plaster. Dornberger felt the building was uncomfortably cold, but his impression might have been a visceral reaction to the business carried out there.

Dornberger intended to take his case to SS General Ernst Kaltenbrunner, chief of the Gestapo. Kaltenbrunner was not available. Dornberger had to settle for a meeting with SS Gruppenfuehrer (lieutenant general) Heinrich Mueller, Kaltenbrunner's subordinate and Himmler's second assistant thug.

Later, when he thought about the encounter, all Dornberger could remember of SS General Mueller were his eyes. They were gray-blue, piercing, cold. They watched him closely, analytically.

Dornberger asked for the immediate release of his men. Mueller countered that thay had not been arrested; they were being held in protective custody. Dornberger did not see the difference. He wanted them freed immediately.

Mueller gulped. Apparently he was not accustomed to challenges to the Gestapo's actions, but he adjusted. He asked Dornberger to present his case.

It was simple, Dornberger said. The three men in "custody" were the key technical people in the A-4 project. They were essential to bringing the missile to operational status—no engineers: no rockets. Dornberger went on to tell of their enthusiasm for space travel and to explain that it in no way conflicted with development of the rocket as a weapon.

There was nothing he could do, Mueller said. The investigation had just begun, and he had not seen any of its results. He would, however, brief the chief of the Gestapo, Kaltenbrunner. Maybe the investigation could be speeded up.

Dornberger had not had any contact with von Braun, Riedel, and Groettrup since their arrest. He asked permission to see them at the prison in Stettin. Mueller granted the request.

Mueller then changed the subject to his visitor. His cold eyes, like icicles, stabbed holes through Dornberger. He told him of the thick file of evidence the Gestapo had gathered against him.

Dornberger asked why the Gestapo did not arrest him also.

Mueller said the time had not yet come; Dornberger was still viewed as Germany's leading rocket expert.

Dornberger told Mueller that his threat of criminal proceedings would not make him happy in his work. Then he got up and left. His only achievement in his meeting with SS General Mueller was getting the last word.

18 MARCH 1944

The wreath of flowers was enormous. It barely squeezed through the doorway under the guidance of the man struggling to keep both himself and the garland upright. It was a gesture of esteem from Adolf Hitler to Albert Speer.

With the aid of his personal physician, Dr. Koch, Speer had left the Red Cross's Hohenlychen Hospital run by Dr. Gebhardt to continue his convalescence near Salzburg in Austria. That day, he had taken up residence on the grounds of Klessheim Palace in the baroque building called the Cloverleaf Palace. Coincidentally, the Fuehrer was also at Klessheim Palace negotiating with Admiral Horthy, the regent of Hungary, for the peaceful capitulation of his country. During a break in the negotiations, Hitler crossed from the main palace to visit his minister of armaments; and he brought with him the absurd, enormous wreath.

It had been ten weeks since they had seen each other, and Speer felt distant from his patron not only in time but also in spirit. Speer was exhausted. He was crumbling under the pressure, the demands, and the reprimands; and his protracted illness added to his depression. He wanted to go back home to his wife and children. Let Hitler and his cronies run the Third Reich—for however long it lasted—and he would re-think his life.

They exchanged pleasantries. Speer found Hitler to be surprisingly cordial. Despite his desire to leave it all, Speer could not resist the opportunity to manage a problem that should have been under his control. He asked why the rocket scientists from Peenemünde, von Braun, Riedel, and Groettrup, had been arrested.

Hitler answered that they had violated Speer's directive by giving peacetime projects precedence over war productions. They had given the fantasy of space travel precedence over development of the desperately needed weapons of vengeance.

Speer explained that the three men were high spirited and naive, but they were not saboteurs or traitors. He asked Hitler to get them released. Hitler agreed, but he claimed that releasing the men would take a great deal of effort on his part. He also agreed that von Braun was to be "protected from all prosecution as long as he is indispensable, difficult though the general consequences arising from the situation" were.

A few hours after Hitler left, Speer received a telephone call from Himmler. Hitler, Himmler said, had ordered that Speer's chosen physician, Dr. Koch, was no longer in charge. Hitler had also ordered that Dr. Gebhardt, in his capacity as a physician, take over the responsibility for Speer's health. In his capacity as an SS group leader, Gebhardt would also be responsible for Speer's safety. Dr. Gebhardt lost no time in assigning a squad of SS guards to "protect" Speer.

Late MARCH 1944

Wernher von Braun spent two weeks in the Gestapo's jail in Stettin without being told of the charges against him. When he was finally brought up for a hearing, it was not before a civil court, but before a court of SS officers. The courtroom was small. There were no lawyers, jury, or spectators. There were only a panel of judges in SS uniforms and Walter Dornberger.

After his unsatisfactory meeting with General Mueller at SS Security headquarters, Walter Dornberger had taken his case to the Counterintelligence Department of the High Command, where he pressed the issue that security at Peenemünde was a military responsibility and not a concern of the SS. He swore under oath that von Braun and the two engineers were essential to the success of the A-4 rocket project. Apparently, Dornberger was unaware of Speer's intercession with Hitler for the release of his men. Now he was finally going to see the ugly business settled, albeit before an SS court.

As expected, the SS tribunal accused von Braun of sabotaging the A-4 project by giving precedence to his dreams of space travel over weapon development. SS spies ostensibly sent to protect the rocket program had overheard comments he made at a party in Zinnowitz, where he, Riedel, Groettrup, and his brother Magnus had speculated on applications of rocket power. The party had been hosted by their friend Hannes Luehrsen and his family, which accounted for their arrests. Furthermore, the court accused von Braun of keeping an aircraft in readiness to fly himself and a treasure of rocket-related documents to England. It was true that he had access to an airplane, a bright blue Messerschmitt 108 Taifun that was on loan from the Luftwaffe. He had regularly piloted the single-engine light plane on business trips throughout Germany with no intention of defecting. Nevertheless, the ghost of Rudolf Hess, Hitler's deputy who had inexplicably flown to England in search of an alliance against Russia three years earlier, haunted the SS and further justified von Braun's arrest.

When the SS court finished reading the charges against von Braun, Dornberger presented the presiding officer with an official-looking document. The man read the paper and immediately ordered von Braun's release. Von Braun left with Dornberger, who had brought along a large bottle of brandy to celebrate the occasion.

Although von Braun and the others were freed, they were to be kept on short leashes. They were freed provisionally for three months, at which time Dornberger renewed his declaration that his men were essential, and the provisional release was renewed for another three months. By the time the second three-month period ended, the SS and Military Counterintelligence had bigger problems on their hands and let the case of the rocket scientists lapse. While on the surface it might appear that they had won the battle, the war was not over. Himmler, through his arbitrary arrests, had made their lives a Kafkaesque drama for two weeks. Himmler could do it again, and with his power growing and Speer's waning, future arrests might lead to a concentration camp or worse.

It is probable that von Braun's arrest by the Gestapo and his mock trial by an SS court had a profound effect on his political perspective. Whatever duty he may have had to the Reich as a Nazi party member and whatever obligation he may have felt to the SS as an honorary member of its ranks were likely to have been canceled by his treatment. Furthermore, his arrest and the charges made against him gave him credibility as an enemy of the Nazis and as one who put the exploration of space ahead of the development of weapons. While neither description was accurate, both would serve him well when the war was over.

CHAPTER 16

The Business of Death

6 MAY 1944

The Mittelwerk was not delivering A-4 missiles according to its production schedule. A major bottleneck was the manufacture of steering mechanisms to guide the rockets on the initial powered segment of their flights. Something more productive than finger pointing had to be done to address the problem.

The general director of the underground factory, Georg Rickhey, chaired a meeting at Nordhausen to find solutions. Among the 28 men who attended the meeting were Walter Dornberger, Wernher von Braun, Ernst Steinhoff, the director of Guidance and Control, Arthur Rudolph, the chief operations director of the underground factory, and SS Sturmbannfuehrer (major) Otto Forschner, commandant of the Dora concentration camp.

Alwin Sawatzki, who was production planner of the Mittelwerk and Rudolph's superior, had for some time complained about the labor shortage at the factory. He had requested of the SS and Lieutenant General Kammler 1,800 more skilled workers to bring production back onto schedule.

SS Major Otto Forschner suggested filling the labor deficit with about 800 Frenchmen. They would be technical specialists, some of them professors of engineering and physics, who would understand the subtleties of the weapon they were to build. Of course, Forschner pointed out, "French workers can only be used if they are clothed." In the parlance of the SS, "clothed" meant that the men would wear the striped uniforms of concentration camp inmates. Forschner was proposing to round up and exploit French political prisoners.

The conditions under which the men would live was no secret to anybody present. Wernher von Braun on his many visits to the underground factory had seen the hell that Kammler and the SS had created. Arthur Rudolph would comment later, "I knew that people were dying." Yet, apparently neither of them objected to the proposal to enslave skilled Frenchmen and work them to death building rockets.

According to the minutes of the meeting, "Major-General Dornberger expressed the hope that this new co-operation would now continue; Germans should keep in mind that the object was to fight the enemy, not each other." The cooperation—both new and old—turned out to be substantial. Both Dornberger and von Braun later estimated that before the A-4 was finally approved for mass production at the Mittelwerk, over 65,000 modifications had been made to its design. The German engineers who ran the factory had to supervise putting every one of these changes into place. The SS also held up their end of the partnership. Within a month after the meeting, over 1,000 French prisoners arrived at Dora to work in the rocket factory; more than 700 of them would die there.

8 MAY 1944

Albert Speer wanted to quit, to give up the battles he knew were lost. He had been away from his office for three and a half months, and during that time he had watched his authority within the Third Reich challenged and eroded. The turning point came not because of the constant inroads made by Himmler and his SS but because of treachery from within his own organization.

Hitler had proposed to remove all construction projects from Speer's ministry, and place them under the control of Speer's deputy, Xavier Dorsch, who would then report directly to the Fuehrer. Hitler wanted Dorsch to supervise construction of a complex of underground factories similar to the Mittelwerk rocket factory. Speer had found such long-range construction projects pointless, believing that German industry would be bombed to oblivion before the caverns were ready. Furthermore, Speer had learned that Dorsch was the Nazi party's secret liaison man in the Ministry of Armaments; Dorsch had betrayed Speer's trust.

On 19 April, Speer had written to Hitler stating at length his objections to Hitler's plans for construction. He concluded the letter with an offer of his resignation if the Fuehrer did not see things his way. That same day

Speer had telephoned Goering, requesting that Goering ask Hitler to dismiss him. On 23 April, he had asked his good friend Luftwaffe Field Marshal Milch to tell Hitler of his intention to resign. Hitler apparently ignored Speer's suggestions, and Speer did not follow through on his half-hearted attempts to resign.

Eventually Hitler did an about-face and left nominal control of construction with Speer, though in reality Dorsch held the power. Now, on 8 May 1944, with his excuse for resigning taken from him and Hitler not inclined to dismiss him, Speer returned to his office in Berlin. Much as he protested, he could not separate himself from the corruptions of power. He would continue to play the role of minister of armaments while his authority, his relationship with Hitler, and the Third Reich all continued their decline.

Late Spring 1944

As the A-4 rockets were being assembled at the Mittelwerk, fuels to power them were being produced at several sites in the Nazi realm. Ethyl alcohol was a relatively simple matter. It was made by the age-old process of fermenting grain or potatoes, then distilling the mash to get the pure fuel. The second fuel, oxygen, was condensed out of air. Producing liquid oxygen was not a complicated business; but keeping it was, since it boils at $-183°C$. Because huge amounts of liquid oxygen would have evaporated during shipment, fuel production and rocket-motor-testing facilities were consolidated into the same site for efficiency.

One of the first fuel production and rocket-motor-testing facilities to be built was at the Redl-Zipf brewery in Austria. In addition to Zipfer beer, the brewery produced ethyl alcohol. A liquid oxygen manufacturing plant was built nearby, in a tunnel 100 feet below the surface. Above the tunnel, but still below ground, was a workshop where rocket motors were examined before being tested. Above that, on the surface, were the rocket engine test stands. The entire complex of oxygen plant, workshops, and test stands was connected and serviced by an elevator shaft.

Bad site planning, leaky plumbing, and managerial incompetence made the Redl-Zipf plant a disaster waiting to happen. Alcohol spilled in the test stand area or leaking from cracked pipes regularly flowed down the elevator shaft, filling the lower levels with highly flammable liquid and vapor. The inevitable explosion wrecked the plant and killed all 27 persons working in the complex.

The disaster at Redl-Zipf would have been lost among the greater tragedies of the war had it not been for the fact that one of the 27 workers killed was Ilse Oberth, the 20-year-old second daughter of Hermann and Mathilde Oberth. The war had taken Oberth's son Julius earlier, and now it had taken a second child. To make the loss doubly bitter, it was an extension of his own research and invention that had caused her death.

31 MAY 1944

Walter Dornberger's control over the A-4 project was beginning to erode. The support he had sought from the Ministry of Armaments had turned into a competitive relationship with Speer's appointee in charge of missile production, Gerhard Degenkolb. The appearance of Hans Kammler as the builder of the Mittelwerk rocket factory further weakened Dornberger's position. Then, the multiple attacks by Himmler and his SS on Zassen and von Braun had nearly taken away from him his two most valuable subordinates at Peenemünde. Now, the army was developing new plans for Peenemünde which did not include him. If he did not do something to re-establish his priority over the A-4 project quickly, all would be lost.

Dornberger sent a memorandum to his direct superior, Colonel General Fromm, head of the Home Army, specifically demanding that he, Dornberger, be given what he had spent 14 years working for and what he believed he deserved. He wanted unequivocal authority over all aspects of the A-4 program, which included development, testing, manufacture, training, and deployment.

Fromm answered Dornberger with a reprimand for his impertinence. The insult was compounded the following day with the injury of the army's decision to turn the Peenemünde establishment into a government-owned, private company.

6 JUNE 1944

When the inevitable day arrived, the German defenses were caught unprepared. The first reports of British and American paratroopers landing in Normandy arrived just after 1:00 A.M.; at 1:30 A.M. the general alarm was sounded. The German generals recognized it for what it was, the beginning of the invasion; but they viewed the action at Normandy as a feint. The main thrust of the invading force was expected at Calais. By dawn Normandy was being pounded by big navy guns, and troops were flooding ashore at three beachheads.

By the time the generals realized that the main force of the invasion was concentrated at Normandy, the Allied forces had penetrated inland from two to six miles. The generals frantically called the High Command at Berchtesgaden for permission to commit two panzer divisions to the fight. The Fuehrer refused permission until he could see what developed, then he went to bed. When he arose at 3:00 in the afternoon, he gave permission for the panzer divisions to join the battle. With the commitment of the additional troops, he gave an impossible order: "The beachhead must be cleaned up by no later than tonight."

13 JUNE 1944

The A-4 that lifted off from Peenemünde was a unique creation. It was being used as a test bed for a radio control guidance system that had been developed for the Wasserfall anti-aircraft rocket. It had a full load of fuel but no warhead. As the missile climbed, a man on the ground directed its flight with a joystick control device. The rocket punched into a high layer of clouds, disappearing from the view of the crew that had launched it and from its ground controller. The test of the guidance system was judged a success, and gravity was left to deal with the now unseen rocket.

About five minutes after liftoff and over 100 miles to the north, the rocket disintegrated in an airburst several thousand feet above the southern countryside of neutral Sweden. Torn sheet metal, twisted pipes, and fragments of electronic gear rained down over a wide area. The Swedish Home Guard swept up as much of the debris as they could find and hauled it off to Stockholm.

The Swedes apparently complained about being bombarded, and Hitler's headquarters called Walter Dornberger for an explanation.

Could the fragments of the rocket be used to deduce how it worked, to infer its size and performance characteristics?

Dornberger answered that it was possible.

Could the missile be reconstructed to an extent that would let the Allies develop a defense against it?

Dornberger thought not. Furthermore, he added, the remnants of the Wasserfall guidance system might lead the Allies astray.

Hitler was not satisfied, and summoned Dornberger to his headquarters at Rastenburg in East Prussia for a reprimand. By the time Dornberger arrived, however, Hitler's temper had cooled. Dornberger was relieved that the Fuehrer no longer wanted to see him. Apparently Hitler had decided that there was merit in letting the Swedes know that Germany could bombard them from a distance. This knowledge might soften up their stance in negotiations.

Before long, word of the strange object crashing in Sweden reached the Allies, and a delegation was sent to Stockholm to crate up the remains of the wayward rocket and return them to London. At about the same time, fragments of A-4s that had been fired from the *Heidelager* site at Blizna in Poland and collected by the underground Polish Home Army also arrived in London. British intelligence experts sifted through the rubble and came up with a picture of the new German weapon. They deduced the basic concept of how the liquid-fueled rocket worked but grossly overestimated the size of the weapon and its explosive warhead. They concluded that the rocket carried a warhead of six to eight tons, significantly greater than the actual weight of one ton. They also inferred an attempt at great accuracy from the radio guidance system found in the wreckage of the rocket that landed in Sweden. While many of the particulars were wrong, the major inescapable conclusion was correct: the Allies and especially London would soon be facing a very dangerous weapon.

16 JUNE 1944

The time had come for Germany to take the offensive. The attack of the "wonder weapons" was to be massive and without mercy. In the first wave of the attack, several hundred Fieseler Fi 103 "flying bombs," each carrying 1,874 pounds of high explosives, would be launched from 55 catapults in France. The attacks would continue day after day, and the result would be devastating. The flying bombs would bring to London terror on a scale that had not been seen even during the Blitz. They would sow confusion and paralysis, and would, ultimately, bring capitulation.

Things went wrong from the beginning. The Allies had observed the launch sites under construction and made them the targets of heavy bombardment. Many had sustained damage, and very few catapults were operational. None of them had been tested. Essential equipment had not arrived, and fuel for the catapults and the flying bombs was not available. The hour of the attack was postponed, then postponed again. When it finally came at 3:00 A.M., the 55 launch sites were able to catapult only ten flying bombs. Four of these crashed on take-off and two more disappeared harmlessly into the English Channel.

The four surviving weapons buzzed through the night at 400 miles per hour with Tower Bridge as their destination. When their fuel was spent, they fell back to earth. The first struck Gravesend on the Thames estuary, 20 miles east of its target. The others fell on Chuckfield, Bethnal Green, and

Sevenoaks, all wide of the mark. Only the bomb that hit Bethnal Green caused casualties, killing six and destroying a railway bridge.

Joseph Goebbels' Ministry of Propaganda made the best of a lackluster performance. In reporting the attack on London, it renamed the flying bomb Vergeltungswaffen-1 (Vengeance Weapon-1), or simply V-1.

17 JUNE 1944

Field Marshal Erwin Rommel had been awake for over 24 hours. When he returned to his headquarters after a 21-hour tour of the front at Normandy, he received the message to report to Battle Headquarters "W II" at Margival, five miles east of Soissons, for a meeting with Hitler. It was 3:00 A.M., and Battle Headquarters "W II" was 140 miles to the rear. Rommel had to leave immediately without making any preparations.

The complex of bunkers at Margival had been built to be the Fuehrer's headquarters during the invasion of England, which had been scheduled for the summer of 1940. Hitler was finally using it. He had come to the western front—or at least to France—to consult with his officers at the scene on how to deal with the Allied invasion.

Rommel, as commander in chief of the invasion front, lectured Hitler on the desperate state of affairs. The German forces were overwhelmed in the air, on the sea, and on land. They were fighting bravely but were doomed if they followed Hitler's orders to give no ground. Rommel demanded approval to fight the battle according to the needs of the hour.

Hitler would have none of it. The turning point had arrived, he asserted, and the Allies would soon be in disarray. The "vengeance weapons," which had been put into use the previous day, were unerringly finding their way to London, bringing with them terror and death. They would be decisive against Great Britain. They would demoralize the enemy and make him sue for peace.

At this point Hitler interrupted the conference to dictate a communiqué to a member of the German press announcing the first use of the V-1 buzz bomb. Hitler had told Rommel that the vengeance weapon would be decisive, and he would tell the German people the same thing through their newspapers and radio.

When Hitler returned to the conference, Rommel proposed that the V-1s be aimed at the Allied beachhead at Normandy, where they might have an immediate effect on the invasion. Artillery General Heinemann, commanding general of the V-weapons, disagreed. He pointed out that the V-1 could not be counted on to fall within nine to 12 miles of its target. A V-1 aimed at the attacking force at Normandy would be as likely to fall on German troops as on the enemy. It needed a target at a safe distance and as big as London.

Rommel was getting nowhere. His only chance of making the Fuehrer see reality was to get him closer to the front where he could talk directly with the field commanders. It was common knowledge that Churchill had already visited the British troops at their beachhead; the Fuehrer should do no less. Hitler finally, reluctantly, agreed to visit the front two days later. The conference ended at 4:00 P.M., and Rommel wearily left to return to his field headquarters.

*   *   *   *

The V-1 shot off its catapult into the French sky. It was on a dead-reckoning flight aimed at London. The flight of the wonder weapon should have taken it over the channel and across the cliffs of Dover. But its gyroscopic stabilizer was humming slightly out of tune, and mile by mile, degree by degree, its direction drifted until it had turned around and was once again over France.

The errant V-1 landed on Battle Headquarters "W II" at Margival. A ton of high explosives quaked through the bunkers. The structures held; there were no casualties, but Hitler was badly shaken. It was the closest he had come to death in the whole bloody exercise of the war. He never went to Rommel's field headquarters as he had agreed. He never did get firsthand knowledge of the situation at Normandy, and he never rescinded his futile order for the German troops to stand and fight the invaders. Hitler ordered his entourage to pack. They left for Germany and did not stop until they reached Berchtesgaden.

Hitler's comment on his excursion to France was said without intended irony: "Rommel has lost his nerve; he's become a pessimist. In these days only optimists can achieve anything."

22 JUNE 1944

The division of responsibility in the underground Mittelwerk factory was clear, but some people were taking actions that were beyond their authority. When German civilian employees came to the Mittelwerk, they were instructed that they were only to supervise construction of the rockets; the SS was in charge of the *Haeftlinge*, the prisoners. Civilians were not to speak to the prisoners about matters other than their work; they were not allowed to discipline the prisoners; and they were to lodge any complaints against the prisoners with the *Haeftlinge* office, which was located within the tunnels. A civilian employee of the *Haeftlinge* office would then relay these complaints to the SS.

The SS did not rely solely on the civilian employees of the Mittelwerk to report challenges to the established order. It was common knowledge that the SS had secret agents in the factory whose job it was to ferret out troublemakers among the slaves. These secret agents might also inform on civilian employees. The spies were part of the SD, the Security Service of the SS; they were known as *Vertrauensmaenner*, or "V-men" for short.

Despite the defined responsibilities and the presence of the V-men, discipline among the civilian employees of the Mittelwerk inevitably deteriorated. The *Haeftlinge* were comical figures in their baggy, striped clown suits. They were emaciated, debased, pathetic foreigners, subhumans—at least not part of the German master race—"zebras." Who could take the slaves seriously even if they were, in theory, the responsibility of the SS?

Civilians were punishing the prisoners or beating them for pure sport. This practice permeated the system of civilian supervision of prisoners building rockets in the Mittelwerk underground factory. Camp Dora's doctor finally complained to those in charge that prisoners were being put into his hospital as the result of beatings and stabbings by civilian employees. He wanted the abuse stopped. Georg Rickhey, general director of the Mittelwerk, and the SS put their warning in writing to Arthur Rudolph and all Mittelwerk personnel. Civilians were in charge of missile production only; punishment of prisoners was the domain of the SS.

EARLY SUMMER 1944

The operational batteries in training at *Heidelager* near Blizna were test firing an average of ten A-4s each day. In addition to training the crews, the launches were intended to gather data on the A-4's accuracy and the destructive force of the one-ton warheads. Instead of punching huge, ugly craters into the Polish soil, however, the missiles scattered torn and twisted chunks of metal over the countryside. Six out of ten broke up in the air upon re-entry. The problem had not been noticed when the rockets were being launched from Peenemünde because they fell into the Baltic out of sight of their builders. Only the green dye stain on the surface of the water indicated the site of impact, and the dye stain would have been there whether the missile struck in one piece or disintegrated in the atmosphere during its descent.

"Our main problem," Walter Dornberger observed succinctly, "is getting the missiles to the target in an unexploded state."

There were two possible causes that had to be given serious consideration. The missile could be torn apart as it slammed back into the unyielding atmosphere. Alternatively, remnants of rocket fuel sloshing around in the bowels of the beast might mix explosively during the buffeting of re-entry. The first step in finding out and correcting the problem was to observe an airburst as it happened.

Wernher von Braun was standing in an open field at Sarnaki, about 160 miles north of Blizna, awaiting the arrival of a missile. "Usually," as he described the incident, "they fell within three or four miles of the designated spot. We always stood right in the center of the target. Our philosophy was that even we could not be that accurate, so that this was probably the safest place to be. We were uncommonly accurate that time though."

The clock at the top of a tower told von Braun that a missile was about to end its five-minute flight. He looked up into the clear blue sky, and . . .

"I was quite frightened. . . . I think I am one of the very few men living who have seen a V-2 [A-4] actually descending. . . . I saw it fall, directly on me, as it seemed."

As fast as he could fall flat on the ground, the warhead exploded a hundred yards away.

"There was a flash of bright light in the sky, then a tremendous fountain of earth. The noise was not great."

The blast lifted him high into the air and dropped him into a ditch. He crawled out of the ditch, dusty but unharmed.

"I was much shaken. It isn't pleasant to be on the receiving end, is it?"

18 JULY 1944

Adolf Hitler finally gave up the idea of using bunkers as bases for attacking England with A-4 rockets. The bunker at Watten near Calais had been turned into a malformed lump of concrete by American bombing a year earlier. The portion of it that could still give shelter from bombing was converted into an installation for producing liquid oxygen to be used by rockets fired from the new bunker built nearby at Wizernes.

The RAF responded to the approaching completion of the supposedly impregnable Wizernes bunker in July 1944 by attacking it and the Watten site with six-ton "earthquake" bombs. The bombs did little damage to the structures themselves, but they put them out of action nonetheless. At Watten they churned the earth around the bunker like an army of monstrous malignant moles. The foundations of the newly installed equipment for liquefying oxygen were undermined and tilted, making the installation useless. At Wizernes the "earthquake" bombs so pulverized the surrounding rock that the bunker and its avenues of access were subject to constant landslides.

With the bunkers out of action, A-4 field operations would use the mobile launchers that Walter Dornberger had championed all along.

CHAPTER 17

The Plot to Kill the Fuehrer

20 JULY 1944

After eleven years of Nazi control, after five years of war, after devastating losses of men and materiel in Russia, after the Allied invasion at Normandy, after daily punishing bombing of the Fatherland, some German Army officers began to realize that Hitler's leadership might no longer be in Germany's best interest. They decided to act.

Little more than a year earlier, Lieutenant Colonel Klaus Philip Schenk, Count von Stauffenberg, had walked into a minefield in Tunisia. He was carried off on a stretcher minus part of his leg, his right hand, part of his left hand, and his left eye. After his discharge from the hospital, he returned to active duty with the army in Berlin and soon found himself chief of staff to General Friedrich Fromm, who was commander in chief of the Home Army and head of army armaments. As Fromm's deputy, Stauffenberg was called to Hitler's Wolf's Lair headquarters as often as two or three times a week to report on the availability of replacements for the decimated units at the fronts. Stauffenberg's assignment gave the conspirators what they needed and had almost despaired of getting: access to the Fuehrer.

Stauffenberg, carrying his briefcase, entered the conference room in the barracks building at Wolf's Lair. At the center of the room was a table, a heavy oak slab supported by two even heavier columns that were almost as wide as the top. Hitler sat at the center of one side of the table, magnifying glass in hand, studying a map of the eastern theater. Standing around the table were 22 high-ranking officers and men of the armed forces and the SS.

Stauffenberg edged his way to the table, and he put his briefcase on the floor, leaning it against the inside of the pillar supporting that end of the table, just a few feet from Hitler. After a few minutes, Stauffenberg left, saying he had to go to a telephone. Another officer, finding Stauffenberg's briefcase in his way, moved it aside, to the far side of the massive oblong column that held up the table.

The conference barracks exploded into a jumble of smoke, flame, flying debris, and bodies. Hitler, it appeared, must be dead, killed by the bomb in Stauffenberg's briefcase; and a large part of the High Command had gone to hell with him.

The conspirators' next move was to take control of the government. They immediately telephoned their fellow conspirators in Berlin and reported the successful assassination of Hitler, then went about cutting off all communication between the Wolf's Lair and the outside world. Colonel Stauffenberg bluffed his way past several checkpoints, and reached the Rastenburg airfield from which he departed for Berlin.

The coup attempt fell apart as Hitler emerged from the shattered barracks burned, lacerated, and bruised. His eardrums were shattered, and his right arm was temporarily paralyzed. One man had been killed outright. A dozen were severely injured, and three would later die of their injuries. Yet Hitler, the target of the attack, was alive; and he was about to take a terrible and bloody vengeance.

The faint-hearted conspirators in Berlin wasted precious hours waiting for confirmation of Hitler's death. They were soon rounded up; and by 10:50 P.M. Colonel Stauffenberg was in the custody of his superior, General Fromm. Not long after midnight, Stauffenberg and three of his co-conspirators were standing before a firing squad. His last words were reported to be "long live our sacred Germany!"

*   *   *   *

General Friedrich Fromm, commander in chief of the Home Army and head of army armaments, had been very energetic in arresting and executing those who conspired against the Fuehrer's life. Many of them, like Stauffenberg, had been his subordinates; and they had undertaken the coup attempt on the assumption that Fromm would give his support after the fact. The close link of many of the conspirators to General Fromm did not escape Hitler's attention. The day after the assassination attempt, Fromm was arrested on Himmler's orders.

Hitler had in the period of that one day developed a justifiable distrust of the German Army. Among his moves to regain control was to give all of General Fromm's authority and responsibilities to Heinrich Himmler. The

SS Reichsfuehrer's realm now encompassed management of the army's weapons development, which included the A-4 program.

1 August 1944

The shock waves from the bomb blast that nearly killed Hitler continued to echo through Germany, and eventually they reached Peenemünde. The decision had been made by the army a month earlier, but now there was no time to waste. Heinrich Himmler was in charge of the Home Army, and the rocket development group headed by Walter Dornberger reported to the Home Army. If something was not done quickly, Peenemünde would soon be under the control of Himmler and the SS.

Managers and supervisors were called to a meeting at the Officers' Club. There they were introduced to a man named Paul Storch, who was on temporary leave from the Siemens Company. Storch confirmed the rumor that had been circulating that the Heeres-Anstalt Peenemünde (Army Establishment Peenemünde), HAP, would, henceforth, be a private concern with the Third Reich as its owner. They were all now employees of the Elektromechanische Werke, or the EKW. Presumably "Electromechanical Industries" was chosen as the name of the new company for security reasons: it said nothing about what the organization did.

Changes in the organizational chart would be kept to a minimum, but there were significant changes at the top. Storch would be the new managing director of the organization. Walter Dornberger, who had built the rocket base as chief of all army rocket development, would no longer be in control of Peenemünde; he was cast into the limbo of undefined responsibilities. Colonel Leo Zassen, the base's military commander whom Himmler had tried to replace the previous year, was assigned to the front. Wernher von Braun as technical director would no longer direct manufacturing and testing; however, he would be Storch's technical deputy. Storch was bright enough not to tinker with a smoothly running operation; and von Braun, because of his seniority, knowledge, experience, and prestige became the de facto leader. If Himmler had gained control of the establishment, he would have undoubtedly followed through on disposing of von Braun as he had tried to do the previous year. Thus, while Dornberger's star was on the wane, von Braun's star—although he may not have realized it at the time—was rising.

8 August 1944

Himmler finally acted, too late to gain control of Peenemünde, but soon enough to seize control of the manufacture of the A-4 and training of troops.

He appointed SS Lieutenant General Hans Kammler as his special commissioner for the A-4 program. General Kammler, Himmler stated in his written order, "acts on my orders and his directions and instructions are to be obeyed." With a swift stroke of the pen, Himmler had destroyed Walter Dornberger. Everything Dornberger had wanted, control of A-4 development, testing, training, and field operations, was denied him. Everything he had created was now owned by a man he viewed as an arrogant, ignorant layman.

Kammler had no use for Walter Dornberger either. Dornberger had learned that a month earlier Kammler had described him to three generals as a public danger who ought to be court-martialed. Kammler had criticized Dornberger for draining off enormous quantities of materials and men for a hopeless project, the A-4 program which Kammler now headed. Dornberger's pride would not let him subordinate himself to the man he loathed. He began to draft a request to the army that it relieve him of his duties relating to the A-4—whatever they might still be—and reassign him elsewhere.

On a Sunday afternoon soon after, Wernher von Braun and Ernst Steinhoff arrived at Dornberger's home in Bansin, on the Baltic shore southeast of Peenemünde, intent on dissuading him of his decision. Dornberger was in for a very long afternoon. Von Braun and Steinhoff presented an argument which Dornberger summarized succinctly: "If we wished one day to have a place in the history of technology and receive recognition from the world for our invention of the long-range rocket, I ought not to desert the ship now."

The A-4 project was in serious danger of collapsing without Dornberger's continued participation; and, with the collapse of the project, everything they had done over the preceding 12 years to develop the rocket would be lost. The entire project was a house of cards with temperamental scientists and suppliers scattered over Germany and the occupied territories. Kammler's heavy hand would inevitably knock it over.

Von Braun and Steinhoff told Dornberger that for the sake of the A-4, he "should even try to help Kammler." Von Braun appreciated the significance of what he was asking Dornberger to do—that he help Hans Kammler. Von Braun had seen how Kammler had exploited slave labor to dig the underground factory and to build rockets; he had seen Kammler's blatant grabs for power and single-minded manipulations to reach his end. Von Braun would later describe Kammler as "the most ruthless man I ever met," which was a significant statement since he had also met Goering, Himmler, and Hitler.

Dornberger knew Kammler's character even better than von Braun, and he countered that Kammler was not open to cooperation. Kammler would give orders and expect them to be carried out.

Steinhoff and von Braun pointed out that Kammler would know whom to blame for failures: themselves.

The Sunday afternoon discussion went on for hours. Absent from Walter Dornberger's account of it were any consideration of using the A-4 rocket in the defense of Germany, the assignment of moral responsibility for exploiting slaves to build the rocket, and the ethical question of using it as a weapon of terror against civilian targets.

Walter Dornberger eventually agreed to stay on, to swallow his pride, and to help the man he despised. He would do it for the sake of the A-4 project and for the glory that would go to the men who built the first long-range rocket.

15 August 1944

The need for skilled workers at the Mittelwerk was unabated, and Wernher von Braun personally sought out men who had the skills desperately needed at the Mittelwerk. On this date, he wrote to Alwin Sawatzki, the production planner of the Mittelwerk, about his efforts to find personnel to staff a workshop to evaluate "ground vehicle test devices." Von Braun wrote as follows:

"During my last visit to the Mittelwerk, you proposed to me that we use the good technical education of detainees available to you at Buchenwald to tackle . . . additional development jobs. You mentioned in particular a detainee working in your mixing device quality control, who was a French physics professor and who is especially qualified for the technical direction of such a workshop.

"I immediately looked into your proposal by going to Buchenwald, together with Dr. Simon, to seek out more qualified detainees. I have arranged their transfer to the Mittelwerk with Standartenfuehrer [Colonel] Pister [Buchenwald camp commandant], as per your proposal."

Von Braun became an active partner with those who would use slave labor by personally selecting top quality technical people to work as slaves on his project. This activity, had it been known at the time, could have made von Braun subject to charges of having committed war crimes, similar to those faced by Albert Speer at Nuremberg.

Hermann Oberth, theoretician of rockets and space travel. (National Archives Photo No. 226-P-25-13)

Albert Speer, Hitler's architect and minister of armaments. (National Archives Photo No. 208–PU–189J–2)

Wernher von Braun, chief designer of the V-2 rocket. (Smithsonian Institution Photo No. 91–7111)

General Walter Dornberger, leader of the German Army's rocket development program. (Smithsonian Institution Photo No. A5347–A)

Heinrich Himmler, Reichsfuehrer of the SS and head of the Gestapo, who saw the potential of the V–2 rocket and eventually brought it under his control.

Adolph Hitler, the Fuehrer of Nazi Germany, who had no faith in the V–2 rocket until he needed it to forestall the inevitable destruction of his empire. (National Archives Photo No. 226–P–25–1854A)

General Walter Dornberger (left front, holding a cigar), Wernher von Braun (right front, with his left arm in a cast), and others after their surrender to the United States Army. (National Archives Photo No. 208–PU–212KK–1)

Two liberated survivors of the Mittelwerk rocket factory. (National Archives Photo No. 111–SC–203416)

Trenches filled with corpses of slaves from the Mittelwerk rocket factory. (National Archives Photo No. 111–SC–203417)

An A–4 rocket, later renamed the V–2, in flight. (Smithsonian Institution Photo No. 86–12191)

United States Army and civilian personnel view a captured V–2 rocket motor. (National Archives Photo No. 111–SC–264020)

The Apollo 11/Saturn V space vehicle carrying astronauts Neil A. Armstrong, Michael Collins, and Edwin E. Aldrin, Jr., on their way to the moon. (NASA Photo No. 69–H–1142)

Apollo 11 mission officials following the successful liftoff on 16 July 1969. Wernher von Braun is the man with binoculars hanging by a strap around his neck. (NASA Photo No. 69-H-1159)

IV

THE ROCKET WAR

CHAPTER 18

Vengeance Weapon-2

29 AUGUST–2 SEPTEMBER 1944

On 29 August Hitler ordered that the rocket bombardment of London should begin as soon as possible from mobile launchers based in Belgium. The following day, SS Lieutenant General Hans Kammler established his headquarters in Brussels.

Field operations of the A-4 missile, now renamed the V-2, were the responsibility of the army's LXV Korps under the command of Major General Richard Metz. Metz was in turn responsible to Army General Heinemann who had command of the entire A-4/V-2 program, including Dornberger's development and training groups. The LXV Korps was preparing to go into action when, on 31 August, notice was received that Kammler had called a meeting in Brussels that night to discuss the opening of the rocket attack. Walter Dornberger was to be present.

The LXV Korps's chief of staff, Colonel Eugen Walter, immediately contacted the High Command for clarification of who was in charge of V-2 field operations, Metz of the army or Kammler of the SS. The High Command's answer to Walter removed any ambiguity in the command structure: The LXV Korps under the command of Major General Metz was exclusively responsible for field operations. Kammler was not to be involved; Dornberger was responsible only for development and supply.

The meeting in Brussels was attended by Kammler, Dornberger, Colonel Walter, and his superior General Metz, among others. When the meeting began, Kammler began issuing orders on the conduct of the A-4 attack as if he were in command. Walter was chagrined that Metz was meekly deferring to the intruder in army affairs. Walter was less reluctant to defend the army's authority. When Kammler turned to him for comments, Colonel Walter coldly read the text of the High Command's answer to his request for clarification of the command structure: Kammler was not to be involved, Dornberger was dangerously close to overstepping his authority, and Metz was neglecting his responsibilities to the Korps.

Kammler was caught off guard. He had assumed that his authority over rocket production would give him credibility, and he had gambled that the army's chastisement after the attempt on Hitler's life would let his grab for control of field operations go unchallenged. Colonel Walter's meddling had thrown Kammler's well-choreographed transfer of power out of control.

He answered to Himmler alone, Kammler told them; and he would contact Himmler for further instructions. Then, in a bullying tone, Kammler advised Colonel Walter that he contact the High Command again for confirmation of the command structure.

It took only two days for Kammler and Himmler to get their way. On 2 September the High Command spinelessly issued new orders that Kammler was to conduct combat action, but that LXV Korps headquarters was to control him and be responsible for his combat actions. Kammler took over but never bothered to report in to the army's LXV Korps headquarters. He was, as he said earlier, responsible solely to SS Reichsfuehrer Himmler; Major General Metz and the meddling Colonel Walter were irrelevant. Thus, SS Lieutenant General Hans Kammler, a man with no front line military experience, took total control of the A-4 offensive.

6 SEPTEMBER 1944

Over 6,300 men and almost 1,600 vehicles in two groups under Kammler's command were deployed in Holland and western Germany in preparation for the A-4 offensive. Group North prepared to bombard London; Group South had as its targets sites in France and Belgium. The opportunity to make history by firing the first ballistic missile in combat was given to 444 Battery of Group South under the command of a Captain Kleiber. The A-4's target was to be Paris, which had fallen to the Allies on 25 August, 13 days earlier. Walter Dornberger probably would have approved of the choice of this first target since he had defined the specifications of the missile on the basis of those of the "Paris Gun" of World War I.

The 444 Battery positioned the A-4 on its firing table early   the morning, and by 10:30 A.M. it was ready to be fired. The rocket engine ignited with a shower of sparks bursting into the preliminary stage of smoke and flame that billowed around the rocket's base. For several seconds the thunder of the engine grew, and its blast churned up a cloud of dust and debris. As the engine reached main stage, the rocket began to rise; then instantaneously the rocket engine cut off. The fully fueled and armed missile fell back onto the firing table with a heavy clank. It wobbled but remained upright: a dangerous dud.

The 444 Battery's second missile was ready to launch at 11:40 A.M. It went through ignition, preliminary stage, and entered main stage; then, just like its predecessor, its rocket engine cut off prematurely. The A-4s were grounded, and history would have to wait while their crews searched the defueled rockets for the defects that caused their failures.

8 SEPTEMBER 1944

The 485th Mobile Artillery Detachment of Group North brought their trucks to a stop just northeast of the Hague in Holland. They raised the rocket from the *Meillerwagen* trailer onto the firing table, then fueled it. At 6:38 P.M. they fired the rocket engine. The missile rose into the evening sky with a deafening roar, climbing higher and higher, then arching over for its trip 200 miles to the west. The A-4's target was an imaginary point 1,000 yards east of Waterloo Station, London.

Radar gave no advanced warning. There was no sound of enemy engines droning in the sky. The people of the London suburb of Chiswick were on their way home from work or already at their dinner tables when a ton of high explosives shattered their evening. Only then did the supersonic double boom of the missile arrive, followed by what those who heard it described as the sound of a large body rushing through the air.

The point of impact was marked by a 30-foot hole torn into the center of the concrete roadway. The blast had destroyed six houses and heavily damaged at least twice as many more. Amid the rubble, three people had been killed and ten severely injured.

News of the rocket attack reached Peenemünde as a headline in a newspaper: "Vergeltungswaffe-2 Gegen London im Einsatz," (Vengeance weapon-2 in action against London). Their Aggregate-4 rocket had been transformed by Joseph Goebbels' propaganda machine into the weapon that would, it said, turn the war around, the V-2. The news report brought about a great deal of initial excitement and enthusiasm among the rocket's developers.

Wernher von Braun is reported to have addressed his team on the occasion. "Let's not forget," he said, "that this is only the beginning of a new era, the era of rocket-powered flight. It seems that this is another demonstration of the sad fact that so often important new developments get nowhere until they are first applied as weapons."

Von Braun is also reported to have quipped about the rocket, "It behaved perfectly but landed on the wrong planet." While it is conceivable that he made this comment at some time, it is not clear that he did so on this occasion or that he believed it the day the first V-2 struck England.

A member of von Braun's team is reported to have described the emotions of the day more objectively. "Don't kid yourself—although von Braun may have had space dust in his eyes since childhood—most of us were pretty sore about the heavy allied bombing of Germany—the loss of German civilians, mothers, fathers, or relatives. When the first V-2 hit London, we had champagne. Why not? Let's be honest about it. We were at war, and although we weren't Nazis, we still had a Fatherland to fight for. . . ."

*   *   *   *

That same day the 444 Battery of Group South recovered from its failure of two days earlier by successfully launching a V-2 against Paris. Their rocket fell near the Porte d'Italie, causing modest damage.

30 SEPTEMBER 1944

For nearly two months Walter Dornberger had tried to live up to his concession to von Braun and Steinhoff to help Hans Kammler deliver the A-4 as an operational weapon. He tried to deal with the barrage of teletyped orders—sometimes 100 in a day—that would arrive from Kammler. Dornberger found most of them uninformed and pointless; he tried to reconcile them and avoid chaos. He watched as the organization he had spent 12 years building began to disintegrate with many of its members shifting their loyalties to the new man in charge, Kammler. In looking back to this time, Dornberger complained about the series of humiliations he had to endure while conveniently forgetting the humiliations handed out as standard operating procedure in the Mittelwerk. At last the opportunity arrived for him to get out from under the ad hoc insanity of the situation and possibly regain control of at least part of his rocket program.

After the attempt on Hitler's life, Army General Fromm, who had commanded the Home Army, was replaced by SS Obergruppenfuehrer (general) Hans Juettner. Juettner was a moderately good-natured, banal man who struggled with getting control of his new assignment. As the new commander in chief of the Home Army, he assumed responsibility for the A-4/V-2 development program and gained General Walter Dornberger as a subordinate and Hans Kammler as a working partner. He finally demanded that Dornberger and Kammler clearly define their respective authorities. The agreement that spelled out their authorities was put into writing and signed on 30 September, first by Dornberger and Juettner, and last by Kammler.

According to the agreement, Kammler would command all firings of the A-4/V-2 in the field, and he retained the authority to decide anything he viewed as a fundamental question. Dornberger was Kammler's "personal representative" at home, inspector of the formation and responsible for training of field units, as well as technical staff officer in charge of development and supply of operational missiles. He was explicitly charged with defining production schedules for the Mittelwerk rocket factory, including the number of rockets to be built and the proportions of the various models. Dornberger took particular satisfaction in knowing that he was not subordinate to Kammler; he would be responsible for his own actions.

The irony of the agreement—though it seems to have escaped Dornberger's notice—was that Kammler, the architect of concentration camps who had no technical or military experience, would be in command of the most sophisticated weapon of war devised by man. Dornberger, the army officer who had combat experience during World War I and who created the ballistic missile, would be responsible for defining the activities of slaves in a concentration camp.

CHAPTER 19

"Compared to Dora, Auschwitz Was Easy!": Death and Survival in the Rocket Factory

DECEMBER 1944–JANUARY 1945

The tragedy that was about to take place in Tunnel No. 2 of the Mittelwerk had been played out many times before on scales large and small. The cast included the wretched slaves, the SS, and many members of the German Army's rocket team. While the drama may have varied from performance to performance, it always reached the same lethal climax.

The drama began hundreds of miles from the Mittelwerk. The rockets produced at the underground factory were continuing to malfunction despite the corrections of engineering problems. Wernher von Braun sent one of his engineers from Peenemünde, Dieter Grau, to the Mittelwerk on a "debugging" mission to find the cause of the continued failures. Grau had been instructed to look for attempts of sabotage by the prisoners, and he found them.

"Those *Haeftlinge*, they were very clever," Grau said later. "They knew where they could tighten or loosen a screw, and this way tried to interfere with the proper function of the missile."

The slaves sabotaged the rockets as an act of defiance to their masters and to save the lives of the intended victims of the weapons. The rockets were complex machines which were vulnerable to simple acts of sabotage. The prisoners loosened screws, removed or left out vital parts, urinated on wiring, produced welds that looked solid but would snap like a cracker under the stress of being fired. Dieter Grau filed a report describing the evidence of sabotage he had discovered. The specific consequences of

Grau's report are not known. However, it is known that standard practice at the Mittelwerk was for Arthur Rudolph, the director of V-2 production, to sign sabotage reports and turn them over to the SS or the SD (the Security Service of the SS).

On 9 November 1944, Arthur Rudolph received an order—he said later that he could not remember who the order came from—to stop all work in the underground factory. He passed on the stop-work order to his department chiefs, and he told them to have all *Haeftlinge* brought together in Tunnel No. 2, the main assembly tunnel. SS troops brought the prisoners to the tunnel.

The focus of attention was 12 men, prisoners who had been accused of planning to blow up the underground plant. Their hands were tied behind their backs, and they had pieces of wood fastened in their mouths. A rope around each man's neck was tied to the traverse boom of an overhead electric crane that was normally used to move rocket components. The crane's boom began to rise slowly, and the bound and gagged men were lifted above the crowd of prisoners, SS guards, and civilian engineers. The tightening nooses strangled the men slowly, their screams and groans stifled by the wooden gags.

Arthur Rudolph arrived on the scene some time after the 12 accused saboteurs had been raised to the top of the tunnel. He could not tell how many of them were already dead, but he did notice that one of them still had the strength to lift his knees.

Afterward, Hans Friedrich, a civilian manager at the underground factory telephoned Rudolph. He asked Rudolph how long the crane would be out of work. Rudolph told Friedrich that the men would be hanging there the last six hours of one work shift and the first six hours of the next work shift so that all *Haeftlinge* could see them.

Hangings of suspected saboteurs within the rocket factory tunnels were, apparently, common occurrences. Three additional mass hangings have been described by witnesses. Hundreds of men were hanged from the overhead crane because they were suspected of sabotage; and many of these victims had been reported to the SS by civilian workers.

12 JANUARY 1945

One man's tragedy can be another man's opportunity. Walter Dornberger's opportunity came when Professor Waldemar Petersen, head of the Long-Range Weapons Commission of the Ministry of Armaments, suffered a stroke. At the time, the commission was wrestling with the problem of protecting Germany from the constant air attacks. With Petersen incapable of working, Dornberger was asked to take his place. At first Dornberger declined the offer. He was unenthusiastic about leading a group of high-level bureaucrats in an attempt to resolve, before the demise of the Third Reich, what he viewed as an insoluble problem.

Dornberger mentioned the offer to Wernher von Braun. His young colleague, always the opportunist, encouraged Dornberger to take on the job, but with some qualifications. He should have the bureaucrats dismissed, and replace them with scientists and engineers who knew the technical capabilities and flaws of weapons systems under development in Germany, and who could quickly reach informed decisions. Dornberger took this counterproposal back to the Ministry of Armaments, and Albert Speer approved it. Arbeitsstab Dornberger (Working Staff Dornberger) was created for the purpose of ending Allied air superiority. Walter Dornberger could finally make decisions about the development of weapons with the full backing of the Ministry of Armaments. The name of the group left no doubt about who was in charge—or so Dornberger thought.

12–19 JANUARY 1945

The surprise Russian offensive began an avalanche of events that rumbled all the way to the rocket factory under the Harz Mountains.

Heinrich Himmler, like any common criminal faced with the possibility of the detection of his crimes, began destroying evidence. Two months earlier, on 2 November 1944, anticipating the imminent loss of his primary extermination camp, Himmler gave orders to stop gassing at Auschwitz-Birkenau. On 26 November, he ordered the destruction of Hans Kammler's crematoriums. A specially formed *Kommando* went about removing the fittings for shipment to concentration camps farther from the advancing Russian front, then it dynamited the remaining concrete and brick structures. The last of the crematoriums at Auschwitz-Birkenau was destroyed in the middle of January.

Himmler's housecleaning caused another problem. Hans Kammler had a solution, albeit an imperfect one, which the commandant of Auschwitz, Rudolf Hoess, commented on: "It now turns out that the armaments industry has an enormous need for manpower, but that they are not making any progress with the construction of lodgings.... Auschwitz is crammed with prisoners waiting to be transported to the armaments camps. New transports by [Adolf] Eichmann are rolling in, stuffing Auschwitz even more...."

Kammler can't work magic . . . and weeks, even months are going by with no essential progress."

The Jews, dissidents, and other social misfits just kept piling up on Hoess's doorstep. Without gas chambers and crematoriums, there was little he could do about it other than put them on trains to other camps as fast as they arrived. The human baggage, in Hoess's view, could become Kammler's problem.

As the Russian armies got closer to Auschwitz-Birkenau and its sub-camps, activities became more feverish. The last rollcall of the complex of camps on 17 January counted a total of 48,340 men and 18,672 women. The following day, tens of thousands of prisoners were marched off by SS guards into the bitter winter toward camps farther behind the advancing Russian front. Prisoners who lagged behind or tried to escape from the death march were shot.

For the SS, fire was to be the great purifier. Records were the first to go into the flames. The SS burned transport lists of all those who had been herded directly to the gas chambers. They were followed by the records of the camp hospitals and clothing and possessions that had been taken from the prisoners. Finally, on 19 January, they set the torch to the barracks. When the flames subsided, all that was left of Auschwitz were six barracks, several thousand prisoners too ill to move, and the ashes of several million men, women, and children.

* * * *

Albert Speer viewed the shipping of prisoners from the extermination camp of Auschwitz-Birkenau to the armaments production camps which included Dora and Nordhausen with ironic optimism: "Kammler, a relent-less but capable robot, . . . threw hundreds of thousands of prisoners into the production process under the harshest conditions. Yet it gave these hundreds of thousands a chance to survive."

One of the Jews who made the trip saw it differently: "Compared to Dora, Auschwitz was easy!" He was, of course, commenting on the work camp rather than the extermination camp at Auschwitz.

Camp Dora was overcrowded even by SS standards. An auxiliary camp for the new arrivals from Auschwitz was needed, and the SS directed their slaves in building it at Nordhausen. This new camp had two distinct sections. One was for those prisoners who were deemed fit to work in the underground factory; the other, without running water or medical staff, was a waiting room for death. Every morning, those fit to work were given assignments at the railway station or in the town of Nordhausen; or they were marched the two and a half miles to the Mittelwerk like the zombies of Fritz Lang's *Metropolis*. Every day, those who had not survived the night were carted to the crematorium at Dora. The Dora-Nordhausen-Mittelwerk complex included at least 40 subsidiary camps scattered throughout the valleys and villages of the Harz Mountains. Many were small and obscure, but some had names that would be heard again, like Bleicherode and Bad Sachsa.

Conditions at Dora had improved after the construction of the above-ground camp from the genocidal to the merely homicidal. With the arrivals from Auschwitz and other camps in the east, the situation inevitably reverted to the genocidal. The new guards who had accompanied the new prisoners from Auschwitz had years of experience herding women and children, the aged and infirm, into gas chambers. Their treatment of the prisoners at Nordhausen confirmed their status as the masters of barbarism. The slaves were fed four ounces of black bread and some thin soup per day, provided these meager rations were not spilled in the dirt by a sadistic guard or stolen by another starving prisoner. Prisoners were dying from starvation, disease, and the noose. Mass hangings, which had taken place in the underground tunnels, now began in earnest. In one day, according to one estimate, 57 unfortunate souls were hanged from the electric crane while the surviving slaves were forced to watch. In the period from 20 January until 3 April 1945, 1,963 emaciated corpses were shipped from the new Nordhausen camp to the crematorium at Dora. Dora and the subordinate camps also contributed their share of deaths.

The factory under the Harz Mountains had grown to be one of the largest and most sophisticated multipurpose manufacturing plants in all of Germany. The Mittelwerk had initially been intended as an assembly plant for the V-2 with components being produced at smaller factories throughout Germany and the occupied territories. As the frontiers of the Third Reich retreated and German industry was pounded to rubble by Allied bombing, production of V-2 components was brought within the realm of the Mittelwerk. Furthermore, since the spring of 1944 the V-1 buzz bomb had also been assembled there, and a portion of the tunnel complex was devoted to the production of Junkers airplane engines.

The maze of tunnels had grown to enormous proportions. The two parallel main tunnels, which Kammler's slaves had drilled through the mountain, were nearly two miles long, 14 yards wide, and ten yards high. They were connected by 47 cross-galleries like rungs on a ladder. The cross-tunnels were about 220 yards long and about the same width and height as the main tunnels, although some were 30 yards in height to accommodate the enormous equipment for the assembly and testing of the rocket. Twenty-seven cross-tunnels at the southern (Dora) end of the complex were dedicated to the production of the V-2 missiles. According to Alwin Sawatzki's original factory plan, raw materials and components were to be brought into the subterranean factory through one of the long main tunnels. They were disgorged into the cross-galleries where they were processed into subassemblies. Final assembly of the V-2 missile took place on an assembly that moved through the second main tunnel. Standard gauge railroad tracks ran through both main tunnels so that raw materials could be delivered and assembled weapons could be loaded and removed efficiently.

With the new arrivals from Auschwitz and other camps in the east, the prisoner population of the Dora-Nordhausen-Mittelwerk complex ballooned to 40,000. About 3,000 SS men guarded the slaves, and another 2,000 German civilian technicians supervised them in the factories. The supervisory personnel at the Mittelwerk included many from Peenemünde, including Arthur Rudolph, the director of the V-2 assembly factory, and Magnus von Braun, who was sent by his brother to supervise gyroscope production.

CHAPTER 20

Final Flights from Peenemünde:
Von Braun Plans for the Future

24 JANUARY 1945

A strange new beast stood on the launching stand at Peenemünde. It had the familiar body of the A-4/V-2, but with broad, swept-back wings drooping from its midsection. It resembled—if anybody were able to recognize the shape—a supersonic aircraft standing on its tail.

Wernher von Braun had not given up on the idea of a rocket-powered airplane, even after the Luftwaffe withdrew support for the army's rocket research in 1939. On 6 July 1939 he had submitted to the Air Ministry a plan for a rocket-powered interceptor that would take off vertically like the A-3 and A-4. Its liftoff would be powered by a 22,400-pound-thrust motor that would take it to an altitude of 25,000 feet where a cruising motor generating 1,700 pounds of thrust would take over. The rocket plane would operate just short of supersonic speed. It would carry four machine guns and a pilot to fire them. The Air Ministry did not support the project. Von Braun submitted a revised version of the proposal on 27 May 1941. The aircraft in the new proposal would take off from the back of a truck, giving it deployment mobility that the rocket plane of the original proposal lacked. There were some modifications in the conformation of the airplane, such as the position of the wings, but the specifications were essentially unchanged. So was the Air Ministry's response: no, thank you.

The concept of a rocket-powered airplane came to life again in 1943 when von Braun and Dornberger had—or at least thought they had—a reliable rocket that could travel a long distance at supersonic speed, the A-4.

They reasoned that if they put wings on the A-4 and launched it through the atmosphere rather than over it, they could significantly increase its range. They calculated the trajectory—actually the flight path—that would give the rocket maximum range. It would fly under rocket power to an altitude of only 12 miles (63,360 feet) with a maximum speed of 2,800 miles per hour. It would coast to an altitude of 18 miles (95,040 feet), then begin a long, gliding descent. The A-4 with wings could theoretically hit a target 342 miles from the launch site, twice the range of the A-4. The trip would take 17 minutes. The winged A-4 was named the A-9.

Von Braun and his engineering group still had some of their impractical dreams, and they designed a variation of the A-9 that was piloted, had a pressurized cockpit, and tricycle landing gear. Then, while they were still dreaming, they designed a two-stage rocket. The booster rocket for the A-9 was designated the A-10. The A-10 would truly be a monster, weighing 87 tons and being propelled by a motor with 200 tons of thrust. It would lift the A-9 for 50 or 60 seconds until it reached a speed of 2,700 miles per hour. The A-10 would then drop away and parachute back to earth for re-use. The A-9 would continue on under its own power to reach a maximum speed of 6,300 miles per hour and an altitude of 35 miles. It would then glide at supersonic speed to a target 2,500 miles away. The two-stage combination of the A-9 and A-10 could carry a pilot or a warhead from Europe to New York in 40 minutes. The rocket scientists spoke of developing the "New York Rocket" or the "American Rocket" as casually as the German artillery had spoken of the "Paris Gun" during World War I.

Evidence that the "American Rocket" was more than talk and blueprints was found in the wreckage of the bunker built for A-4/V-2 preparation and launching at Wizernes in France. Before the bunker had been bombed out of action, an analyst had found that the orientation of the launch site pointed within half a degree of the great circle bearing on New York. While the apparent orientation of the Wizernes bunker might have been fortuitous, the ruins could not be dismissed as easily. The five-foot-thick bomb-proof doors and the rocket-handling equipment had been built to accommodate a rocket twice the size of the V-2. Had Germany been able to defeat England with rockets fired from Wizernes, it would have had a launching site from which it could threaten America with the "American Rocket," presuming the weapon was built.

When in the summer of 1943 the design deficiencies of the A-4 became apparent, work on the A-9 and A-10 was set aside. In October 1944 as the western front advanced toward Germany, and the A-4/V-2 launching sites were pushed farther and farther from their targets, von Braun and Dornberger dusted off the blueprints for the rocket with double the A-4/V-2's range.

The version of the A-9 that was actually built was designated the A-4b to take advantage of the priority given to the A-4. The "A-4 bastard," as it was called by von Braun and Dornberger, was in essence an A-4 with enlarged tail fins and two sharply swept-back wings fused to its midsection. The wings had a span of about 18½ feet and a surface area of 145 square feet.

Dornberger and von Braun had often watched with admiration and, possibly, envy as the rocket-powered Me 163s flew from the Luftwaffe base at Peenemünde West. Now they had a challenger in both speed and power to its supremacy of the air. While the A-9 had almost as much wing area as the rocket plane—the Me 163B interceptor had 211 square feet of wing area—its rocket motor developed about 18 times the thrust. The A-9, if it had a pilot, would have been a technical leap ahead of the tiny airplane.

The first winged rocket was launched from Peenemünde on 8 January 1945. It rose normally to about 100 feet above the firing table; then, as Dornberger described the event, "the control failed." Now, on 24 January 1945, a second A-9 was ready for flight.

The firing of the winged missile went as planned. It climbed vertically above Peenemünde, until it reached a speed of 2,700 miles per hour and an altitude of 50 miles. Then, its fuel spent, it curved over and began its shallow glide back to earth. The A-9 had gone through the liftoff and the beginning of its descending glide rock stable; but as it began to plow back through the upper atmosphere, a wing tore off. The rocket plane tumbled out of control back to earth.

Despite the abrupt end to the flight of the A-9, its builders were delighted with its performance. They had built and flown the first, unpiloted, supersonic airplane. They had demonstrated that it could be done. What was left was to systematically solve the technical details and to work through the fine points of development. All they needed was time, which they did not have.

27 JANUARY 1945

Hans Kammler could not help but react to the formation of Working Staff Dornberger, which functioned under the sponsorship of Minister of Armaments Albert Speer. For more than three months, Walter Dornberger had been conveniently under the SS general's thumb as his liaison to the V-2 development, supply, and training groups in Germany. Working Staff Dornberger was an opportunity for Kammler to add to his growing empire, if only he could keep control of Dornberger. Kammler began by persuading Hermann Goering to appoint him his special commissioner for breaking the air terror. Since Kammler's new position and Working Staff Dornberger had the same mission, it was only logical for Kammler to appoint Dornberger and his group as his technical staff. Kammler's influence had grown, and Dornberger was once again subordinate to him.

As much as Walter Dornberger claimed to despise Hans Kammler, he was nonetheless pleased at once again being appointed Kammler's deputy. Albert Speer and the Ministry of Armaments had given Dornberger authority over civilian authorities and industry. Hans Kammler was now giving him similar control over military authorities with the backing of the SS.

On 27 January, Working Staff Dornberger assembled in Berlin under the joint sponsorship of Speer and Kammler for its first meeting. The ten-member panel reviewed the status of anti-aircraft weapons programs and found them often redundant and ill conceived. It quickly decided that Germany's only hope would be to focus its efforts on four guided anti-aircraft rockets: the subsonic "Butterfly" being developed by the Henschel Aircraft Works, a similar missile that operated at supersonic speed, the small X-4 wire-controlled rocket of the Ruhr Steel Company, and the large radio-controlled Wasserfall, which was being developed by Dornberger's former group at Peenemünde. Working Staff Dornberger recommended that all centers and factories involved in developing these small missiles be relocated to the Nordhausen area of central Germany, where they would be less vulnerable to enemy attack. With the backing of the Ministry of Armaments and of the SS through Kammler, Dornberger now had the power to make this recommendation a reality.

*   *   *   *

During the morning of 27 January, the SS made its final effort to destroy the evidence of its crimes at Auschwitz-Birkenau by blasting what was left of Kammler's gas chambers and five crematoriums. At about three in the afternoon the First Ukranian Front reached the 40-square-kilometer complex of camps. The retreating German forces had left behind about 7,000 prisoners, the majority of them women who were incapable of marching, and a few doctors and nurses. The evil history of Auschwitz had come to an end, but the work of the Nazi regime would continue at Dora and Nordhausen and other camps in the heart of Germany.

28 JANUARY 1945

With the approval of Adolph Hitler, Hans Kammler assumed control of the V-1 buzz bomb offensive, which had slipped through the hands of various Luftwaffe and army commanders. Kammler, who had started his military career in the SS construction department and had been the architect of Auschwitz-Birkenau, was now directing the operations of Germany's most advanced weapons, the V-1 and V-2, as well as exerting substantial control over their production at the Mittelwerk.

END OF JANUARY 1945

With their former commander, General Walter Dornberger, shunted off into a position with responsibilities to the Ministry of Armaments and the SS, the thousands of workers at Peenemünde, especially the civilian workers, looked to Wernher von Braun for leadership. As the Russian cannons boomed on the advancing front now only 50 miles away, von Braun changed from chief engineer to leader of men, from loyal German to independent agent. The man who was a member of the Nazi party, who had flown with the Luftwaffe, who was an officer in the SS, and who had been honored by his Fuehrer and his Fatherland with a titular professorship took his first step toward the age that would follow the Third Reich.

Wernher von Braun called a secret meeting of a small group of his closest and most trusted staff members. They met in the parlor of the Inselhof Hotel in Zinnowitz. Present at the meeting with von Braun were Ernst Steinhoff, Eberhard Rees, Ernst Stuhlinger, engineer Werner Gengelbach, and Dorette Kersten, von Braun's secretary. It was clear to everybody that before long Peenemünde would fall to the Russian troops then streaming across eastern Germany. They could decide to wait for the arrival of the Russians, or they could move to a position where they could turn themselves over to another of the Allies. Von Braun asked for a vote. The choice was unanimous. They would deliver themselves and their knowledge of rockets to the Americans. Defection to Germany's enemy would be a group exercise. The rocket team would be kept together with the full intention of continuing rocket development work into the unforeseeable future.

31 JANUARY 1945

Although Peenemünde would inevitably be in the hands of the Russians, von Braun's plan to leave it with its staff, equipment, and records would be a risky maneuver. Even talking about it was dangerous. Several engineers from Peenemünde had spoken openly about abandoning the facility. They were arrested by the SS and summarily shot. So that their lesson would not be lost on their surviving colleagues, the bodies of the executed men were hung from trees along major roads. They carried signs that read "I WAS TOO COWARDLY TO DEFEND THE HOMELAND."

While acting on the decision to abandon Peenemünde was dangerous, not to act might be even worse. In the chaos of Germany's collapse, every local bureaucrat and warlord felt free to issue orders to von Braun and his team. Quite understandably the local Nazi party *Gauleiter* (district leader) and Gestapo chief ordered them to stay and defend Peenemünde with their lives, as did the army commander at the retreating front. Then von Braun received a teletype ordering him to do what he wanted to do all along. He seized the opportunity.

Von Braun summoned his section chiefs, department directors, and those in his immediate circle to his office for an urgent meeting. He had an announcement to make. He told them that SS General Hans Kammler had just ordered that all of the most important defense projects be relocated to central Germany. Von Braun added for emphasis, this was not a suggestion; it was Kammler's order.

If anybody disagreed with Kammler's order—the engineers of Peenemünde, the local Nazi party Gauleiter and Gestapo chief, the army commander facing the advancing Russians—they could take it up with SS Lieutenant General Hans Kammler, who had shown in the past his lack of patience with those who questioned his orders with a terrible, swift retribution.

It is unlikely that many of von Braun's group knew that Kammler's order implemented the recommendation of Working Staff Dornberger, which had been constituted along lines proposed by von Braun. Although the membership of Working Staff Dornberger remains obscure, it is hard to imagine the group without von Braun as a leading participant; and if von Braun had been a member of the group, then he had also been involved in the genesis of Kammler's relocation order. While the evacuation of Peenemünde would not immediately deliver the rocket team into the hands of the Americans as they wished, it would put them closer to their goal and at a safe distance from the advancing Russians.

After the exclamations died down, von Braun continued. He told them that they would have to identify who would go, and in what order. Priority for relocation would be as follows: first, those who supported rocket production at the Mittelwerk; second, those working on improving the V-2's range and accuracy; and, finally, those developing the Wasserfall anti-air-craft rocket. Von Braun gave them two hours to draw up their lists. Those who did not make the lists would be reassigned or, regrettably, be released to the military to become cannon fodder in defense of a lost cause.

3 FEBRUARY 1945

Wernher von Braun assembled his staff again for a final planning meeting. This time his department heads, many of their administrative assistants, and representatives of the army were present. He asked his personnel manager for the current tally of personnel. The manager was prepared, and he read from his list, breaking it down according to project and support function. There were a total of 4,325 people in the rocket research group. About 30 percent of them were not deemed essential to the project and would be released to the military or reassigned to armaments plants in the area.

Von Braun's civilian staffer gave his report on the status of transportation. All railroad cars were being kept at the rocket base for the evacuation. Motor vehicles were also being organized to carry equipment from the workshops, laboratories, and offices to the railroad siding.

Somebody pointed out that there still were not enough railroad cars available to carry them and their equipment to central Germany.

Von Braun agreed. Then he added that they would have a number of ships and barges at their disposal, which could be towed very close to their destination in central Germany.

The juggernaut was in motion. There was no turning back.

17 FEBRUARY 1945

Preparation to relocate to central Germany was now the primary activity of the rocket development group. Documents had been sorted and packed. Equipment and furniture were being loaded onto trucks and barges. Everything was color coded according to department to simplify sorting at their destination. Personnel with their families and some light equipment were the first to move out by train.

Travel was limited both by the ravages of war and by bureaucracy. Refugees escaping from the invading Russians clogged the roads. The SS had extended its control over Germany by dotting the countryside with checkpoints where they could stop deserters, spies, or anyone else whose travel might be viewed as not in the best interests of the Third Reich. The key to travel in Germany was the possession of the right documents.

Authorizations and orders on imposing letterheads with high-ranking sig-
natures and multiple-stamped impressions could take one anywhere.

Von Braun's group prepared their own passes and authorizations. Their
original plan was to identify themselves as being under the command and
orders of the SS, specifically Walter Dornberger's new SS-sponsored
counterpart to Working Staff Dornberger, the BzbV Heer. When the station-
ery came back from the printer, one meaningless jumble of letters was
transposed into another: VZBV. It was too late to change the letterheads, so
they changed the name of their organization. VZBV, they decided, stood for
Vorhaben Zur Besondern Verwendung (Project for Special Disposition).
The meaningless acronym began to appear in bold letters several feet high
on the sides of boxes, trucks, and wagons. The organization was supposed
to be top secret, so there was no problem if nobody had ever heard of it or
understood what its obscure name meant. They were traveling with the
authorization of Army General Walter Dornberger, SS General Hans
Kammler, and SS Reichsfuehrer Heinrich Himmler; the documents with the
VZBV letterhead said so.

Wernher von Braun also said so when their authority was in doubt.
Despite his arrest and provisional release by the Gestapo, he was still a
major in the SS. "The only time I made use of my SS rank," he said later,
"was during the evacuation of the rocket development facilities from
Peenemünde to Bleicherode (Central Germany), in order to prevent them
from falling into the Russian hands. Since at that time (early 1945) the
communication and traffic system in Germany was almost completely
disorganized, this move was only possible by issuing very strict transportation orders. In issuing these orders, I turned my SS rank into account in
order to put more steam under these movements."

On 17 February the first train left under the protection of the fictitious
VZBV carrying 525 people, members of the rocket team and their families,
and a few boxcars of materials. Nobody interfered with them or any of the
others that followed. All essential personnel and most of their equipment
arrived safely in central Germany.

At about the same time the Peenemünde group was in transit, Walter
Dornberger and his staff were leaving their headquarters at Schwedt on the
Oder River. Their destination was Bad Sachsa, a resort village about a dozen
miles north of Bleicherode, the village that would soon be von Braun's
headquarters. Both groups would be within the range of sub-camps that
were part of the Dora and Nordhausen concentration camps, which supplied
slave labor to the Mittelwerk rocket factory.

19 FEBRUARY 1945

The last missiles fired from Peenemünde arced over the gray Baltic. In the preceding two and a half years, 264 A-4/V-2s had been fired from there and nearby sites; 147 of these had been built at Peenemünde and 117 at the Mittelwerk. The success rate had jumped rapidly in the spring of 1944 when most of the missiles tested had been built at the underground factory. The increased success rate was undoubtedly a consequence of the development group at Peenemünde having solved the major problems in the operation of their rocket and assuring the quality of manufacture by their close cooperation with the builders of the rockets at the Mittelwerk.

27 FEBRUARY 1945

Wernher von Braun returned to Peenemünde to brief his department and section heads on what awaited them in central Germany. The weapons development groups that were already in central Germany and those from Peenemünde, which were being relocated there under the direction of Working Staff Dornberger, would operate as part of a central cooperative development group. Von Braun would be the overall technical director of the new organization. It would have been a great opportunity, a major promotion if not for the fact that—as everyone knew by then—Germany was racing toward the precipice. Von Braun and the rest of them could only hold on for the ride and hope the fall would be a short one.

Von Braun also told his department and section heads that test sites were planned for all of the projects, including large test stands for their Wasserfall and the A-4/V-2. He said it as if he believed it himself and expected them to believe it. Their job was to pick up where they had left off, just as if enemy bombing was not turning industry into rubble and Germany was not collapsing into chaos. Well, if that was what von Braun wanted, if that was how they would keep the rocket team together, they would play along.

A few days later, von Braun left Peenemünde forever, and the rest of his group was not far behind.

WINTER 1945

In all that has been recorded about Hans Kammler, there is no indication that he was motivated by Nazi ideology or German patriotism. There is no indication that he was mindlessly following orders like the commandant of Auschwitz, Rudolf Hoess. Kammler cheerfully built concentration camps, destroyed the Warsaw ghetto, and drove slaves, not for the benefit of the

Third Reich, but to satisfy his own ambition. He was not a zealot, but he was a fanatic. As the enemy advanced, as he climbed higher and higher in the Nazi hierarchy, his personal charm eroded. He no longer had the time to be diplomatic nor the need to be cunning. He had the power to drive others, and his lunacy was law.

Kammler refused to believe that the war was being lost or that the Third Reich would soon collapse. He dashed back and forth across Germany, directing the V-weapon assaults, supervising weapons production, and keeping a tight grip on the strings of his empire.

On one occasion, Colonel Herbert Axster, Walter Dornberger's chief of staff, was acting as a liaison between the rocket development group and troops training for field operations. As Axster was examining V-2 firing positions, Hans Kammler drove up in his staff car.

"You have nothing more to do with this program," Kammler screamed at Axster. "It's my business now. I don't need you anymore."

Thereafter, the army colonel decided that it would be prudent to stay out of the way of the SS general.

Walter Dornberger, having agreed to serve the devil, did not have the option of avoiding him. Kammler was constantly summoning Dornberger to conferences at impossible hours in improbable places.

Kammler's and Dornberger's cars stopped on the autobahn under the midnight sky. Dornberger, his nerves strained to their limit by the pressure and tension, minced no words. Still, Kammler poured out his pointless orders with a final warning: obey them or they would all be doomed. Dornberger knew that Germany was already doomed.

Kammler had said his piece. It was time for him to move on. He pulled out his tommy gun and broke the stillness of the night with a burst of bullets.

"No need for *them* to sleep!" he said of his officers who had dozed off in exhaustion. "I can't sleep either!"

Victory and survival were no longer the issues. Kammler had lost sight of the goal but demanded that the effort be doubled. All that mattered was his manic obsession. No time to sleep, no chance to think. Just exhausting, nerve-wracking, futile resistance, building a dike of sand to hold back the pounding waves. The "berserk warrior," as Dornberger described him, returned to Holland to press the attack with the V-2.

MARCH 1945

The records of executions at Dora are sketchy at best, but those that do exist indicate a terrible toll as the end of the war drew near. On 12 March,

58 prisoners were hanged. On 20 March, the gallows took another 30; and, on 23 March, yet another 30 unknown slaves were hanged. There were more executions than just these, of course. One estimate claims about 300 executions took place after early March. Many men died on the gallows; some died more quickly with a bullet to the back of the head.

For the most part the men had been accused of sabotage. It is possible that they were in fact saboteurs since there were organized efforts to disrupt production at the Mittelwerk. Theirs were acts of brave defiance with no hope of recognition other than on the gallows. The men died as unarmed, unknown soldiers in a doomed battle against a vicious enemy.

16 MARCH 1945

It should have been an uneventful trip to Berlin. Wernher von Braun, along with his driver, in one car was being followed by Hannes Luehrsen, his chief architect, and Bernhard Tessmann, his chief designer of test facilities, in a second. They were on their way to the Ministry of Armaments to ask for funds to build a new laboratory. The laboratory was superfluous as far as the Third Reich was concerned, but planning for it was an essential exercise if von Braun wanted to keep his team together.

They left Bleicherode at 2:00 A.M. so they could drive the 150 miles to Berlin under cover of darkness. Daytime travel was out of the question because of the constant strafing by Allied fighters. The compact Hannomag Storm sped toward Berlin with a civilian driver at the wheel and von Braun dozing in the adjacent seat. Luehrsen and Tessmann followed the dimmed lights of von Braun's car on the dark, monotonous autobahn.

Wernher von Braun was soaring. He had the strange sensation that he was soaring through the peaceful, cobalt blue sky high above Grunau. He was back in the days of youth and innocence, before the Nazis, before the war, in a glider catching the rising air currents above Silesia. The sensation lasted only a fraction of a second; and von Braun found himself awake, sprawled inside an automobile in the dark. He pushed open a door and groggily got out.

There was a man in the front seat of the car, the driver. The man was unconscious. For some reason, it did not seem to be a good idea to leave him there. Von Braun began to drag the unconscious man out of the car. He was pulling only with his right hand; his left arm was not working. Von Braun kept pulling and the man came out of the car and onto the ground; then von Braun slowly dragged the unconscious man away from the wreck.

Von Braun's senses were beginning to work. He felt a warm stickiness of blood leaking over his lips. A searing pain cut through his left arm. He looked down to see that his left hand was hanging below his knee. A bright orange light crackled through the night air; the car was on fire. Then everything went black as von Braun slumped to the ground.

Luehrsen and Tessmann had watched in horror as the taillights of von Braun's car swerved off the pavement, flew over the embankment, and crashed into a railroad siding below. They stopped their car and scrambled down the embankment in the flickering light of the burning car. They found von Braun and his driver unconscious on the ground. Luehrsen and Tessmann gave what first aid they could, then went for help. Four hours later an ambulance arrived to take the two injured men to the hospital.

Von Braun awoke to find his chest and left arm encased in plaster. His shoulder had been shattered and his arm broken in two places. The gash in his upper lip had been stitched. The man he had pulled from the burning wreck, the driver, had sustained a fractured skull; but he too was alive.

CHAPTER 21

Scorched Earth:
Hitler's Solution to Defeat

19 MARCH 1945

The situation conference in Hitler's bunker had just ended. It had begun in the late evening and had gone past midnight. Albert Speer approached the Fuehrer with a thick memo in his hand.

Hitler asked his orderly to bring over a small package. It was a flat, red leather case stamped with the Fuehrer's emblem. Hitler handed the case to Speer with best wishes on his Minister of Armaments' 40th birthday. Inside the case was a silver-framed photo of Hitler with an inscription to Speer thanking him for his years of support and reassuring him of their lasting friendship. Hitler's handwriting was barely legible, showing the effects of his shaking hand and deteriorating nerves. Hitler had given similarly inscribed photographs to most of his close associates; but somehow, in the 12 years of their relationship, he had never presented one to Speer.

Speer had asked Hitler's adjutant to tell the Fuehrer that he would like such a gift as a 40th birthday present. It was Speer's circuitous way of telling Hitler that he valued their relationship and that he was still a loyal member of the team. Speer needed to reassure himself as well. Several weeks earlier, he had schemed to free Germany of Hitler's failed leadership by assassinating him. Speer had planned to release poison gas into the bunker through the ventilation system, thereby killing Hitler and all those with him. The plan failed, however, when Hitler himself ordered that the air intakes be modified to specifically remove the risk of a gas attack. His opportunity lost, Speer accepted Hitler's gift in lieu of forgiveness; and was moved by what he perceived to be unusual warmth on the part of Hitler during the presentation.

Having laid the groundwork of good fellowship and trust, Speer gave Hitler the 22-page memo he had been holding while the Fuehrer presented him with the birthday gift. In the memo, Speer analytically presented his prediction of the final collapse of Germany and his view of steps to be taken to preserve its industrial capacity for the survival of the German people after the war. He had not seriously objected to Hitler's policy of leaving only scorched earth for the enemies as they retook the conquered territories. After all, factories left behind could make weapons that could be turned against Germany. Now, he argued strongly against blowing up bridges and destroying factories in Germany. The extension of this destructive policy to the Fatherland was nothing less than national suicide. Nevertheless, as Speer left Hitler, he felt somewhat awkward at having used the moment of fellowship as an opportunity to challenge Hitler's policies.

While Speer was arranging transportation to leave Berlin, Hitler summoned him for a parting comment.

"This time you will receive a written reply to your memorandum," Hitler said. The warmth of moments earlier had turned to ice. "If the war is lost," he continued, "the people will be lost also. It is not necessary to worry about what the German people will need for elemental survival. On the contrary, it is best for us to destroy even these things. For the nation has proved to be the weaker, and the future belongs solely to the stronger eastern nation [i.e., the Soviet Union]. In any case only those who are inferior will remain after the struggle, for the good have already been killed."

Hitler's reply was not just to Speer, but to all of Germany. Before the day was out, he issued a general order for the destruction of all military, industrial, transportation, and communication facilities to prevent them from falling into the hands of the enemy. Let the enemies of the Reich inherit the scorched earth.

27 MARCH 1945

At 7:20 A.M. a ton of high explosives shattered a block of flats in Stepney. As the smoke and dust cleared, the double boom and sound of a body rushing through air identified the cause of the explosion. Over 130 people were killed that morning by a V-2. At 4:45 in the afternoon of the same day, the last V-2 fired at England fell with little significant effect at Orpington in Kent. Hans Kammler's battalions, which fired the weapons, quickly packed up their equipment and retreated from the advancing Allied front. London was safely out of range.

During the seven-month period in which the V-2 was used as a weapon, over 1,300 rockets were fired at England with 518 falling on London and 537 falling elsewhere in the country. Over 2,700 people were killed and over 6,000 seriously injured by the missile attacks. On the continent, 1,265 V-2s fell on Antwerp. Since that city was in the war zone, statistics on deaths and destruction were not gathered as rigorously as in England. While the deaths and injuries caused by the V-2 were unquestionably personal trage-dies, the numbers killed and the destruction were, in the context of the vast losses of the war, insignificant.

*　　*　　*　　*

The Luftwaffe was a shambles. The Allies dominated the skies, and the only weapon the Luftwaffe had that could retake them, the turbojet-powered Messerschmitt 262, was in short supply. Hitler needed a man who would not let the collapsing state of German industry stand in the way of producing more aircraft. He appointed Hans Kammler as the "Plenipotentiary of the Fuehrer for Jet Engine Aircraft." Hitler had put Kammler in charge of the manufacture and transport of jet aircraft to the airfields and also of con-struction of new airfields. He made Kammler the superior of Albert Speer and Hermann Goering in this area. Then Hitler explicitly ordered Speer and Goering to countersign the decree and thereby acknowledge their subordi-nate role to Kammler.

Kammler's new responsibilities were accompanied by a rank worthy of them. He was promoted from the rank of SS Gruppenfuehrer (lieutenant-general) to Obergruppenfuehrer (general).

30 MARCH 1945

Good Friday, the day of Redemption . . . for some.

"As far as the Luftwaffe is concerned," Joseph Goebbels wrote in his diary, "the Fuehrer has now given SS-Obergruppenfuehrer Kammler ex-traordinary wide plenary powers. In the matter of air armaments the Fuehrer wishes to carry through quite a small programme which, however, must be pursued with the utmost energy. Whatever happens, it must be completed. As a result of the powers given to Kammler, Goering feels that he is being by-passed but there is nothing to be done about that. The Fuehrer refuses any blame for failure to appoint Kammler earlier. Kammler only came to his notice in the organization for employment of the V-weapons. He is the right man to activate the Luftwaffe at its reduced level. . . . Should the

Luftwaffe generals object to Kammler's orders, the Fuehrer will react with courts martial and shooting. In any case he is determined to put some order into the Luftwaffe now. I think that he will succeed, for the Luftwaffe generals, after all, are cowards just like the army generals, and, as soon as they realize that they have a master over them, they will do what they are told."

1 APRIL 1945

Easter Sunday. The day of Resurrection. For the man buried in the Berlin bunker, it was April Fool's day.

American tanks had advanced as far as Muehlhausen, only 12 miles south of von Braun's headquarters at Bleicherode. Several members of von Braun's staff gathered at his temporary home for a strategy session. There was no question about it: they would have to move again. To stay would risk being caught in the middle of a battle. Besides, there was the awkward possibility of having to explain what they were doing in the proximity of the concentration camp that was building the rockets they had designed. A safe surrender to the Americans could only be helped by distancing themselves from the Mittelwerk. Von Braun decreed that no equipment be taken and that all engineering documents and plans be hidden somewhere in the mountains until they could be retrieved and used again.

One of those present, Dieter Huzel, wondered who would retrieve and use the documents, the Americans or the Russians?

Dieter Huzel was a 32-year-old electrical engineer who had been taken by the draft from a comfortable career with Siemens-Schuckert in Berlin and sent on a less-promising mission as a private on the eastern front. After a year in jobs behind the lines, he had the good fortune of being transferred to Peenemünde, where he rose rapidly in von Braun's organization. In the summer of 1944 Huzel became Wernher von Braun's technical assistant, replacing Magnus von Braun who had gone to the Mittelwerk to take over gyroscope production.

Von Braun, his mobility seriously restricted by the upper body and arm cast that encased his broken arm and shoulder, delegated to Dieter Huzel the responsibility of gathering together and hiding the rocket program's most valuable documents.

2 APRIL 1945

Dieter Huzel rose early and began the job of alerting everybody to prepare their essential documents and records for storage. He found it to be a monstrous task because of the disorganization resulting from the move from Peenemünde.

Von Braun called him to his office to find out how it was going. Huzel told him, and von Braun was not surprised. He gave Huzel a letter of safe conduct and told him that as far as finding a place to hide their documents was concerned, he and the rest of the staff would not be much help. Von Braun suggested that Huzel contact the local mining authorities. Possibly they could locate a suitable old mine or cave. Von Braun then gave Huzel what help he could. He told Huzel that he had assigned Bernhard Tessmann to assist him, that the car pool would give him a three-ton truck, and that the army would give him a corporal and eight or ten men to do the manual labor. Then von Braun emphasized the seriousness of the matter, saying there was no time to lose.

Huzel went back to the telephone to finish alerting the rocket development staff to gather together their most important papers for storage. Everything else was to be burned.

3 APRIL 1945

Joseph Goebbels made the following entry in his diary: "The Fuehrer has had very prolonged discussions with Obergruppenfuehrer Kammler who now carries responsibility for the reform of the Luftwaffe. Kammler is doing excellently and great hopes are placed on him." Hermann Goering was, in effect, replaced by a man with no experience in aerial warfare.

Hans Kammler was at the apex of an extraordinary career that had started in the extermination camps. His power had grown at the expense of concentration camp slaves, Albert Speer, the army, and now Hermann Goering. Unfortunately, the base of his power, Nazi Germany, was disintegrating under his feet. He would have to adapt to the fortunes of war.

*   *   *   *

It was night when the telephone rang for Lieutenant Colonel Herbert Axster, Walter Dornberger's chief of staff. SS General Hans Kammler's adjutant was on the line with an order from the general.

"You have a list of four hundred of the top men. You, as chief of staff, are responsible to gather these people together and are to move them to Oberammergau at the earliest possible time. There, at the Messerschmitt installation, will be a part of Kammler's staff. They will take over. You know that this is an order from Kammler."

It was not possible to get the men and their equipment together on such short notice, Axster objected.

"I will be expecting to hear from you in twenty-four hours."

They were being sent to Oberammergau in the "Alpine Redoubt." The Alpine Redoubt had never been planned by Hitler because the Third Reich was not supposed to have its back up against the wall, but it was a convenient fiction that was quickly adopted as an alternative to humiliating defeat at the hands of the Allies. According to the fantasy, the Fuehrer with his loyal SS divisions would regroup in the impenetrable mountains before counter-attacking, and then gaining final victory.

One did not have to be a rocket scientist to know that retreating to the Alpine Redoubt was futile. The Third Reich was crumbling, and all that was possible was a suicidal last stand.

4 APRIL 1945

Lieutenant Colonel Axster broke the news to Wernher von Braun before dawn. The team had to be assembled immediately. There would be no room for equipment or families. Anyone who refused to follow Kammler's order and stayed behind with his family ran the risk of being shot by the SS.

Despite the threat behind the evacuation order, von Braun may have welcomed it. He would be leaving behind many of his engineers and most of their records and equipment, but he would also be leaving behind Dora and the Mittelwerk. If he were captured by the Allies in their vicinity, von Braun, as an SS officer and the chief designer of the V-2 rocket, might be held responsible for the crimes committed at the Dora concentration camp and at the subterranean factory where slaves assembled the weapon he had created. He could hope to receive a warmer reception from the Americans if he surrendered himself and the keys of German rocket technology at an innocent distance from Dora and the Mittelwerk.

They would travel to Oberammergau aboard the "Vengeance Express." It was a train that had been with the rocket team for over a year. It had been at the A-4 test site at Blizna in Poland, where it had served as headquarters and dormitory for the launching crew officers. Most recently, it had been parked on a railroad siding at a potassium mine two miles outside of Bleicherode, where it was being used as a dormitory by the refugees from Peenemünde. The train had a powerful locomotive, a dozen sleeping cars, and a diner stocked with food and liquor. The Vengeance Express also had, as the 400 engineers discovered as they crowded on board, close to 100 armed SD guards, members of the Security Service of the SS. The guards were there, the engineers were told, for their protection. The guards could also have been there to see to it that no matter what happened, the rocket scientists did not fall into the hands of the enemy.

The Vengeance Express chugged out of Nordhausen on its twisting journey to the Alpine Redoubt, 400 miles to the south, and to an unknown future.

*   *   *   *

Not all of the rocket men were aboard the train. Wernher von Braun, because his upper torso and left arm were still encased in an awkward and uncomfortable cast, was permitted to travel to Oberammergau by automobile. When his car left Nordhausen, it was followed by a convoy of about 20 cars and trucks. Von Braun wanted means of transportation independent of the SS, just in case the need arose.

*   *   *   *

A third convoy formed in Bleicherode. Dieter Huzel, with a uniformed soldier behind the wheel, was in the lead car. Behind it were three panel trucks, two of them pulling trailers. Bernhard Tessmann and seven soldiers filled the cabs of the trucks. In the trucks and trailers were 14 tons of documents, all the technical treasures and knowledge needed to start a rocket development program at the stage where that of the Third Reich had been cut off. Everything that was not essential had been burned. Huzel's convoy drove off into the Harz Mountains in search of a place to bury the treasures.

*   *   *   *

Himmler had ordered that all prisoners of the Dora/Nordhausen complex of camps be herded into the subterranean factory and gassed. But Himmler, as Hans Kammler had tried to point out to him three years earlier, did not understand the technical difficulties of mass murder. The Dora/Nordhausen complex held tens of thousands of men on the brink of death, but the SS did not have the means to kick them into the abyss. The tunnel openings would have to be sealed, which was no minor task. In addition, the area within the tunnels was so vast that there was not enough gas available to do the job. Furthermore, with the arrival of American troops imminent, there was not enough time. The only thing to do was to make the prisoners somebody else's problem.

On the morning of 4 April, the SS guards told the prisoners to take their daily rations and a blanket—if they could find one—and march. The men, starved and sick with dysentery, were herded with the encouragement of truncheons, gun butts, and boots to the railroad station where they were loaded into open wooden wagons. They had seen other prisoners taken away in the trains before, men too sick or too feeble to work. Those who left never came back. The prisoners wondered if now they too would be joining the "Heaven Kommandos." When evening came, the trains finally began to move. An icy rain started to fall, and it soon soaked the pitiful men. The fourth convoy left the subterranean rocket factory on its miserable journey into the unknown.

EARLY APRIL 1945

Hans Kammler had come to see Albert Speer in Berlin to say good-bye. It was a strange thing for him to do in view of their competitive relationship. Kammler seemed to lack his usual arrogant elan. Speer thought he seemed insecure and slippery. Perhaps Kammler's demeanor was caused by the strain of carrying on as if victory was imminent. The charade was necessary, of course. To admit to the reality that the Reich was disintegrating all around them would invite an accusation of being a saboteur, and that would invite summary execution by SS men even more zealous than he was. So Kammler had promised Hitler everything and put on a good show for Goebbels and the rest of Hitler's entourage.

Kammler's conversation with Speer snaked around the current rumor on its way to the point. There were some in the SS who were making plans to get rid of Hitler, he said. Kammler, of course, was not involved. He had other plans. He intended to contact the Americans. Kammler would trade Germany's technical treasures for his freedom. He was in a position to do it because he was in control of jet plane production and rocket development, which included, as he pointed out, the "transcontinental rocket" (i.e., the "American Rocket"). Kammler had already begun to assemble the booty. He was, he said, gathering together in upper Bavaria all of Germany's key technical experts. Speer was welcome to participate in Kammler's proposed deal with the Americans. It would certainly work out in Speer's best interest. Kammler was about to leave for Munich. Perhaps it would be wise for Speer to join him in moving south.

Speer could be one more pawn in Kammler's trade. Speer was not interested.

5–7 APRIL 1945

The sun had been down several hours when Dieter Huzel stopped the truck at the mouth of the inactive mine near the small village of Doernten in the foothills of the Harz Mountains. Bernhard Tessmann was in the seat beside him. The rest of the men were locked in the back of the truck with the boxes. If questioned later, the men would be able to say truthfully that they did not know where they had left the 14 tons of documents. Huzel let the men out of the back of the truck. An electric battery-powered engine with several small flatcars was parked on a siding that ran into the mine. The men immediately began transferring the boxes of documents from the truck and the trailer behind it to the flatcars. When they had finished, Huzel drove off to his staging point at Goslar, many miles away, to get the second truck.

The small engine pulled the cars loaded with treasures into the tunnel, past several side galleries, for a distance of about 1,000 feet into the hillside. A side shaft led gently upward for about 100 yards and ended at an ironclad door. Behind the door was an empty room about 25 feet wide by 25 feet deep and 12 feet high. The old caretaker of the mine had told Huzel that when the mine had been in operation, the room was the powder magazine. The men began stacking the boxes of documents in the room.

Three hours after he had left, Huzel returned with the second truck. He waited for his crew for about two hours. They finally emerged from the mine, took a brief rest, and began loading the boxes from the second truck onto the flatcars. Then Huzel was off for the third and last truck. When he got back to the mine, it was nearly dawn. They hauled the last of the boxes into the vault at 11 A.M., and they were bleary eyed and dead tired.

The caretaker of the mine saw to it that before they left they all got showers and a meal of bean soup. Then Huzel and his crew drove off in search of beds and a long night's rest.

Huzel and Tessmann drove back to the mine the following day to inspect the caretaker's handiwork. He had promised to dynamite the tunnel leading to the vault. The old man had blasted a substantial piece of the tunnel's roof into a barricade, but someone with curiosity and dedication could still have climbed over the jumble of rocks to find the vault. The caretaker said he would take care of it. Huzel and Tessmann were long gone when the second dynamite blast sealed the tunnel, and only they and the old caretaker knew there was anything of value behind the wall of broken rock.

9 APRIL 1945

Dieter Huzel, with his driver, in an empty truck was returning to Nordhausen, threading through the gauntlet of crumbling Germany on the way to rejoin von Braun and his group at Oberammergau. As they approached Nordhausen they heard fierce anti-aircraft fire cutting through the night sky, followed by the concussion of bombs. Brilliant flares floating over the city and the flash of exploding bombs made a lethal celebration. They pulled to the side of the road to watch the deadly fireworks and to wait for the bombing to end.

*   *   *   *

The people of Nordhausen fled to the only place they knew was safe, the only place where the falling bombs could not touch them: the underground rocket factory three miles away. They got in the way of what was to be the SS's last activity there. The SS guards had assembled the remaining slaves—those who had not been shipped out by rail or died—in the tunnel near the entrance for a general roll call. They had positioned a battery of machine guns at the entrance to the tunnel facing the prisoners. The SS guard had orders from Hitler, relayed via Himmler, that all prisoners should "share the annihilation" rather than fall into the Allies' hands. Before Himmler's order could be carried out, hundreds of German civilians from Nordhausen arrived in lorries and flooded into the tunnel. Women and children mingled with the wretched remnants of the prisoner work force. There was no way to selectively machine gun the slaves. Their misery could last a little longer.

11 April 1945

The smoking ruins of Nordhausen were taken and occupied by Combat Command B of the United States Army's 3rd Armored Division under the command of Brigadier General Truman Boudinot. The door-to-door cleanup was to be carried out by the 104th "Timberwolf" Infantry Division, which followed in the wake of the tanks. The United States Army groups made discoveries that would shock and sicken the most battle-hardened veterans, then amaze them.

The concentration camp at Nordhausen had been abandoned by its SS guards. What was left behind to be found by the liberating armies was described in an official history of the Third Army: "Hundreds of corpses lay sprawled over the acres of the big compound. More hundreds filled the great barracks. They lay in contorted heaps, half stripped, mouths gaping in the dirt and straw, or they were piled naked like cordwood." By one estimate there were 5,000 corpses in varying stages of decomposition.

Amid the stench of human decay and the unbelievable filth were about 1,000 survivors, those who had been too far gone to be evacuated a week earlier. They had starved till they were just skin-covered skeletons, but they had not yet cut the last thread that connected them to life and freedom. Their prison uniforms hung on their shrunken bodies loosely; some were so filthy that the vertical stripes could no longer be seen. The skeletons were aged men and 14-year-old boys. They tottered and weaved among their liberators in a delirium of euphoria and exhaustion, speaking a babel of tongues, the languages of the enemies of the Third Reich.

With Nordhausen secured, the United States Army units moved along the road and railroad line toward the village of Niedersachswerfen about two and a half miles to the northwest. As they approached the village, they were met on the road by more of the emaciated, hollow-eyed men. They were shouting and waving toward the mountain. There was something the Americans must see, something fantastic, important.

What they found was fantastic: another concentration camp as evil, malignant, and repellent as the one discovered in Nordhausen just hours earlier. The camp was an open cesspool brimming with filth and stinking of excrement and decomposing bodies. Corpses were everywhere. Hundreds had been dumped on the ground adjacent to a low building part way up the hill, the crematorium. In the days before liberation, thousands had died of starvation and cholera. Bodies had been fed into the ovens four at a time day and night, but the bodies piled up faster than the ovens could consume them. When the liberators arrived, the ovens were still warm.

The walking skeletons at Camp Dora were ecstatic that their liberators had arrived. One group tried to lift an American officer onto their shoulders, but could not do it. The freed slaves were too weak. Before long, United States Army medical units arrived and moved the survivors out of the camps and into improvised hospitals.

The wraiths had not meant Camp Dora when they told their liberators of something fantastic. To them death was as common as dirt. They took the officers of the Armored group beneath the earth into the two parallel tunnels that ran over a mile into the mountain. One tunnel was occupied by a factory for building V-1 buzz bombs of the type that had rained down on England; the other tunnel held a factory for building giant rockets, the V-2s. The two main tunnels were connected by cross-tunnels filled with tools and precision machinery. Everything seemed to be in working order, as if the workers had just taken a break.

If the good Germans of Nordhausen had been ignorant of the atrocities that had taken place in their city, they were to learn about them quickly. About 100 people from Nordhausen and captured SS men were conscripted under guard to clear the camps of the decaying bodies.

The Nordhausen and Dora concentration camps were the first major slave labor camps to be liberated. The grainy newsreel was proof of the unimaginable depravity of the Third Reich. The starved wraiths leaned out of their filthy bunks to stare blankly at the camera. Hundreds, thousands, of corpses appeared to be skeletons thrown into filthy sacks as they lay in orderly rows in a vast courtyard. The corpses were dragged off and thrown like so much rubbish into mass graves. These images caught on film caused shock and repulsion. They burned into the conscience of Western civilization and made a lasting impact in history. The cavern where the pitiful men slaved and died and the factory that built the fantastic rockets were soon forgotten.

CHAPTER 22

The Alpine Redoubt: A Refuge and a Trap

11 APRIL 1945

As Wernher von Braun described it, "the scenery was magnificent. The quarters were plush. There was only one hitch—our camp was surrounded by barbed wire!" When they had arrived at Oberammergau in the foothills of the magnificently scenic Alps, the core group of 400 rocket scientists took up residence in a former army camp. Half of the camp was already occupied by engineers from the Messerschmitt factory who had been brought there earlier. Von Braun's team went through the motions of solving problems, and designing the next generation of rockets. Why not? There was nothing else to do, and the SS guards kept them from leaving.

Hans Kammler had summoned Wernher von Braun to meet him at what was known locally as the "House of Jesus." It was, more formally, the Hotel Alios Lang, bearing the name of its owner who played the part of the Savior in the local Passion Play. Lang was a Nazi, as were all other members of the cast, except, ironically, the man who played Judas.

Kammler's mood, as described by Wernher von Braun, was quite different from that of the intense and insecure man who had said good-bye to Albert Speer only a few days earlier. Presumably, von Braun did not know about Kammler's farewell visit to Speer or his scheme to trade the Third Reich's technical treasures to the Americans for his freedom, a plan remarkably similar to von Braun's. Did von Braun, caught up in the intensity of the moment, simply misread Kammler? Had something happened during the intervening days that von Braun did not know about?

Did von Braun hold back some of the details? We have only his account of the event.

Von Braun was told to wait in the lobby of the hotel until he was called to his meeting with Kammler. Von Braun waited, uncomfortable in his upper body and arm cast. As he waited, he caught bits and pieces of a conversation between two familiar voices. The voices came from the adjacent room, the tavern. He could make out some words: "Ettal," "Ettaler Klosterlikor." Ettal was a town three miles south of Oberammergau and was the location of a fourteenth-century Benedictine abbey and its rococo church. Ettaler Klosterlikor was the popular liqueur distilled by the monks at the abbey. So, von Braun thought, they were drinking.

Why don't you burn that uniform, put on civilian clothing, go to the monastery at Ettal, and become a monk, one voice said. Von Braun recognized it as that of Kammler's chief of staff, SS Major Starck.

The idea has merit, Kammler replied, carrying on what von Braun thought was a joke.

Kammler continued. The monastery would be an excellent place to hide out, and there certainly would be enough liquor to drink. Who knows, maybe he could bring some good business sense to the management of the operation, make a career of it.

At that point, an SS guard escorted von Braun into the tavern and the presence of Kammler and his chief of staff, Starck. Starck had his machine pistol at the ready, leaning against his right thigh. Kammler sat next to him.

The Bavarian ambience must have agreed with Kammler, or perhaps it was the liquor. He was in a surprisingly relaxed mood. He asked von Braun to sit down and offered him a glass of the Etaller Klosterlikor. Then he asked von Braun about his broken arm and shattered shoulder. He was concerned about von Braun's well-being. And what about von Braun's team? Were they being well taken care of? And were they still working?

Von Braun assured Kammler that his team of engineers was carrying out the meaningless exercise.

Good. Kammler was pleased. Then he reminded von Braun that he had more to concern himself with than the rocket builders. He was also "Plenipotentiary of the Fuehrer for Jet Engine Aircraft." He was about to "leave Oberammergau for an indeterminate period." It seemed he had a meaningless exercise of his own to take care of.

In his absence, SS Major Kummer would be in command. Kammler hoped that von Braun and his men would be as cooperative with Kummer as they had been with him.

Final victory is still attainable, Kammler said. He had played out his charade for von Braun. Von Braun was dismissed.

It was the last time anybody of any consequence or with any credibility reported seeing Hans Kammler.

12 APRIL 1945

Hans Kammler left Oberammergau as he said he would. Those members of his staff who stayed behind did not know or would not say where he had gone, but two things were still certain: the 400 men of von Braun's rocket development group were still confined within the old army camp, and the SS was on the outside in charge of their fate. It was time for von Braun to meet and size up Kammler's appointed successor, Major Kummer.

Von Braun and his old friend and colleague Ernst Steinhoff went to introduce themselves to their new keeper. Major Kummer was handsome in his black SS uniform. He was polite and genial to his two visitors; but he was clearly not cut from the same cloth as his superior, Kammler. He was somehow uneasy, possibly insecure. Perhaps this man could be reasoned with.

Von Braun and Steinhoff were pleased to be under his protection here in Germany's Alpine Redoubt, they told Major Kummer. They appreciated the seriousness of his responsibilities; but of course, there was the problem of the Jabos, the American P-47 Thunderbolts. The Jabos owned the sky; and they would continue to do so until General Kammler, the "Plenipotentiary of the Fuehrer for Jet Engine Aircraft," was able to clear them of the enemy. Until then . . . well, there was the constant danger that their bombing and strafing could seriously harm those under Major Kummer's protection. They conjured up the image of a bomb falling on the camp and wiping out everybody there. Kummer, they said, would be held responsible.

Von Braun and Steinhoff could almost see Kummer weighing the dilemma in his mind. He had orders to keep the rocket development team in the camp. If he disobeyed the orders, he would be in deep trouble. On the other hand, the American pilots could attack the camp and cause casualties among his charges, possibly kill them all. Then his troubles would be much worse.

He understood the problem, he admitted, but there was nothing he could do about it. Just then a flight of Jabos screamed overhead.

Von Braun proposed a solution. Scatter the men among the neighboring villages. Then no single attack could seriously harm the whole team.

Kummer made his last feeble arguments. He was responsible for their safety, and he could not guarantee it if the rocket scientists were dispersed. Besides, he did not have access to transportation for their dispersal.

That was no problem, von Braun smiled. While the majority of his men had come to Oberammergau by rail on the "Vengeance Express," he had ordered a small contingent to drive about 20 cars and trucks to the Alps.

But what about fuel? Kummer protested.

They had some gasoline and a virtually unlimited supply of ethyl alcohol rocket fuel. They could easily mix a serviceable concoction. To sweeten the deal, they offered Major Kummer a private sedan with all the fuel he could use. What was a little corruption after all that had gone before?

Still, Kummer was not sure. He had the option of following orders or making a decision; and German officers, especially SS officers, excelled at following orders. Time ticked by with agonizing slowness as Kummer considered the proposal.

Then the American Jabos whined overhead again. Major Kummer made a decision. The rocket engineers would be dispersed.

The following day, SD guards took the rocket engineers in small groups to their new residences in the neighboring villages. True, the engineers were still under the protection of the SS; but the chances of the whole team being annihilated by an enemy bombing raid or the quirky, arbitrary action of the SS was greatly reduced.

13 APRIL 1945

The last pointless and depraved scene of the Dora-Nordhausen-Mittelwerk drama was acted out near Gardelegen, about 80 miles north of Nordhausen. A convoy of 2,500 to 3,000 prisoners had spent six days and nights in wagons and on foot before finally reaching the area. They were housed temporarily in an old cavalry school located in the middle of Gardelegen. The commandant of the town along with officers of the German Army and the Luftwaffe took two more days to decide how to dispose of this human baggage.

The prisoners were marched out of their quarters in the town to Isenschnibbe, outside Gardelegen. They were guarded by about 100 men from the SS, the army, the Luftwaffe, the Home Army, and parachutists, and about 25 German prisoners who had been outfitted in SS uniforms complete with death's head emblems on their caps and rifles in their hands. At 7:00 P.M., over 1,000 starved and exhausted men were herded into a barn. The floor of the barn had been covered with straw, then soaked with gasoline. The guards locked the doors of the barn and set fire to it. The screams of the dying men were soon lost in the roar of the flames, which lasted seven hours.

When American troops reached the area a day and a half later, they found 1,016 bodies in the remains of the barn and in an unfinished mass grave. Only four of the victims could be identified by name and 301 by their number; 711 bodies were unidentifiable. Less than 20 men had survived the flames by taking shelter in holes they had dug or under the charred corpses of their less fortunate fellows. The murderers had, of course, disappeared leaving behind scorched earth as Hitler had ordered.

15 APRIL 1945

Oberammergau was dangerous. The SS was everywhere; and, with the end in sight, they might do something Wernher von Braun would regret. Von Braun decided it was time for him and the last few members of his team who were still with him to move higher into the mountains to Oberjoch near the Adolf Hitler Pass. Walter Dornberger had taken refuge there after the mass exodus from the Mittelwerk, and he had with him the remnants of his staff. The company of about 150 army men would be a protection, albeit a small one, against the SS.

They left Oberammergau quietly and separately. The sun had set long before the last of them reached Oberjoch. They found Dornberger and his staff staying at Haus Ingeborg, a large, three-story hotel. The hotel was already crowded, but the army found room for them. Walter Dornberger and Wernher von Braun were together again; but their team, which had breathed life into the giant rocket, had now dwindled to just a handful: Dieter Huzel, Bernhard Tessmann, von Braun's younger brother Magnus, and a few others.

17 APRIL 1945

They must have thought he had gone mad when they received Kammler's message at SS Headquarters.

"According to the Fuehrer's order, jet planes have priority over military planes. Am therefore not in position to release desired truck." Kammler had sent a secret wire to SS Headquarters from Munich in response to an attempt by the SS to confiscate a truck from the Junkers aircraft firm. "Work on expediting jet aircraft production is progressing in accordance with the Fuehrer's orders."

The Third Reich was collapsing on all fronts, the homeland had been penetrated deeply by the enemy, and Kammler was still building jet fighter planes for which there was no fuel. On top of that, he lectured headquarters on priorities so that he would not have to turn over one truck. Why did he make such a big deal out of one lousy truck?

They never found out, because it was the last time they heard from Kammler, or about the truck. Yet, the truck was important, at least to Kammler. He may have needed it to haul something. Documents? Blueprints? Test records? His own personal records of the deployment and operations of the superweapons? One could imagine Kammler at the wheel of the disputed truck, driving his load of technical treasure into the waiting arms of the highest bidder and into the safety of an anonymous future.

V

DEFEAT AND TRIUMPH

CHAPTER 23

Twilight of the Trolls:
The Death of the Third Reich

23–24 APRIL 1945

The tiny Fieseler/Storch artillery-observation plane touched down on the broad boulevard and rolled to a stop just in front of the Brandenburg Gate. The pilot stayed with the aircraft while the tall passenger stopped a passing army vehicle and persuaded its driver to take him to the Reich Chancellery, less than a mile away. Albert Speer had come to Berlin to say good-bye to his mentor and his friend.

Despite the conciliatory nature of his visit, Speer was uneasy about seeing Hitler. He had disobeyed his Fuehrer by refusing to execute Hitler's "scorched earth" policy, wanting to save as much of Germany's industry as possible for the difficult days of rebuilding that would follow the war.

Speer entered Hitler's study. He had hoped for and expected a warm greeting from Hitler, but he was disappointed. Hitler was cool and unemotional. He was burned out, empty, and preoccupied with his own impending doom. Hitler began to talk about Admiral Karl Doenitz. What did Speer think about Doenitz's approach to his job? Speer had the impression that Hitler was gathering opinions about his possible successor, and he gave Doenitz a cautious endorsement.

Then Hitler abruptly changed the subject. He asked Speer if he should stay in Berlin or fly to Berchtesgaden. Stay in Berlin, Speer advised Hitler. What would he do at Obersalzberg? When Berlin is lost, the war will be over. Hitler agreed, saying he only wanted Speer to confirm his own thinking. Then he talked about ending his life, that of his mistress, Eva Braun, and that of his dog, Blondi.

Speer's awkward meeting with Hitler ended when the army chief of staff, General Krebs, arrived to give the situation report. It was a dreary meeting that gave no hope but merely charted the approaching end. Hitler tried to find cause for optimism in the report, but his colleagues were quietly unconvinced. The meeting ended abruptly.

Hermann Goering's radio message had arrived in the evening. It was addressed not to Hitler, but to Reich Minister Joachim von Ribbentrop. In it Goering stated that since Hitler was trapped in Berlin and was no longer free to lead the Reich, he, Goering, was assuming the role of leadership. Goering then ordered von Ribbentrop to fly to Berchtesgaden to join him.

Goering had blundered magnificently and disastrously. Not only had he been caught in a naked grab for power—what little of it there was left in Germany—he had insulted the Fuehrer by directing his message to a subordinate.

Martin Bormann, secretary to the Fuehrer, drafted a telegram for Hitler's approval. The message immediately stripped Goering of his right of succession and accused him of treason to the Fuehrer and of betrayal of National Socialism. The telegram offered Goering immunity from further penalties if he would resign all his offices immediately because of failing health. Within half an hour Goering's reply arrived. He was resigning all of his offices, he said, because he had suffered a severe heart attack.

Goering's resignation left a vacancy for commander in chief of the Luftwaffe. A logical replacement would seem to be SS General Hans Kammler, who Hitler had recently given sweeping responsibilities over the Luftwaffe. However, Kammler had simply disappeared a week earlier. Hitler would have to find somebody else to replace Goering.

At three o'clock in the morning, Speer sent word to Hitler that he was about to leave and wished to say good-bye. Hitler was once again unemotional and detached. Speer grasped his cold hand for the last time.

"So, you're leaving? Good. *Auf Wiedersehen.*"

Speer's composure began to crumble. He stammered something about coming back, the old friends could be together again. Hitler could see that it was a lie. He turned his attention to other matters. Speer was dismissed.

25 APRIL 1945

At 4:40 P.M., American and Russian troops met on the banks of the Elbe at Torgaun, 75 miles south of Berlin. Nazi Germany was now cut into two parts: the northern retreat centered around Berlin, and the mythical Alpine Redoubt lay in the remote south.

*   *   *   *

Wernher von Braun was a physical wreck. He had been the de facto leader of the rocket development organization since the previous July when Dornberger was reassigned, and he had been on the move and constantly under pressure to save his team since late January. On top of all that, his broken shoulder and arm were not healing properly. He was told that if he did not have his arm re-set soon, he might lose it. So with a good part of his team left behind in the Harz Mountains and the rest scattered throughout Bavaria, with meaningful work at a standstill, he agreed that it was time to consider his own health. He went to a hospital at Sonthofen, 40 miles west of Oberammergau.

The hospital had an excellent orthopedic staff with plenty of experience repairing the fractured bones of skiers and mountain climbers. Von Braun was told that he needed two operations about four days apart to re-break and re-set his fractures. Since medical supplies were in short supply and used only for the most serious cases, he underwent the first procedure without benefit of an anesthetic. He was returned to bed in traction with instructions not to move.

As von Braun lay in bed recovering from his ordeal, a flight of Jabos appeared. The fighters strafed and bombed Sonthofen. While other patients were taken to safety in the basement, von Braun remained in his room tied to his bed. The attack shattered nearby buildings and took its toll on von Braun's nerves, but it left the hospital intact.

In the afternoon of von Braun's third day in traction, a soldier driving an ambulance and wearing a Red Cross armband arrived at the hospital. He had been sent by Walter Dornberger.

Get dressed, he said. I've brought an ambulance to take you away.

Why?

The French are near. They could be here in an hour.

If von Braun stayed and he was lucky, he had one more bone-setting procedure to go through, again without the aid of an anesthetic. If he was unlucky, the French Army would arrive and separate him—possibly for ever—from Dornberger and the remnants of the rocket team. The choice was easy.

A doctor untied him from his bed and put his left arm in a massive plaster cast. His arm was bent at the elbow and raised to shoulder height so that it looked like a bird's wing frozen in place before the bird could leap into the air and fly. They dressed von Braun and put him in the ambulance. Before the day was over, von Braun was back in the relative safety of Oberjoch with Dornberger and his inner circle.

26–29 APRIL 1945

Hitler's last two visitors arrived in a bullet-riddled Fieseler Storch that was leaking gasoline from its wing tanks as it rolled to a stop on the East-West Axis just short of the Brandenburg Gate. On board was General-aloberst (colonel general) Robert Ritter von Greim, the man Hitler had chosen to be Goering's successor in leading the Luftwaffe. Von Greim, who had been piloting the light plane, had been wounded, his foot shattered by an armor-piercing bullet. His companion who took over the controls, was, like him, fanatically loyal to Hitler and willing to die for the crumbling Reich. She was von Greim's lover, the erstwhile Luftwaffe test pilot, Hanna Reitsch.

Von Greim's wound was treated when they reached Hitler's bunker. Then Hitler told his guests why he had ordered them on their perilous journey. He promoted von Greim to field marshal and appointed him Goering's successor as commander in chief of the defeated Luftwaffe. Von Greim was honored by the appointment, and he and Hanna Reitsch asked their Fuehrer for the ultimate honor, to be allowed to stay with him in the bunker until the end. Hitler agreed.

Two days later, Hitler changed his mind. He had learned that Himmler had betrayed him by trying to cut a deal with the Allies for a favorable end to the war. He gave von Greim and Reitsch a twofold mission. They were to stop Himmler and to rally the Luftwaffe to the defense of the beseiged city of Berlin. Although they were devastated at being deprived of the honor of dying with their Fuehrer, they obeyed his order.

In the early hours of 29 April, von Greim and Reitsch left the bunker amid a hail of Russian artillery shells to begin their fool's mission. When they reached the East-West Axis, they squeezed into a two-seat Arado 96 trainer with a Luftwaffe pilot. The aircraft sped down the broad boulevard and then lifted off over the Brandenburg Gate. It climbed over the shattered, burning city through the smoke and the glare of searchlight beams, and into the safety of the clouds. It carried the last people to escape the city before its fall to the Russians.

29–30 APRIL 1945

The remaining core of the rocket team from Peenemünde waited for the end at Haus Ingeborg in Oberjoch near the Adolf Hitler Pass. The surroundings had never been touched or even approached by the war, but its arrival was expected soon in the form of American or French troops.

There is disagreement about the mood of the group during its last few days at Oberjoch. According to Walter Dornberger, they were peaceful days in the pristine beauty of the high mountains. Below them spring had arrived, turning the pastures on the hills a brilliant green. The snow on the mountains sparkled under the clear blue sky, and wildflowers were beginning to push their buds up through the melting snow. The war was over for Dornberger and his companions. Their rocket development work had ended. They had left the Mittelwerk long ago and were free of Kammler and his cronies. They lay out on the hotel terrace quietly reflecting on the years of hard work, on their incredible achievement, and on the opportunities that had been lost with the war.

Dieter Huzel remembered the last days as being filled with uncertainty, tension, and hysteria. The vacuum of information was filled with rumors. The enemy was approaching. Were they French or American? French. Worse than that: Moroccans. The Moroccans had gained a reputation among the Germans as being fierce and merciless fighters. When under the influence of liquor, they were murderous. About the time the residents of Haus Ingeborg heard the rumor about the Moroccans, they discovered the wine cellar. The liquor had to be gotten rid of. If the Moroccans ever found it, they would all be dead. They formed a bucket brigade to pass the bottles to the trucks. A few bottles were opened along the way, and their contents fueled the frenzy. The men filled the trucks with 5,000 bottles of wine and liqueur, then carried the deadly cargo to a nearby military hospital. Let the unsuspecting casualties of war deal with the liquor and the Moroccans.

Then there was the lingering specter of their former collaborators, Kammler and the SS. Those murderous zealots could not be trusted. They might trade the Dornberger-von Braun team to the enemy in exchange for their own escape. If a trade could not be worked out, they might kill them all, destroy Germany's greatest treasure, just to keep them from falling into the hands of the Allies. Not surprisingly, many of the rocket scientists had quietly slipped away in search of a safer haven or a way home.

1 MAY 1945

The morning was a dreary gray with an occasional sprinkling of cold rain. The boredom of the afternoon was interrupted by the radio. "Stand by for an important announcement," it said.

This is it, they thought. Surrender.

A few moments later the announcement came. "The Fuehrer was killed yesterday, April 30, in combat in his headquarters in Berlin."

It was, somehow, totally expected and anticlimactic. Nobody had much to say afterward, and they all went back to their solitary pursuits. Not until much later did they learn the truth, that Hitler and his companions had committed suicide. Describing their reactions to that day, Dieter Huzel wrote, "A little man, who had long since ceased to matter, had died." It was melancholic news, but trivial in the light of the suffering he had brought upon Germany. What the misfits of the Third Reich would have wanted to romanticize as the *Gotterdammerung*, the twilight of the gods, turned out to be the twilight of the trolls.

2 MAY 1945

After the betrayals by Goering and Himmler, in one of his last acts before he took his own life, Adolf Hitler named Admiral Karl Doenitz as his political successor. The new chief of state was faced with the thankless and hopeless task of putting Germany out of its misery.

As the final bits of the Third Reich were swept away by the Allies, Albert Speer, who had recommended Doenitz to Hitler, looked to the future. Hitler was gone, and the rest of the Nazi leadership would soon follow. Speer, however, had no intention of being one of those to go. He thought about his future in postwar Germany, and he planned to begin writing his memoirs without delay. It never occurred to him that the victors would hold him accountable for his crimes as a leader of the Third Reich.

*   *   *   *

Each survivor of the Third Reich had his own way of dealing with matters of honor and survival. Wernher von Braun and General Walter Dornberger decided on the path of surrender.

Their options seemed limited. They could wait for the French troops who were reportedly approaching the area to take them into custody. They could wait for some zealous and trigger-happy SS men to make their options and choices irrelevant, or they could contact the Americans. Magnus von Braun, Wernher's younger brother, was chosen to make the first contact because he spoke English better than anybody else in the group.

The younger von Braun left Haus Ingeborg in Oberjoch by bicycle in the morning on his way through the Adolph Hitler Pass toward Austria, where they believed American troops were in control. He had gone no more than four kilometers when he reached the Austrian border town of Schattwald and was taken into custody by a group of American soldiers. Between his broken English and the rudimentary German spoken by one of the Americans, he got across his story. He was one of 150 German rocket personnel who were lodged a short distance away behind the German lines. His brother Wernher, who had led the group that had invented the V-2 rocket, and the others wanted to surrender.

The Americans thought his story fantastic; but, nonetheless, they took Magnus von Braun to the command post of the United States Army's 44th Division Counter-Intelligence Corps, which was in Reutte, 26 kilometers to the east. At Reutte, Magnus repeated his story to First Lieutenant Charles L. Stewart. He said that the group of rocket men wanted to join the Americans because they felt the Americans would support their continued rocket development work. He added that his group wanted to surrender immediately because they felt their lives were in danger from the zealous remnants of the SS who did not want them to fall into the hands of the enemy.

Lieutenant Stewart was willing to listen to more and to accept the surrender of the German rocket scientists—if, in fact, the young German was telling the truth. He gave Magnus a pass that would allow him and the key people of the German rocket group to safely cross into Austria and the area controlled by the American army.

Magnus had returned to Haus Ingeborg by 2:00 P.M., and the group of rocket men who would surrender to the Americans began to assemble. The German Army's rocket team had eroded catastrophically in just four months. The 4,325 who had worked at Peenemünde had been pared down to about 3,000 who had been relocated to the Mittelwerk. The group had been whittled down again to 400 key people who had taken the Vengeance Express to Oberammergau, then eroded to the loyal few who had stayed with Wernher von Braun and Walter Dornberger at Haus Ingeborg. Of the 150 who were there, the large majority were from Dornberger's military staff and were not rocket scientists as Magnus may have implied to Lieutenant Stewart. Walter Dornberger and Wernher von Braun selected the final seven members of the team who would immediately turn themselves over to the Americans.

At 4:10 P.M. a somber procession of three field-grey BMWs left under an equally gray sky. Magnus von Braun, Walter Dornberger, and Bernhard Tessmann were in the lead car. Wernher von Braun and Dieter Huzel were in the middle car. Hans Lindenberg, chief propulsion engineer of the team, and Herbert Axster, Dornberger's chief of staff, brought up the rear. All seven men, including General Dornberger and Lieutenant Colonel Axster, had dressed in civilian clothes. A light sleet had begun to fall, accentuating the somber mood as they drove into their uncertain future.

When they finally arrived in Reutte it was dark. Lieutenant Stewart and his staff briefly questioned the Germans, assigned them to rooms in the mansion they were occupying, then fed them dinner. The long day had ended for both the rocket scientists and their American hosts.

There was something about the dynamics of the group of Germans which Lieutenant Stewart noticed but did not understand. The lead was taken by the 33-year-old, blonde engineer who unashamedly claimed responsibility for having designed the V-2 rocket, the weapon that had brought terror, destruction, and death to England and the Low Countries in the final months of the war. He was outgoing, full of information, and strangely jovial. Major General Walter Dornberger, the ranking member of the group, was reserved to the point of being subordinate. What Stewart did not understand or appreciate was that von Braun was a civilian with knowledge and skills to sell to his hosts. Dornberger was, for the second time in his life, a defeated warrior with an indefinite stay in a prisoner-of-war camp as the only certainty in his future. He had no reason to be in a good mood; the war had ended for him—not with a bang, but with a humiliating whimper.

3 MAY 1945

The storm had passed, and the morning was clear but cold when the seven defectors arose. Their American hosts led them to a temporary building which was being used as a mess hall. There they were treated with unexpected deference to a regulation G.I. breakfast of eggs, toast, cereal, and coffee. When they had finished, they were taken outside for an even greater surprise: a press conference.

The photograph taken at the time shows seven men in overcoats standing on the muddy ground. They were unsmiling, uncertain, possibly apprehensive about their futures, and uncomfortable about being put on display. The two men placed prominently at the center of the picture were Walter Dornberger, his features partially hidden in the shadow of his hat brim, and Wernher von Braun. Von Braun's left arm was encased in plaster and jutted out horizontally from under his coat; it bent at the elbow placing his hand over the center of his chest in a mysterious salute.

The center of attention at their introduction to the press was not the senior member of the group, Walter Dornberger. He was, after all, just another defeated German general; and there were more than enough of them already. One of the reporters, a sergeant writing for an army newspaper, found his story in the 33-year-old man with his arm encased in plaster. Von Braun, who had spent his entire professional career in the obscurity of military secrecy, apparently loved the new-found attention.

The army reporter described von Braun as being jovial and nonchalant as he told his story. He claimed to be the technical director of the group that designed and built the V-2 rocket. He had, according to the reporter's account, conceived the idea of the fantastic new weapon while a student in Berlin over 13 years earlier. If they had had two more years, von Braun boasted, the V-2 missile would have given the victory in the war to Germany. Of course, the victory would have also required production of 200 missiles a day, and von Braun glossed over the facts that Germany had neither the time nor the missiles. Dornberger's contributions as the man who interested the German Army in rockets, who built the research organization, and who defined the specifications of the weapon were somehow overlooked.

Not having a technical background, Lieutenant Stewart did not know what to make of these seven Germans; but he listened to their story and thought they might have dropped into his lap a major intelligence coup. Not only that, they said it was important that they be taken to Eisenhower as soon as possible. Stewart telephoned his superiors at Seventh Army headquarters for instructions on how to proceed.

They told him to find out if his seven guests were Nazis.

Stewart lost his patience. "Screen them for being Nazis! What the hell for? Look, if they were Hitler's brothers, it's beside the point. Their knowledge is valuable for both military and possibly national reasons."

Before long, the American authorities would accept Lieutenant Stewart's point of view. The bombardment of London and Antwerp would be forgiven. The Mittelwerk and the tens of thousands who slaved and died there would be forgotten. Nothing but the rockets and their creators would matter.

5 MAY 1945

Infantry of the White Russian Army under the command of Major Anatole Vavilov took the prize of Peenemünde. It had been crippled by Allied bombing raids, stripped of anything worthwhile in the winter evacuation, and then the remaining bones blasted by the German Home Army. Major Vavilov said that the base his men captured was "75 percent wreckage." He was ordered to destroy the rest. By the end of spring, the establishment at Peenemünde, the birthplace of missile warfare and the space age, was no more.

Joseph Stalin, who was humorless in the best of circumstances, was in an exceptionally foul mood when he learned how little of German rocket technology was to be his booty. "This is absolutely intolerable," he fumed. "We defeated Nazi armies; we occupied Berlin and Peenemünde, but the Americans got the rocket engineers. What could be more revolting and more inexcusable? How and why was this allowed to happen?"

7 MAY 1945

Grand Admiral Karl Doenitz performed the only significant act of his brief career as leader of the Third Reich by authorizing an unconditional surrender to the Allied forces. The surrender was put into writing at Eisenhower's headquarters at Reims, France, and again the following day at the Soviet headquarters near Berlin. The war in Europe was over.

*   *   *   *

Several days after their surrender, von Braun and the others were taken to Garmisch-Partenkirchen, a resort area in Bavaria that had hosted the 1936 Winter Olympics. There they joined several hundred other members of their rocket team who had already been rounded up for questioning and the inevitable waiting. Although Walter Dornberger was there, von Braun now assumed the position as head and spokesman for the group.

While the others may have brooded over lost glories, Wernher von Braun was planning for the future. With time on his hands, he began to prepare a paper on rocketry for the edification of the Americans. He ambitiously titled it " 'Ubersicht' uber die bisherige Entwicklung der Flussigskeitsrakete in Deutschland und deren Zukunftsaussichten" ('Survey' of Previous Liquid Rocket Development in Germany and Future Prospects). In the document, von Braun presented his thesis that the liquid-fueled rocket was a new means of transportation that would revolutionize the future, much as the airplane had changed the world after World War I. He characterized the development of the V-2 as "an intermediate solution conditioned by this war"; and he concluded that "when the art of rockets is developed further, it will be possible to go to other planets, first of all the moon."

Wernher von Braun no longer presented himself as the designer of the world's most sophisticated weapon; he was back on track as the young visionary with the exploration of space as his true goal. Furthermore, he and his team of experienced rocket scientists were available to the Americans to make the journey a reality. With their genius and the Americans' wealth, anything was once again possible.

9 MAY 1945

Although details of the incident varied, three of the four accounts agreed on the date.

Version 1. The German Red Cross search of master files in Munich records that Hans Kammler, according to the statements of comrades, died in Austria in April. The names of Kammler's comrades, the cause of death, the exact date of death, the location, and the site of burial were, somehow, omitted from the dossier.

Version 2. The trial of six of Kammler's subordinates in December 1958 presented an opportunity for the telling of a second story. Three of the group were ultimately found guilty of the mass murders of Russian and Polish workers attached to the V-1 operation during its retreat from Holland early in 1945. Kammler's whereabouts became an issue during the trial because the defendants asserted their innocence on the basis that they were only following Kammler's orders.

A witness at the trial who held the rank of SS Untersturmfuehrer (second lieutenant), claimed that he had served as Kammler's adjutant. He told of how, on 9 May 1945, Kammler and his entourage had been driving between Pilsen and Prague. Kammler ordered the car to stop, and he walked into a group of small trees. When he did not return, his companions searched for him and found his body. Between his teeth was the crushed glass of a cyanide capsule. The witness claimed to have buried Kammler's body in a "makeshift grave."

The name of the witness was obscured in the court record, but a reporter who covered the trial determined that his name and rank were different from the man identified by others as Kammler's adjutant, Major Starck.

Version 3. The reporter who had covered the war crimes trial of Kammler's subordinates decided to take the direct approach to finding those who could give a detailed description of the last moments of Kammler's life. He advertised for witnesses in the periodical of Waffen SS veterans, *Die Friewillinge.* He assembled this version from the testimony of two men claiming to have been Kammler's aides.

By early May, Kammler had found his way to the last SS stronghold, Prague. No sooner had he arrived than the Czech population rose up to finish off the last of the Nazi forces. Kammler with his aides escaped Prague and fled the advancing Russian forces back toward Germany. On the morning of 9 May, the band of fugitives found themselves near the German border. Kammler gathered his group around him to address them. He told them that it was no longer possible to follow their Fuehrer's orders, that they were all relieved of their duties, and that they were free to find their ways back home. When he had finished addressing his entourage, he walked into the woods. Moments later the sound of a single shot broke the peace of the countryside. Kammler's companions found his body and immediately buried him near where he lay.

The reporter noted that his witnesses were unable to remember where the bullet had entered Kammler's body or whether he was dead or dying when he was found, although their memories were quite good on details of their other experiences of that period.

Version 4. The version of Kammler's death which has been retold the most—possibly because of its dramatic quality—places the elusive general in Prague on 9 May. Kammler and 20 to 25 other SS men found themselves in a bunker as the anti-Nazi uprising swept the city. As 600 Czech partisans—one report has it as a Russian patrol—attacked the bunker, Kammler charged out to meet them, laughing and firing his machine pistol. Ten paces behind him, his adjutant, SS Major Starck, fired his own machine pistol into the back of Kammler's head. The variations of this version disagree on whether Starck was following Kammler's orders or acting on his own initiative.

Curiously, this version can be traced to Walter Dornberger who is reported to have heard it from eyewitnesses. The witnesses who knew the players and survived the siege remain unknown.

CHAPTER 24

Weapons for the Next War

MAY 1945

That there would be spoils of war was never in doubt. The only issue was how they would be divided. The spoils of the A-4/V-2 program could be divided into four components: completed rockets, the factory where the rockets had been made and more might be built, the mountain of documents containing plans and test results, and the personnel who designed, built, and fired the rockets. As the war ended, the victors began scrambling for the pieces of the rocket system. Nobody worked harder at collecting the components of the V-2 program than a small group of American army officers.

The American effort to exploit German rocketry was ad hoc, bordering on chaotic, with numerous teams questioning interned personnel and rummaging through captured materiel. The most productive actions were done under the direction of Colonel Holger N. Toftoy, chief of United States Army Ordnance Technical Intelligence in Europe. Toftoy was a 41-year-old West Point graduate. He was tall, lean, and wore steel-rimmed glasses. His expertise was in submarine mines, not rockets. As Nazi Germany fell, Toftoy had received a request from Colonel Gervais Trichel, chief of the rocket branch in the Ordnance Department at the Pentagon, to acquire and ship 100 operational V-2s to the White Sands Proving Ground in New Mexico for testing. Soon after the capture of the area around Nordhausen and the Mittelwerk, Toftoy set up Special Mission V-2 to do the job. He put Major William Bromley in command of Special Mission V-2; Bromley reported back to Colonel Toftoy through Major James P. Hamill, who was responsible for shipping the weapons from Nordhausen to Antwerp, and from there to New Orleans.

Special Mission V-2 was in trouble even before it began. At the Yalta Conference, Roosevelt, Churchill, and Stalin had carved up Germany into zones of future occupation. During the final days of the war, the American troops had pressed far beyond the imaginary line of demarcation drawn at Yalta. The area they occupied beyond the line stretched about 400 miles from north to south and was 120 miles across at its greatest width. Nordhausen and the Mittelwerk were within this area, which, according to the Yalta agreement, was to be turned over to the Soviets. Although there had been no official announcement, it was commonly accepted that withdrawal to the positions agreed upon by the three leaders was to take place on 1 June. Furthermore, the agreement of the winning powers required that all physical assets, such as factories, supplies, and weapons, were to be turned over intact with the captured territory. Thus, in the overall scheme of postwar planning, the Allied Powers had given the rocket factory as well as the rockets and components that remained at the assembly site to the Soviet Union.

Formal notice of the content of the Yalta agreement was never passed down the chain of command to Toftoy and his Special Mission V-2. In the absence of orders to the contrary, they proceeded to do what they viewed as being in the best interest of their country. There was not much that Toftoy's group could do about the underground factory; it would come under Soviet control within a month. But they could attempt to ship 100 V-2s to White Sands. They quickly learned that there were no operational V-2s in Germany. Walter Dornberger had found that the performance of the rockets deteriorated quickly after they had been built, and he had insisted that they be fired as soon as possible. Furthermore, most of the rockets that had been assembled but not fired had been damaged in one way or another. The best Toftoy's group could hope to do would be to gather up the parts needed to assemble 100 rockets, and that approach encountered two other problems. There was no parts list, and there were no instructions for assembly of the rockets. They would deal with these issues later.

The foul underground tunnels and cross-galleries of the Mittelwerk were full of parts and subassemblies. Major Hamill hired 150 former prisoners of the Dora and Nordhausen concentration camps to re-enter the cavern as free men to do the backbreaking work for honest wages. They started by clearing one of the tunnels so that they could bring rail cars into the factory. Then the former slaves and a group of United States Army enlisted men began collecting parts—100 of everything—crating them, and loading them onto the cars.

Fortunately for Special Mission V-2, hundreds of railroad cars had been stranded in and around Nordhausen when Allied bombing destroyed most of the bridges in the area. Major Hamill hired German crews who were desperate for any kind of work to run the trains. The first train was assembled and its load of rocket parts left Nordhausen for Antwerp on 22 May. On each of the following days, another train rolled out of Nordhausen; the trains averaged 40 cars in length. The last train left Nordhausen on 31 May at 9:30 P.M., just three and a half hours before the Soviets were initially to take over. As luck would have it, the withdrawal to the zones of occupation had been delayed, and the haste turned out to be unnecessary.

Special Mission V-2's cargo arrived at the docks at Antwerp, where it was loaded onto Liberty ships for transport to New Orleans and then on to White Sands. The rocket factory may have been lost to the Soviets, but the rocket parts had been salvaged. They might be turned into operational V-2s if the Americans could find the documents that described the components they had salvaged and the people who knew how to assemble them into rockets and fire them.

*   *   *   *

Colonel Trichel of the Ordnance Corps at the Pentagon, the man who had given Colonel Toftoy the job of shipping 100 V-2s to White Sands, assigned another officer to the job of compiling a list of key German rocket engineers and scientists to be found and questioned. Major Robert Staver began his job in London, and he used information gleaned from British intelligence to produce a "black list" of key personnel. The list was headed by Professor Dr. Wernher von Braun.

When Nordhausen and the Mittelwerk were captured, Staver attached himself to Colonel Toftoy's group to gain access to the area. He roamed through the Harz Mountains for two weeks without locating a single person who would admit to being part of the rocket team. Then on 12 May, following a tip, he located Karl Otto Fleischer in Nordhausen. Fleischer had been general business manager of the Elektromechanische Werke and—although Staver did not know it at the time—was also the man in Nordhausen whom Dieter Huzel had told of the location of the buried cache of documents. With Huzel, Tessmann, von Braun, and the others being held at Garmisch, he was the only person in Nordhausen who knew the location of the buried treasures.

Now that the Third Reich had faded into history, Fleischer was willing to cooperate with the victors; but he was also cautious about what he would tell. Fleischer led Major Staver to Dr. Eberhard Rees, who had been director of prototype production. Rees in turn led Staver to other key participants in the rocket program who had stayed in the area around Nordhausen.

Staver's luck held; and, on 14 May, he located Walter Riedel in a jail at Saalfeld, 60 miles north of Nordhausen. Walter Riedel had been the second man—after Wernher von Braun—hired by Walter Dornberger 12 years earlier; and Riedel had become chief of the rocket motor and structural design section at Peenemünde. United States Counter-Intelligence agents had arrested Riedel, mistakenly believing that he had worked on poison gas and bacteriological weapons; and Riedel had somehow lost several front teeth during interrogation. Nevertheless, he was willing to talk to Major Staver; and the army officer finally began developing a picture of the German rocket team.

It was not until 19 May that Staver convinced Karl Fleischer that von Braun and the other leaders of the rocket team wanted him to reveal the location of the documents to the Americans. The documents were buried in an abandoned mine about 30 miles from Nordhausen, Fleischer told Staver. Huzel had given him a description of the mine and told him approximately where to find it, but Fleischer was not familiar with the area and was unsure of the mine's exact location. He asked Staver if he and Eberhart Rees might search for the mine the following day without being accompanied by an American. He implied that the presence of an American might make it harder to get cooperation from Germans. Staver decided to take the chance. He gave them gasoline and passes.

Two days later, on 21 May, Staver was tired of waiting. He went to Fleischer's lodgings in Bleicherode to learn what the two had found.

Fleischer said that he and Rees had found the documents, but only after a long search, and only after convincing the caretaker of the mine that they really were representatives of the group that had hidden the cache in the first place. They persuaded the caretaker to hire some men to immediately clear the rubble-filled tunnel.

With this minor success came a major problem. Staver learned that as of 10:00 A.M. on 26 May, the area containing the village of Doernten, where the mine was located, would be turned over to the British. They had less than five days to clear the mine tunnel and remove the documents. Staver had to deal with the delays and bureaucratic bungling he had come to expect; but, on the morning of 26 May, he and his men began loading the 14 tons of documents into six two-and-a-half-ton trucks. The convoy crossed into the American occupied sector just as the British began setting up their roadblocks.

The parts needed to build 100 V-2s and the technical documents were now in American hands.

10 JUNE 1945

Charles Lindbergh became the quintessential world hero when in 1927 he flew nonstop from New York to Paris; but the future was to be an age of villains, and Lindbergh's glory could not avoid being tarnished. In April of 1941 before a crowd of 30,000 he spoke in opposition to U.S. involvement in the war in support of the British. Lindbergh had known violent death and loss. His own son had been kidnapped and murdered. In a war, if it came, everyone's son could be taken and brutally killed. The Germans certainly had the machines to do it; he had seen them. He had spent the years after the loss of his son in self-imposed exile in Europe, some of it in Germany; but he had not seen the horrors that were already taking place in Germany and would inevitably take place elsewhere in Europe under the domination of Nazi Germany.

Two days after Lindbergh's naive public pronouncement, President Roosevelt accused him of being a defeatist and an appeaser. Before the week was out, Lindbergh angrily resigned his commission as a colonel in the United States Army Air Corps Reserve. When the war finally came, he served unobtrusively as a consultant to aircraft manufacturers and the United States Army Air Force.

Lindbergh and his army escort arrived by jeep at Camp Dora in the late afternoon. The prisoners were gone—or at least they seemed to be. They had been replaced by displaced persons (D.P.'s), refugees of all nations of Eastern Europe. The D.P.'s seemed to be adequately clothed for the season, and they were not emaciated. The barracks were full of them, and those who could not fit in built shelters for themselves in the cavernous tail sections of rockets laid on their sides. As they passed through Camp Dora, Lindbergh noticed the odor, the "mouse smell." It was the smell of urine and rotting garbage, and worse.

Before they would be allowed into the underground factory, they learned, they would have to get a pass from the local army unit headquarters on the other side of the mountain. Since they had to make the detour, they decided to enter the tunnel system from the far side of the mountain. They drove their jeep into the tunnel along the railroad track, past side tunnels, past machinery, rocket motors, and rocket parts. The factory, which had once writhed with slaves like anonymous drones in an anthill, was empty of people; Lindbergh and his companion had it all to themselves. They stopped halfway through when their way was blocked by a boxcar. Then they worked their way through the labyrinth on foot, zigzagging back and forth between the two main tunnels by way of the cross-tunnels and past more machinery and rocket parts. They came across an assembled V-2 rocket that had been crudely cut lengthwise to reveal its cross-section. The job had been done, presumably, by one of the Allied teams that had looted the liberated factory.

They knew they were getting closer to the entrance at the Dora end of the tunnels by the smell, that mouse smell of urine and garbage and disease. Decaying litter surrounded them. They found a cross-tunnel with two tiers of small rooms built of wood. Lindbergh surmised that it had been a combination office and hospital tunnel. They explored the rooms and found paperwork and files dumped on the floors everywhere. Lindbergh found personnel cards, thousands of them, each with a description of the worker and his photograph. Just like the parts to the rockets, the workers had been carefully inventoried and efficiently used.

11 JUNE 1945

Words heard over breakfast: "The prisoners were so badly starved that hundreds of them were beyond saving when the Americans came. They're still dying."

Lindbergh had planned to finish exploring the underground factory, but decided to visit Camp Dora first. He and his military escort drove the few miles from Nordhausen to the camp. They saw on the mountainside above the camp a small, low, factorylike building. It had a brick smokestack that appeared to be unusually broad for its height. They could not find a road leading up to the building, so they put the jeep into four-wheel drive and went straight up the hillside, weaving back and forth between the trees as they went.

At one end of the low building, they saw a stack of stretchers, probably two dozen in all, dirty and stained with blood. One of them held the dark-red outline of a human body. The doors to the building were open, and they went inside. Through another doorway on their left they saw two crude coffins and between them a form carelessly draped with canvas. It had the shape of a body.

They moved into the main room of the building and saw the two large cremating furnaces, now empty and cold. The steel stretchers for holding the bodies stuck out through the open furnace doors.

A figure entered the room, a wraith dressed in a baggy prisoner's uniform. He was a boy, Lindbergh thought. He had starved until he was a walking skeleton, his bones held together by his shrunken skin.

The boy pointed to the furnaces. He spoke in German and Lindbergh's companion translated. "Twenty-five thousand in a year and a half."

They asked the boy who he was and how old he was. He said he was a Pole, 17 years old. Then the boy motioned for them to follow him. They walked back to the room where they had seen the crude coffins. The boy pulled back the canvas to reveal a corpse curled up on a stretcher. The body was skin and bones, dressed in a striped prisoner's uniform. He could have been the boy's twin.

The boy said, "He was my friend, and he is *fat!*"

Lindbergh noticed the dead man's face. The eyes were dark and burning, but the features were serene. After living in the subterranean hell, he had found peace on earth. He had died a free man. He would enjoy the privilege of a coffin and escape the terminal insult of going up the chimney as smoke.

They went outside, and the boy led them to a corner of the building. Lindbergh's mind was still inside, pondering the furnaces and the dead man, the people and the system that were responsible for the horror.

The boy spoke again, and Lindbergh's escort translated. "Twenty-five thousand in a year and a half." The boy cupped his hands to show a measure. "And from each one there is only so much."

Only then did Lindbergh realize that they were standing beside a pit that was overflowing with ashes. He estimated the pit to be about six feet by eight feet. Nearby he saw two oblong mounds of about the same dimensions, which at one time may also have been pits.

Later he wrote about what he had seen. "Of course, I knew what was going on; but it is one thing to have the intellectual knowledge, even to look at photographs someone else has taken, and quite another to stand on the scene yourself, seeing, hearing, feeling with your own senses. . . . It seemed impossible that men—civilized men—could degenerate to such a level. Yet they had."

Lindbergh remembered man's long history of pogroms, riots, lynchings, and the burning of witches at the stake. He recalled witnessing the savage treatment of Japanese soldiers and the desecration of their dead by Americans in the Pacific. "It is not the Germans alone, or the Japs," he wrote, "but the men of all nations to whom this war had brought shame and degradation."

19–21 JUNE 1945

Wernher von Braun, still encased in plaster, his left arm in an awkward salute, arrived in Bleicherode on 19 June. Several thousand members of his team had been left behind when the Vengeance Express with its selected passengers pulled out for Oberammergau over two months earlier. The Americans had asked von Braun to help find missing members of his team, and he was pleased to be able to help. Those they could not find or could not convince to move west would be lost to the Soviets when the Americans withdrew according to the Yalta agreement. The withdrawal was scheduled to take place in two days.

The day after von Braun arrived, Major Robert Staver and his staff had rounded up nearly 1,000 former members of the Peenemünde rocket team. Each was allotted 100 pounds of luggage. They boarded the last train scheduled to leave before the arrival of the Soviets, and they were soon 40 miles to the southwest in the American Zone.

In the morning of 21 June, Major Robert Staver continued to search for buried treasure despite the fact that the Soviets were scheduled to take over at noon. With the aid of a land mine detector, his men found the last of the V-2 documents which Walter Dornberger had buried at Bad Sachsa. Five crates of papers weighing 260 pounds were loaded onto a truck which sped off at top speed to the west.

At noon, the American army pulled back, abandoning Nordhausen, Dora, and one of the biggest prizes of the war, the world's only factory for building long-range rockets.

5 JULY 1945

After some delays, Soviet forces occupied the Mittelwerk. It was soon back in business generating technical information and producing rockets for the Soviets to evaluate. Production was now in the hands of German civilians and second-rate rocket scientists. The highest-ranking member of the German staff was Helmut Groettrup, one of the engineers arrested with Wernher von Braun.

19 JULY 1945

The United States Joint Chiefs of Staff established Operation Overcast to gather the technological spoils of war. Their secret memorandum stressed that the purpose of Overcast "should be understood to be *temporary* military exploitation..particularly that which will assist in shortening . . . the Japanese war." The German civilian scientists who would be part of Overcast were to be given short-term contracts to work in the United States. There was no intention that the positions would become permanent or that they would bring their families or take up permanent residence. The army began recruiting specialists in the applied sciences with an emphasis on aeronautics and rockets.

There is no evidence to indicate that on this day the Joint Chiefs of Staff considered developing the German long-range rocket as a delivery vehicle for the atomic bomb which had been secretly and successfully tested in New Mexico three days earlier. Nevertheless, they knew about both weapons, and they authorized the recruiting of the rocket scientists. The pieces would inevitably come together.

AUGUST 1945

Kransberg Castle was in the Taunus Mountains near the Rhine. In 1939 Albert Speer had supervised the rebuilding of the castle, including the addition of a modern two-story wing, so that it could be used as a headquarters by Hermann Goering. The Americans were now using the castle as a site for the controlled questioning of Germany's most powerful and imaginative technical experts. The prisoners were housed in the new wing, but they had the freedom to roam the entire castle. They were relatively well fed, being given the same rations enjoyed by the American troops. Among those residing in this gilded cage were Albert Speer and the highest-ranking members of his Ministry of Armaments, Wernher von Braun and many of his team members, and Hermann Oberth.

The questioning was chaotic. German technical experts were quizzed, then quizzed again over the same material by different interrogators. Some interrogators lacked technical expertise; others were simply inept and offensive. Many German tempers were short. They wanted the Americans to finish and set them free. Perhaps they were apprehensive that they might be asked embarrassing questions about the Mittelwerk. Apparently the subject did not come up. In any case, they were rocket scientists; the Mittelwerk was the business of the SS.

Hermann Oberth was a burnt out, 51-year-old man; the war had taken an inordinately heavy toll on him and his family. His son Julius had been lost at Stalingrad, and his daughter Ilse had been killed in the explosion of a liquid oxygen plant. His brother Adolf Gustav had been killed in action in 1943, and his father had committed suicide at the age of 84 because he could not stand the conditions after the Communists took over Rumania. In addition, Oberth had lost his property in Rumania, and his adopted country had been destroyed. He had been pushed aside, kept "on ice," while his best ideas were exploited by others. Now the victors wanted to exploit him again.

Maybe he did not have answers for their questions. Maybe he did not care. Possibly he lost his patience with the obtuse interviewers. Whatever the reason, whether Oberth intended to or not, he made a poor impression.

One of his interrogators, Dr. Fritz Zwicky, summarized his impression of Hermann Oberth: "Oberth belongs to the class of unfortunate amateur-type individuals who pick up an idea early, who advocate the idea, and who find no response. Later, when the idea is taken up and developed by competent professionals, there remains nothing for the original advocate but to reminisce on the past."

When he was finally released, Oberth returned to his wife and their family home in Feucht near Nuremberg. Within a month, Albert Speer, too, would go from Kransberg Castle to Nuremberg, but not as a free man. He would stand trial for his part in the crimes of Nazi Germany.

*   *   *   *

Colonel Holger Toftoy, who had conceived Special Mission V-2, which brought components of 100 missiles to the United States, was back in Germany after a brief visit to the Pentagon. He returned as chief of the Army Ordnance Rocket Branch, replacing his former boss, Colonel Trichel, who had been reassigned to the Pacific. Toftoy had authorization to hire no more than 100 rocket scientists under the umbrella of Operation Overcast. The men were to be brought to the United States under six-month contracts during which time they would be exploited for their knowledge of rockets.

Toftoy began with Wernher von Braun. Not only was he the chief engineer of the rocket team, he was the only one who could make sense of the résumés of the rocket scientists and could put together a coherent working group. The two men developed an easy rapport. The scope of Operation Overcast quickly expanded—at least in the mind of von Braun—beyond the six-month contracts. According to von Braun's account, Toftoy asked him, "Do you think you could become a loyal citizen of the United States?"

He said he would like to try.

"You realize, Mr. von Braun, that I can promise you nothing about your future in my country. How long you stay, what work you do, and where you are assigned will depend on many things, including your cooperation."

Wernher von Braun would be cooperative with his new employer just as he had been with the Nazi regime in Germany. Toftoy relied on his help to whittle down the stack of résumés to a lean core of 118 rocket experts who would eventually go to the United States under the auspices of

Operation Overcast. The number had swollen slightly from Toftoy's original authorization.

Between 50 and 80 percent of the scientists and engineers brought to the United States for exploitation after the war were members of the Nazi party. Generally, they claimed to have been only nominal Nazis; they joined the party, they said, as the result of tremendous pressure and out of concern for their own safety. Nevertheless, party membership had paid off for them in positions of esteem and honor. Among those who accompanied von Braun were the following:

Arthur Rudolph, chief operations director of the Mittelwerk rocket factory. Not only had he set the schedules by which prisoners were worked to death; but, it was later discovered, he had reported instances of suspected sabotage by prisoners to the SS that led to their subsequent executions.

Kurt Debus, a rocket launch expert. Like von Braun, Debus joined the SS in 1940. It has been reported that Debus displayed his loyalty by regularly wearing his SS uniform at Peenemünde and that in 1942 he denounced a colleague to the Gestapo as anti-Nazi.

Lieutenant Colonel Herbert Axster, Walter Dornberger's chief of staff. In civilian life he had been an attorney, not a scientist or engineer. According to testimony of witnesses, he beat foreign slave laborers who worked on his estate in Germany.

Georg Rickhey, director general of the Mittelwerk. Rickhey was an engineer, though not a rocket scientist.

Magnus von Braun, Wernher von Braun's younger brother, who had supervised gyroscope production at the Mittelwerk.

Notable by their absence were *Hermann Oberth*, *General Walter Dornberger*, and *Helmut Groettrup*, one of von Braun's companions in the Gestapo prison in Stettin. Oberth had offered his services to the Americans, but was rejected by them, probably because he lacked current information and presented himself poorly at interviews. Dornberger was interned in Britain for the two years following the war and was never invited to join the team. Groettrup went to work for the Russians, first, as director of the reopened underground missile factory and, later, as one of hundreds of German specialists conscripted to work in the Soviet Union.

The following year, 1946, "Operation Overcast" was renamed "Project Paperclip." A policy regarding the eligibility of scientists and engineers to be utilized was developed and approved by President Truman. The policy explicitly forbade recruitment of war criminals or those active in Nazism. It stated in part, "No person found . . . to have been a member of the Nazi party and more than a nominal participant in its activities, or an active supporter of Nazism or militarism shall be brought to the U.S. hereunder." The directive was too late; von Braun and his team were already in the United States preparing to test fire the V-2 at White Sands in New Mexico.

CHAPTER 25

Aged Rocketeers and Astronauts

16 JULY 1969

"T minus fifteen seconds. Guidance is internal."

Miles away across the salt marsh, the rocket stands like a tower of ice against the electric-blue Florida sky. Spectators, thousands of VIPs with personal invitations, watch in silence.

"Twelve."

Hand-selected witnesses . . .

"Eleven."

Of the timed-to-the-second . . .

"Ten."

Choreographed to the nth degree . . .

"Nine."

Historical event in the making.

"Ignition sequence starts."

The last of the rocket warriors are there.

"Six."

Wernher von Braun, full of confidence and success . . .

"Five."

Whose will kept the dream alive . . .

"Four."

For nearly 40 years . . .

"Three."

Through peace and war and secret crimes . . .

"Two."

Who led the team that designed and built . . .

"One."

The Saturn V booster.

"Zero."

The pillar of ice becomes a geyser of fire.

"All engines running."

An avalanche of snowy exhaust billows across the salt marsh, and the rocket thunders to life.

"Liftoff. We have a liftoff. Thirty-two minutes past the hour."

An old man with white hair and a bushy white moustache stands proudly under the Florida sun. After a life filled with failures, Hermann Oberth watches his dream become real . . .

"Liftoff of Apollo 11."

Carrying three men to the moon.

EPILOGUE

CHAPTER 26

Time's Vengeance on the Nazi Rocketeers

WALTER DORNBERGER (6 SEPTEMBER 1895–JUNE 1980)

After his surrender and initial questioning by the American army, Dornberger was held as a prisoner of war in England for two years. He was finally released when the English decided not to try him for his participation in the rocket bombardment of London and lost interest in him.

In 1947 Dornberger came to the United States to work as a consultant to the air force on missiles. Like most of the German rocket scientists who found themselves in the United States after World War II, he applied for U.S. citizenship. In 1950 he left the employ of the air force for the Bell Aircraft Corporation of Buffalo, New York. He eventually held the position of vice-president and chief scientist of Bell Aerospace Corporation, from which he retired in 1965. He died in West Germany in 1980.

Dornberger gave his account of the German rocket program in his book *V-2*, which was published in 1954. The book was honored for its technical contributions to the history of rocket development. It is, perhaps, not surprising that Dornberger in his history made only a few oblique references to the underground Mittelwerk factory, he did not mention the Dora concentration camp, he failed to write about the tens of thousands of slave laborers who built the rockets and died at the Mittelwerk, and he ignored the additional thousands who died as a result of V-2 rocket bombardments.

HANS KAMMLER (26 AUGUST 1901–?)

There are no reliable reports of Kammler's whereabouts or his fate after his disappearance on 17 April 1945.

Hermann Oberth (25 June 1894–28 December 1989)

After being released from the internment camp at the end of the war, Oberth returned to his country home at Feucht. "All my attempts to find a job as a teacher at a university, high school, or even public school, were futile," he said of this time. "I can do nothing better than grow cabbage and turnips in my little vegetable garden."

In 1950 the Italian Admiralty hired him to finish development of the ammonium nitrate-powered rocket he had been working on at WASAG in Wittenberg. When the project was completed in early 1953, he returned to Feucht in Germany. There he completed the book *Menschen im Weltraum*, published in 1954, which restored some of his past credibility as a theoretician of space travel.

His former student, Wernher von Braun, once again at the top as director of rocket research and development for the United States Army, invited Oberth to join his team as a research engineer at the Redstone Arsenal in Huntsville, Alabama. Oberth worked there from 1955 until 1958 when he returned to his home in Feucht to retire on the modest pension he had earned as a German civil servant.

In the years following the war, Oberth received many awards, honorary memberships in learned societies, and even the doctorate degree (from Iowa Wesleyan College) that had been denied him for so long. At the time of the first manned flight to the moon, Oberth made the following melancholic comment on the event: "Sometimes I feel like an unmusical person who attends a concert and doesn't really understand what seems to excite everybody. On other occasions I feel like a mother goose who has hatched a brood and now, somewhat perplexed, watches the flock going off into the water. It is only very rarely that I have the satisfaction that everybody believes I ought to feel."

Albert Speer (19 March 1905–1 September 1981)

Speer was tried at Nuremberg for having used millions of prisoners of war and for having conscripted laborers from the conquered countries as slaves in armaments plants in violation of both the Hague and Geneva conventions. Speer, alone among the Nuremberg defendants, accepted full responsibility for his actions and the crimes of Nazi Germany. Although the Soviet Union wanted him executed for his crimes, he was sentenced to 20 years in Spandau Prison.

After his release from Spandau on 1 October 1966, Speer produced three books based on the experiences of his life: *Inside the Third Reich* (1969),

Spandau: The Secret Diaries (1976), and *Infiltration: How Heinrich Himmler Schemed to Build an SS Industrial Empire* (1981). His efforts at writing history—and exorcising his ghosts—have been greeted by critics with terms that ranged from "objectivity," "insight," and "revealing" to "one-sided," "self -vindication," and "shrill."

WERNHER VON BRAUN (23 MARCH 1912–16 JUNE 1977)

Wernher von Braun went with his hand-picked team to Fort Bliss, Texas, in 1945. They worked under the obscurity imposed by military secrecy while test firing V-2s from the nearby White Sands Proving Ground. In 1950 the German rocket team moved to the United States Army's Redstone Arsenal in Huntsville, Alabama, where von Braun became director of research and development at the Army Guided Missile Center. He and many of his German colleagues became U.S. citizens in 1955. Unlike the other German rocket scientists who preferred obscurity, von Braun enjoyed the public eye. He became America's leading publicist of rockets and advocate of the exploration of space.

The achievements of von Braun and his team include development of the Redstone intermediate-range ballistic missile and a variant of it, the Jupiter C booster. The latter was used to launch the first U.S. satellite into orbit and to propel the first Mercury astronaut into space in a suborbital flight. When the Army Guided Missile Center was turned over to NASA in 1959, it became the Marshall Space Flight Center with von Braun as its director. Von Braun led that organization in developing and building, among other giant rockets, the Saturn V booster, which sent the American astronauts to the moon.

In 1970 von Braun left Huntsville for Washington, where he became NASA's deputy associate administrator for planning. He left government service for private industry two years later.

On the day in 1977 that Wernher von Braun died, President Jimmy Carter said of him, "To millions of Americans, Wernher von Braun's name was inextricably linked to our exploration of space and to the creative application of technology. . . . Not just the people of our nation, but all the people of the world have profited from his work. We will continue to profit from his example." Apparently Carter did not know the rocket warrior's full story.

*   *   *   *

After the defeat of Germany, the occupying United States Army tried individuals accused of war crimes committed at concentration camps. Dora/Nordhausen was represented by 24 individuals who were tried under a general charge of "violation of the laws and usages of war" and of specific charges ranging from assault to torture to murder. The trial took place at the site that had been the Dachau concentration camp. Most of the defendants were low-ranking SS men and *Kapos*, inmate guards. The highest-ranking defendant and only free civilian tried was Georg Rickhey, general director of the Mittelwerk.

Rickhey had been brought to the United States with Wernher von Braun and his rocket team, but his stay was cut short when he was returned to stand trial. Wernher von Braun, Magnus von Braun, and Arthur Rudolph submitted lengthy depositions for the defense in which they characterized Rickhey as an uninvolved figurehead; the control of the Mittelwerk was, they claimed, in the hands of Alwin Sawatzki, who derived his authority from Hans Kammler. The depositions, although their authors would be reluctant to admit it, showed extensive knowledge of the Mittelwerk's history and operation.

At the Dora/Nordhausen war crimes trial in 1947, 19 of the defendants were found guilty; one of these, an SS first lieutenant, was sentenced to death and eventually executed. Georg Rickhey was one of the five acquitted; however, he did not rejoin the rocket scientists in the United States after his release.

*   *   *   *

Most of the 118-man German rocket team headed by von Braun and brought to the United States by the army stayed, brought their families, and became citizens. Arthur Rudolph, who had been operations director at the Mittelwerk underground rocket factory, was one of the most successful of the group. He became the director of NASA's Saturn V program, which built the 364-foot-tall rocket that carried Apollo astronauts to the moon and Skylab into orbit. For this achievement, NASA awarded Rudolph its highest honor, the Distinguished Service Medal, in 1969.

In 1984, a Justice Department investigation of war criminals residing in the United States implicated Rudolph in crimes committed at the Mittelwerk. At the age of 77, Rudolph renounced his U.S. citizenship and returned to Germany rather than face charges that he had hidden his Nazi past and possible participation in war crimes when he applied for citizenship. He did, however, retain his pension for service to the United States government as an employee of NASA. No legal action has been taken against any of the other rocket team members, although an estimated ten to 15 of them had worked at the Mittelwerk, and others, like Wernher von Braun, hid their Nazi involvement and distanced themselves from the crimes committed at the underground rocket factory.

References and Notes

Abbreviations for the most often cited and important references:

Dornberger: Walter Dornberger, *V-2*, Viking Press, New York, 1954.

FBI-vB-FOI: FBI files on Wernher von Braun obtained through the Freedom of Information Act.

Huzel: Dieter K. Huzel, *Peenemünde to Canaveral*, Prentice-Hall, Inc., Englewood Cliffs, N.J., 1962.

Ley: Willy Ley, *Rockets, Missiles, and Men in Space*, Viking Press, New York, 1968.

McGovern: James McGovern, *Crossbow and Overcast*, William Morrow & Co., Inc., New York, 1964.

Michel: Jean Michel, *Dora*, Holt, Rinehart and Winston, New York, 1979.

Ordway & Sharpe: Frederick I. Ordway III and Mitchell R. Sharpe, *The Rocket Team*, Thomas Y. Crowell, New York, 1979.

Shirer: William L. Shirer, *The Rise and Fall of the Third Reich*, Simon and Schuster, New York, 1960.

Speer-Infiltration: Albert Speer, *Infiltration*, Macmillan Company, New York, 1981.

Speer-Inside: Albert Speer, *Inside the Third Reich*, Macmillan Company, New York, 1970.

USA-vB-FOI: United States Army Intelligence and Security files on Wernher von Braun obtained through the Freedom of Information Act.

USAvAndrae: *United States of America v. Kurt Andrae et al.*, National Archives Microfilm M1079.

vB-Reminiscences: Wernher von Braun, "Reminiscences of German Rocketry," *Journal of the British Interplanetary Society*, May 1956, reprinted in Arthur C. Clarke, ed., *The Coming of the Space Age*, Meredith Press, New York, 1967.

vB&O-History: Wernher von Braun and Frederick I. Ordway III, *History of Rocketry and Space Travel*, Thomas Y. Crowell Company, New York, 1966.

vB&O-Rockets: Wernher von Braun and Frederick I. Ordway III, *The Rockets' Red Glare*, Anchor Press/Doubleday, Garden City and New York, 1976.
Sources of quotations are noted parenthetically. Sources of dates of events are noted parenthetically if the source is not obvious or if multiple references confirm the date.

PART I: DREAMS AND ILLUSIONS

1. When Space Travel Was Science Fiction

15 October 1929: *Lang*: Peter Bogdanovich, *Fritz Lang in America*, Frederick A. Praeger, Inc., 1969, pp. 125–126. *Tsiolkovsky*: K. E. Tsiolkovski, "K. E. Tsiolkovski: An Autobiography," *Astronautics*, May 1959, reprinted in Arthur C. Clarke, ed., *The Coming of the Space Age*, Meredith Press, New York, 1967, pp. 100–104. *vB&O-History*, pp. 40–43. *Oberth: Ley*, pp. 114–120 (date) and 259. Hermann Oberth, "Hermann Oberth: From My Life," *Astronautics*, June 1959, reprinted in Clarke, op. cit., pp. 113–121. United States Army Security and Intelligence files on Hermann Oberth obtained through the Freedom of Information Act (henceforth called U.S. Army Oberth FOI files), various assessments of Oberth's personality. *vB&O-Rockets*, pp. 128–131. Helen B. Walters, *Hermann Oberth: Father of Space Travel*, Macmillan Company, New York, 1962, pp. 63–69. *Goddard*: Robert H. Goddard, "Robert H. Goddard: An Autobiography," *Astronautics*, April 1959, reprinted in Clarke, op. cit., pp. 105–113. "A Severe Strain on Credulity," *The New York Times*, 13 January 1920, reprinted in Clarke, op. cit., pp. 66–67. *vB&O-History*, pp. 43–47.

17 May 1930: *Ley*, p. 125 (date). *vB&O-Rockets*, pp. 132–133 (date).

Spring 1930: *Ley*, p. 123. *vB&O-Rockets*, p. 131 (date).

23 July 1930: *Ley*, pp. 123–124 (date, quote). *vB-Reminiscences*, pp. 33–55. *vB&O-Rockets*, pp. 131–132.

2. The P. T. Barnum of Rockets

27 September 1930: *vB-Reminiscences*, p. 35. *Ley*, pp. 126–127 (date).

Fall 1930–Spring 1931: *Ley*, pp. 122, 125–130, 132–134 (date). *vB-Reminiscences*, pp. 35–37. Ley assigned credit for the design of the Mirak to Nebel while von Braun gave it to Riedel. I have accepted Ley's version since he was more intimately involved in the operation of the VfR, and since the design is so in keeping with Nebel's personality.

Fall 1931: *Ley*, pp. 133–134, 139.

Spring 1932: Erik Bergaust, *Reaching for the Stars*, Doubleday & Company, Inc., New York, 1960, p. 50 (date).

Also in Spring 1932: FBI files on Walter Dornberger obtained through the Freedom of Information Act (henceforth called FBI Dornberger FOI files), "Dossier for German Scientist Walter Dornberger," Joint Intelligence Objectives Agency (physical description). *Ley*, p. 143. *vB-Reminiscences*, pp. 37–38. *vB&O-Rockets*, pp. 136–137 (date).
August 1932: *Dornberger*, pp. 31–32 (date). *Ley*, p. 143. *vB-Reminiscences*, p. 38. Von Braun stated that the rocket was a Mirak II and gave the date as July 1932.

3. The Baron's Son and the Soldier

Summer 1932: The date is inferred from the following references: Michel Bar-Zohar, *The Hunt for German Scientists*, Hawthorn Books, Inc., New York, pp. 16–17 (quote: von Braun). Bergaust, *Reaching for the Stars*, op. cit., pp. 39–41. "Von Braun, Wernher," *Current Biography*, 1952, pp. 607–609. Jozef Garlinski, *Hitler's Last Weapons*, Times Books, New York, 1978, p. 4 (friendship of Becker and Baron von Braun). Willy Ley, *Rockets: The Future of Travel beyond the Stratosphere*, Viking Press, New York, 1944, pp. 151–152 (Count von Braun and information about the army's rockets that von Braun gave in 1932). *Ordway & Sharpe*, pp. 93–94 (quote: Ley describes von Braun). *vB-Reminiscences*, pp. 38–40 (quotes Becker and Nebel). *vB&O-Rockets*, p. 138. Helen B. Walters, *Wernher von Braun, Rocket Engineer*, Macmillan Company, New York, 1964, p. 3 (inspired by Verne's *From the Earth to the Moon*).
Summer–Fall 1932: "Dornberger, Walter R(obert)," *Current Biography*, 1965, pp. 125–127. *Dornberger*, pp. 26–27. *McGovern*, p. 23 (powder rocket explosion).
21 December 1932: *Dornberger*, pp. 23–26 (date). *vB-Reminiscences*, p. 40.
January 1933: *vB-Reminiscences*, p. 40.

4. The Birth of the Third Reich and the Death of Conscience

5 March 1933: Bogdanovich, op. cit., p. 128. "Einstein, Albert," *Current Biography*, 1941, 257–259. "Lang, Fritz," *Current Biography*, 1943, pp. 424–428. Otto Friedrich, *Before the Deluge*, Harper and Row, New York, 1972, pp. 394–395 and 405–407. Ley, *Rockets: The Future of Travel beyond the Stratosphere*, op. cit., p. 122 (Oberth joins the Nazis). *Shirer*, pp. 194–200 (date). *USA-vB-FOI*, "Affidavit of Membership in NSDAP of Prof. Dr. Wernher von Braun," pp. 170–171 (memberships in various Nazi-affiliated organizations). Walters, *Wernher von Braun*, op. cit., p. 37.
Sometime 1933: Peter Carey, "Nazi Rocket Scientist Says He Was Fair to Slaves," *San Jose Mercury News*, 17 April 1985, pp. 1A, 5A. *Dornberger*, pp. 29–30. *Ordway & Sharpe*, p. 22 (date, quote).
Late 1933: Date is inferred from the chronologies of the following and other references: *Dornberger*, pp. 32–33, 36. *vB-Reminiscences*, p. 41.

27 July 1934: Bergaust, *Reaching for the Stars*, op. cit., p. 55. *USA-vB-FOI*, intelligence report, p. 559 (date).

2 August 1934: *Shirer*, pp. 226–227.

Summer 1934: *Ley*, pp. 147–148.

4 September 1934: Leni Riefenstahl, *Triumph des Willens* (Triumph of the Will), Leni Riefenstahl Produktion, 1935, Embassy Home Entertainment videotape, 1986. *Shirer*, p. 230 (date). *Speer-Inside*, pp. 58–62.

December 1934: *Dornberger*, p. 36. *vB-Reminiscences*, pp. 40–41 (date).

5. Rockets for the Reich

January 1935: *vB-Reminiscences*, p. 43 (date). *vB&O-Rockets*, p. 142. *Shirer*, pp. 49, 282, 283 (background on Goering and the Luftwaffe).

Summer 1935: *Dornberger*, p. 124, described the event but stated it took place in spring 1936. *vB-Reminiscences*, p. 43, described a similar event, though differing in some details, that he said occurred in summer 1935. Von Braun's date fits nicely into the overall chronology while Dornberger's does not. Dornberger's details, however, seem more in keeping with preceding and subsequent events.

7 March 1936: *Shirer*, pp. 291–293.

March 1936: *Dornberger*, pp. 47–50.

Spring 1936: *Dornberger*, p. 125 (date). *vB-Reminiscences*, pp. 36–37.

April 1936: *Dornberger*, pp. 39–41 (date). *Ley*, pp. 181–182. *vB-Reminiscences*, pp. 43–44 (quote of Becker). *vB&O-Rockets*, pp. 142–143.

May 1936: Erik Bergaust, *Wernher von Braun*, National Space Institute, Washington, 1976, p. 107 (von Braun's enlistment in the Luftwaffe). *FBI-vB-FOI*, von Braun's application for civil service commission, 14 July 1952. *USA-vB-FOI*, intelligence reports on pp. 105, 168 (Office of Military Government of Germany [U.S.] NSDAP records check dated 23 April 1947).

April 1937: *Dornberger*, p. 125. David Masters, *German Jet Genesis*, Jane's Publishing Company Limited, London, 1982, pp. 13, 37 (date).

1 May 1937: *USA-vB-FOI*, pp. 168 (date), 170–171 (quote). FBI Dornberger FOI files, "Dossier for German Scientist Walter Dornberger," Joint Intelligence Objectives Agency.

6. Rocket City: The Secret Base at Peenemünde

May 1937: *Dornberger*, p. 53 (date). *Ley*, p. 186 (quote, von Braun on Nebel). *Ordway & Sharpe*, pp. 30–33. *vB&O*, p. 143, gives the date of the move to Peenemünde as April 1937. I have used Dornberger's date as the time of completion of the move.

Spring 1937: Walters, *Hermann Oberth*, op. cit., pp. 86–87.

Summer 1937: *Dornberger*, p. 126. Masters, op. cit., pp. 13, 37 (date).

December 1937: *Dornberger*, pp. 42–46, 54–56 (date). *Ley*, pp. 187–188. *vB-Reminiscences*, pp. 41–42. *vB&O-Rockets*, pp. 141–142 (date).
12 March 1938: *Shirer*, pp. 322–350 and other sources.
Sometime 1938: *Ley*, pp. 202–203 (date). Oberth, op. cit., p. 120 (date).
30 September 1938: *Shirer*, p. 420 (quote).
9–10 November 1938: Michael Bar-Zorah, *The Avengers*, Hawthorne Books, Inc., New York, 1967, pp. 5 (date), 19. *Shirer*, pp. 581–582 (date).
Early 1939: *Ordway & Sharpe*, p. 30.

PART II: WAR ASCENDING

7. Casualties of the Blitzkrieg

23 March 1939: Bergaust, *Reaching for the Stars*, op. cit., pp. 69–79. *Dornberger*, pp. 64–67.
1 September 1939: *Shirer*, pp. 597–599 (quote, date). *Speer-Inside*, p. 167.
October 1939: *Dornberger*, pp. 58, 60–63 (date). *vB-Reminiscences*, p. 46. Von Braun stated the first launch was under a cloudy sky; Dornberger recalled a bright, sunny day.
February 1940: *Dornberger*, p. 69. Jeffery L. Ethell, *Komet, The Messerschmitt 163*, Sky Books Press, New York, 1978, p. 41 (date). *Ley*, pp. 199–200. *Speer-Inside*, pp. 232, 241.
Sometime 1940: *Ley*, pp. 202–203 (quote). Oberth, op. cit., p. 120 (date).
1 May 1940: *FBI-vB-FOI*, El Paso office field report No. 77-594 and New York office field report No. 116-447851 cite informants who claim to have seen von Braun in SS uniform. *Speer-Inside*, p. 369. *USA-vB-FOI*, p. 168 (date), 170–171 (quote).
April–December 1940: Various sources.
Sometime 1941: *Ley*, p. 203. Oberth, op. cit., pp. 120–121 (date).
Summer and Fall 1941: Various sources.

8. The Architects of Destruction: The Men Who Built Armaments and Auschwitz

7 February 1942: *Speer-Inside*, pp. 191–197. Speer, Hitler, and Goering are quoted from pp. 195–196.
13 June 1942: *Dornberger*, pp. 3–17. Ethell, op. cit., pp. 56, 153. *Ley*, pp. 200, 500 (date). *Speer-Inside*, p. 367 (date). *vB&O-History*, p. 106.
17–18 July 1942: Tom Agoston, *Blunder! How the U.S. Gave Away Nazi Supersecrets to Russia*, Dodd, Mead & Company, New York, 1985, pp. 7–9, and captions to illustrations between pp. 70 and 71. Gerald Astor, *The "Last" Nazi*, Donald I. Fine, Inc., New York, 1985, pp. 48–49. Jozef Garlinski, *Fighting Auschwitz*, Julian Friedmann Publishers, Ltd., London, 1975, pp. 146–147 (date). Rudolf Hoess,

Commandant of Auschwitz, The World Publishing Company, Cleveland and New York, 1959, pp. 233–239.
16 August 1942: *Huzel*, p. 8. Von Braun is quoted from the introduction. David Irving, *The Mare's Nest*, Little, Brown and Company, Boston, 1965, p. 21 (date). *Ley*, pp. 200, 500 (date).
15 September 1942: Raul Hilberg, *The Destruction of the European Jews*, Quadrangle Books, Chicago, 1961, pp. 596–597. *Speer-Infiltration*, pp. 16, 20 (date).

9. The First Spaceship and the Fuehrer's Dream

3 October 1942: *Ley*, pp. 200–201, 500. *Dornberger*, pp. 3–17 (date, Dornberger quoted p. 17). *vB&O-Rockets*, p. 147. *Ordway & Sharpe*, p. 42 (quote of Oberth and award to von Braun).
11 December 1942: Bergaust, *Wernher von Braun*, op. cit., p. 134 shows a photograph of the Hearth Room. *Dornberger*, pp. 180–181 (quotes of Himmler and Fromm, date given as beginning of April 1943). *McGovern*, photograph with caption between pp. 120 and 121. Michael J. Neufeld, *The Rocket and the Reich*, The Free Press, New York, 1994, p. 176 and references cited. *Speer-Infiltration*, p. 203 and notes, p. 353 (date given as mid-December).
8 January 1943: *Dornberger*, pp. 73–78 (date). Irving, op. cit., p. 30 (von Braun's reaction to Degenkolb). *Ordway & Sharpe*, pp. 60–61. *Speer-Infiltration*, p. 203 and notes, p. 353 (Stegmaier's communications and Himmler's actions).
29 January 1943: Helmut Krausnick, Hans Buchheim, Martin Broszat, and Hans-Adolf Jacobsen, *Anatomy of the SS State*, Walker and Company, New York, 1968, pp. 101–102 (date and quote). Hoess, op. cit., 214 (first use of crematoriums).
31 January 1943: *Shirer*, pp. 925–932 (date). *Speer-Inside*, pp. 247–250. Walters, *Hermann Oberth*, op. cit., pp. 109, 132.
March 1943: *Dornberger*, p. 91 (quote). Irving, op. cit., pp. 26–27.

10. The Missile Arsenal: Demonstrations for Leaders of the Reich

29 March 1943: Irving, op. cit., p. 29.
26 April 1943: *Dornberger*, pp. 182–185 (date and quote). *vB-Reminiscences*, p. 51. *Speer-Infiltration*, p. 203.
26 May 1943: *Dornberger*, pp. 93–96 (date). Irving, op. cit., pp. 23 (date, quote of Speer), 58–59. *Ley*, pp. 206–207.
28 May 1943: *Dornberger*, p. 98.
23 June 1943: *McGovern*, p. 13, photograph and caption between pp. 120 and 121.
28 June 1943: Associated Press, "Rocket Scientist Used Slave Labor, Report Says," *San Francisco Chronicle*, 21 Aug. 1993 (repeats a story from the *Frankfurter Rundschau* reporting that Professor Reiner Eisfeld of Osnabrueck University discovered a document signed by Arthur Rudolph requesting slaves from the SS in

June 1943). *Dornberger*, pp. 186–194 (date given as 29 June 1943). Irving, op. cit., pp. 73–74 (date given as 28 June 1943). Neufeld, op. cit., p. 185 (Rudolph and slave labor). *USA-vB-FOI*, p. 168.
29 June 1943: *Dornberger*, pp. 194–195. Irving, op. cit., pp. 73–74 (date given as 29 June 1943). *Ley*, p. 500.

11. A Command Performance for the Fuehrer

7 July 1943: *Dornberger*, pp. 100–107 (date, quotes). *Speer-Infiltration*, p. 203 (Himmler's recommendation). *Speer-Inside*, p. 368 (date, quotes). *Ley*, p. 208. Neufeld, op. cit., p. 139 (20 August 1941 meeting).
Summer 1943: Hilberg, op. cit., pp. 317–327 (date on p. 327). Agoston, op. cit., illustrations between pp. 70 and 71.
Early July 1943: *Dornberger*, pp. 110–113 (date). *Ley*, p. 500. Neufeld, op. cit., p. 195 (Dornberger and slave labor).
25 July 1943: Irving, op. cit., pp. 88–90 (Hitler quote and date). *Speer-Infiltration*, p. 205 (date). *Speer-Inside*, p. 365.

PART III: TERROR AND COUNTERTERROR

12. The Flames of Peenemünde

17 August 1943: *Dornberger*, pp. 147–155 (date). Irving, op. cit., pp. 101–103. *McGovern*, p. 24.
18 August 1943: *Dornberger*, pp. 155-168 (date). Irving, op. cit., pp. 103–115. *Ordway & Sharpe*, p. 114 (list of those present).
19 August 1943: Neufeld, op. cit., p. 199 (dates of factory bombings). *Ordway & Sharpe*, pp. 64–65. *Speer-Infiltration*, p. 205 (date). *Speer-Inside*, p. 369.

13. Rockets Rising from the Ashes

20 August 1943: Hauptman Hermann (pseudonym), *The Luftwaffe, Its Rise and Fall*, G. P. Putnam's Sons, New York, 1943, pp. 113–114 (Milch quoted). Krausnick et al., op. cit., p. 588 (Kammler joined the SS). *Speer-Infiltration*, pp. 12 (Kammler ran construction division of the Air Ministry), 205–207 (date, quote of Himmler). *Speer-Inside*, p. 373 (Kammler at the Air Ministry).
21 August 1943: *Speer-Infiltration*, pp. 12, 207–208.
23 August 1943: *Michel*, pp. 61–62.
27 August 1943: *Dornberger*, pp. 176–177. Irving, op. cit., pp. 27–28, 123–124 (date), 142.
6 September 1943: *Dornberger*, pp. 196–199 (date). Irving, op. cit., p. 123.
10 September 1943: Irving, op. cit., pp. 136–137 (date). *Ordway & Sharpe*, p. 66. *Speer-Infiltration*, p. 217.

September 1943: Carey, op. cit., pp. 1A, 5A (quote of Rudolph). *Dornberger*, p. 209 (firings from Blizna). Linda Hunt, "Arthur Rudolph of Dora and NASA," *Moment*, April 1987, pp. 32–36. *Huzel*, p. 61 (no reconstruction at Peenemünde). Oberth, op. cit., p. 121. *Ordway & Sharpe*, pp. 69 (date), 117 (Oberth's departure). Thomas O'Toole and Mary Thornton, "Road to Departure of Ex-Nazi Engineer: Documents Implicate Rudolph," *Washington Post*, 4 November 1984, pp. A1, A25 (requisitioned slaves from Dora). *USAvAndrae*, Defense Exhibit 39A. Rudolph states he began working at the Mittelwerk on 1 September 1943. Walters, "Hermann Oberth," pp. 116–117.
5 November 1943: *Dornberger*, pp. 208 (Kammler), 214–215 (first Blizna firing).

14. The Nazi "Metropolis": A Subterranean Rocket Factory

Fall 1943: *Michel*, pp. 41–43, 62–63, 67 (conditions at Dora), 66 (Kammler quoted). O'Toole and Thornton, op. cit., pp. A1, A25 (quote of Dr. A. Poschmann at the Nuremberg trials).
10 December 1943: James P. O'Donnell, *The Bunker*, Houghton Mifflin Company, 1978, p. 119 (Speer warned to stay away from Auschwitz). *Speer-Infiltration*, pp. 210–211 (date, Speer quoted). *Speer-Inside*, pp. 370–371 (date).
17 December 1943: *Speer-Infiltration*, p. 219.
31 December 1943–1 January 1944: *Ordway & Sharpe*, p. 72.
18 January 1944: *Speer-Infiltration*, pp. 211 (date), 224–226. *Speer-Inside*, pp. 318–320, 323 (date), 327.
25 January 1944: *Dornberger*, pp. 215–216. Hunt, "Arthur Rudolph of Dora and NASA," pp. 32–36 (von Braun quoted p. 34). Irving, op. cit., p. 204 (date). *Michel*, p. 89. *USAvAndrae*, Defense Exhibit 38A (von Braun's testimony on his visits to the Mittelwerk).
January 1944: Krausnick et al., op. cit., p. 588.
February 1944: *McGovern*, p. 43.
10 February 1944: *Speer-Infiltration*, pp. 224–226 (date). *Speer-Inside*, pp. 330–332 (Koch quoted).

15. Dangerous Occupations: Rockets and Politics in the Third Reich

Dates of events described in this chapter are estimates; other sources may give different dates.
21 February 1944: Irving, op. cit., pp. 205-206 (date). *vB-Reminiscences*, pp. 51–52 (quotes). *USA-vB-FOI*, pp. 168 (SS ranks), 170 (membership in SS riding school).
15 March 1944: Bergaust, *Reaching for the Stars*, op. cit., p. 92. *Dornberger*, pp. 200–201. *Ordway & Sharpe*, pp. 46–47 (those arrested named). Wernher von

Braun, "Why I Chose America," *The American Magazine*, July 1952, pp. 15, 112, 114–115.

16 March 1944: *Dornberger*, pp. 201–203.

17 March 1944: *Dornberger*, pp. 203–206.

18 March 1944: *Speer-Inside*, pp. 333–335, 371–372.

Late March 1944: Bergaust, *Wernher von Braun*, op. cit., p. 107 (von Braun's Messerschmitt 108 Taifun). *Dornberger*, pp. 206–207. *McGovern*, pp. 52–53. *Ordway & Sharpe*, pp. 46–47.

16. The Business of Death

6 May 1944: Bower, op. cit., pp. 112–113 (quote of Rudolph). Hunt, "Arthur Rudolph of Dora and NASA," op. cit., pp. 32–36 (quote of von Braun). Irving, op. cit., pp. 221, 260 (quote of Dornberger), 282 (65,000 modifications). O'Toole and Thornton, op. cit., pp. A1, A25 (quote of Forschner).

8 May 1944: *Speer-Infiltration*, pp. 231–233. *Speer-Inside*, pp. 328, 336–343, 346 (date).

Late Spring 1944: *Ordway & Sharpe*, pp. 84–86. The approximate date of the Redl-Zipf disaster is inferred from information given by these authors. Walters, *Hermann Oberth*, op. cit., pp. 122, 156–157.

31 May 1944: *Dornberger*, pp. 208–209.

6 June 1944: *Shirer*, pp. 1037–1038.

13 June 1944: *Dornberger*, pp. 262–263. *Huzel*, pp. 100–101 (date). *Ordway & Sharpe*, pp. 130–159.

16 June 1944: Irving, op. cit., pp. 232–233. *Speer-Inside*, pp. 355-356 (date).

17 June 1944: Erwin Rommel, *The Rommel Papers*, edited by B. H. Liddell Hart, Harcourt Brace and Company, New York, 1953, pp. 478–479. *Speer-Inside*, p. 356 (quote). Hans Speidel, *Invasion 1944*, Henry Regnery Company, Chicago, 1950, pp. 92–99.

22 June 1944: Hunt, "Arthur Rudolph of Dora and NASA," op. cit., p. 34 (date). *USAvAndrae*, Prosecution Exhibit 127, deposition of Hans Rudolf Friedrich (rules for civilian conduct, V-men); Defense Exhibit 38A, deposition of Wernher von Braun (V-men).

Early Summer 1944: Bergaust, *Reaching for the Stars*, op. cit., pp. 95–96 (date). Irving, op. cit., p. 220 (Dornberger quote). *USA-vB-FOI*, von Braun's comments recorded by Frederick Cook, p. 376.

18 July 1944: *Dornberger*, pp. 176, 179. Irving, op. cit., pp. 148, 246–247 (date).

17. The Plot to Kill the Fuehrer

20 July 1944: Shirer, pp. 1044–1045, 1048–1069 (date, quotes of Heusinger and Stauffenberg). *Speer-Infiltration*, p. 213. Robert Wistrich, *Who's Who in Nazi*

Germany, Macmillan Publishing Co., New York, 1982, pp. 298–300 (personal history of Stauffenberg).

1 August 1944: *Dornberger*, p. 209, states that the Peenemünde establishment actually became a private concern on 1 June 1944. *Huzel*, p. 106 (date of the announcement). *Ordway & Sharpe*, pp. 53–54.

8 August 1944: *Dornberger*, pp. 211 (date, Himmler quoted), 236–238 (date, Dornberger quoted). *Shirer*, pp. 1069–1071 (date). *Speer-Inside*, p. 395. Von Braun, "Why I Chose America," op. cit., p. 112 ("most ruthless man" quote).

15 August 1944: Neufeld, op. cit., pp. 228 and 325 quotes a memo from von Braun to Sawatzki in the files of the National Air and Space Museum, FE694/a.

PART IV: THE ROCKET WAR

18. Vengeance Weapon-2

29 August–2 September 1944: *Ordway & Sharpe*, pp. 193–194 (dates).

6 September 1944: Basil Collier, *The Battle of the V-Weapons 1944–45*, William Morrow & Company, New York, 1965, p. 109. Irving, op. cit., p. 284 (date).

8 September 1944: Bergaust, *Reaching for the Stars*, op. cit., pp. 115–116 (quote: "Don't kid yourself . . ."). *Huzel*, p. 119 (headline and quote: "Let's not forget . . ."). Irving, op. cit., pp. 285–286. *Ley*, p. 217. *Ordway & Sharpe*, p. 195 (444 Battery attacks Paris). Walters, *Wernher von Braun*, op. cit., p. 76 (quote: "It behaved perfectly . . .").

30 September 1944: *Dornberger*, pp. 238–239 (date). Christopher Simpson, *Blowback*, Weidenfeld & Nicolson, New York, 1988, p. 29.

19. "Compared to Dora, Auschwitz Was Easy!": Death and Survival at the Rocket Factory

December 1944–January 1945: This date is approximate and is inferred from the depositions of Rudolph and Friedrich cited here. Ralph Blumenthal, "German-Born NASA Expert Quits U.S. to Avoid War Crimes Suit," *New York Times*, 18 October 1984, pp. A1, A12. Susan Faludi, "In the Rockets' Glare," *Atlanta Journal* and *Atlanta Constitution: Atlanta Weekly*, 26 May 1985 (first part of Grau quote). Hunt, "Arthur Rudolph of Dora and NASA," op. cit., pp. 32–36 (second part of Grau quote). O'Toole and Thornton, op. cit., pp. A1, A25. *USAvAndrae*, Prosecution Exhibit 126, deposition by Arthur Rudolph, stated he witnessed hangings "about the fall of 1944." Prosecution Exhibit 127, deposition of Hans Rudolf Friedrich, stated the men were hanged because they plotted to sabotage the Mittelwerk on 9 November 1944.

12 January 1945: *Dornberger*, pp. 258–260.

12–19 January 1945: *Auschwitz*: Garlinski, *Fighting Auschwitz*, op. cit., pp. 260–262 (dates). Hoess, op. cit. (quoted from *Speer-Infiltration*, pp. 236–237). Krausnick et al., op. cit., p. 100 (date Himmler ordered end of gassing). *Speer-Infiltration*, p. 236. *Dora-Nordhausen-Mittelwerk*: Agoston, op. cit., p. 29 (prisoners' rations).

Huzel, p. 117 (Magnus von Braun to Mittelwerk). Konnilyn G. Feig, *Hitler's Death Camps: The Sanity of Maddness*, Holmes & Meier Publishers, New York, 1981, p. 232 (subcamps and prisoner population). *Michel*, pp. 64 (the tunnel system), 96 (57 hanged), 225 (arrivals from Auschwitz and new camp at Nordhausen), 226 (deaths at Nordhausen). *Ordway & Sharpe*, p. 75 (the tunnel system), 76 (civilian supervisor population). *Speer-Infiltration*, p. 238. The total prisoner and guard populations in the Third Reich given in this reference were used to calculate the SS guard population.

20. Final Flights from Peenemünde: Von Braun Plans for the Future

24 January 1945: *Dornberger*, pp. 141–143 (A-9/A-10 design), 250–251 (date). Irving, op. cit., pp. 219–220 (Wizernes bunker and New York Rocket). Masters, op. cit., pp. 37–39 (von Braun interceptors). *Speer-Infiltration*, p. 210, used the term "American Rocket." *Vb&O-History*, p. 119.

27 January 1945: *Dornberger*, pp. 260, 264–266 (Kammler and Working Staff Dornberger; date). Garlinski, *Fighting Auschwitz*, op. cit., p. 262 (Auschwitz; date). *Speer-Infiltration*, p. 326, confirms Dornberger's account of Kammler's involvement in the "Working Staff" and states that Kammler formalized the relationship with a directive dated 6 February 1945. John Toland, *The Last 100 Days*, Random House, New York, 1965, pp. 10, 11.

28 January 1945: *Ordway & Sharpe*, p. 184.

End of January 1945: *Ordway & Sharpe*, p. 255. *vB&O-History*, p. 114 (date).

31 January 1945: *Huzel*, pp. 133–135. *McGovern*, pp. 90–91. Von Braun, "Why I Chose America," op. cit., pp. 15, 112, 114–115.

3 February 1945: *Huzel*, pp. 135–137.

17 February 1945: *Dornberger*, p. 266. *Huzel*, pp. 138–139 (date). *USA-vB-FOI*, Affidavit, p. 170 (von Braun quote).

19 February 1945: *Huzel*, pp. 128–129.

27 February 1945: *Huzel*, pp. 139–140.

Winter 1945: Date is inferred; no dates were given for these events. *Dornberger*, pp. 266–267 (Kammler-Dornberger meeting). *Ordway & Sharpe*, pp. 199–200 (Kammler-Axster exchange).

March 1945: Garlinski, *Hitler's Last Weapons*, op. cit., pp. 143–144. For estimates of deaths, the author refers to *Yad Vashem*, Jerusalem: Department of Court Records, Landgericht Essen, Utreil, Catalog No. TR-10/769.

16 March 1945: Bergaust, op. cit., p. 109. *McGovern*, pp. 94–95.

21. Scorched Earth: Hitler's Solution to Defeat

19 March 1945: *Shirer*, pp. 1103–1105 (date). *Speer-Inside*, pp. 436–440 (date, quote).

27 March 1945: Agoston, op. cit., illustration between pp. 70 and 71 reproduces Hitler's directive giving control of jet aircraft production to Kammler. *Ley*, pp. 217–

218. Irving, op. cit., p. 295. *Speer-Infiltration*, p. 240 (date; Kammler's new position and promotion). *Speer-Inside*, p. 450.

30 March 1945: Joseph Goebbels, *Final Entries, 1945: The Diaries of Joseph Goebbels*, edited by Hugh Trevor-Roper, G. P. Putnam's Sons, New York, 1978, p. 279 (quote).

1 April 1945: *Huzel*, pp. 149–154.

2 April 1945: *Huzel*, pp. 152–153.

3 April 1945: Goebbels, op. cit., p. 310 (quote). *Ordway & Sharpe*, p. 264 (quote of Axster's telephone conversation). *Dornberger*, p. 271, states he recieved the order to relocate on this date. *USAvAndrae*, Defense Exhibit 38A; von Braun describes receiving orders to relocate to Oberammergau.

4 April 1945: *Dornberger*, p. 271. *Michel*, pp. 258–259 (date; prisoners taken from Dora). Hoess, op. cit., p. 182, footnote (Himmler ordered gassing of prisoners). *Huzel*, p. 154 (date inferred from the text; documents convoy left Bleicherode). *Ordway & Sharpe*, pp. 264–265. There is disagreement on the date the "Vengeance Express" left the Nordhausen area. Huzel implies that the train left shortly before his group on 4 April. Dornberger claims his group left on 6 April. Secondary sources give other dates.

Early April 1945: *Speer-Infiltration*, p. 243.

5–7 April 1945: *Huzel,* pp. 158–162 (dates inferred from the text).

9 April 1945: Goebbels, op. cit., p. 327 (date). *Huzel*, p. 163. *Michel*, p. 278. *Speer-Infiltration*, p. 238 ("share the annihilation" quote).

11 April 1945: Agoston, op. cit., pp. 27–29 (quote of Third Army history). Hunt, "Arthur Rudolph of Dora and NASA," op. cit., pp. 35–36 (date). *McGovern*, pp. 120–122 (date). Simpson, op. cit., 30.

22. The Alpine Redoubt: A Refuge and a Trap

11 April 1945: This date is inferred from the references and is approximate. Wernher von Braun, *American Weekly*, 27 July 1958, quoted by Bergaust, *Reaching for the Stars*, op. cit., p. 110. *McGovern*, pp. 130–132.

12 April 1945: This date is inferred from the references and is approximate. Bergaust, *Reaching for the Stars*, op. cit., pp. 110–111 (quotes). *McGovern*, op. cit., pp. 132–134.

13 April 1945: Hunt, "Arthur Rudolph of Dora and NASA," op. cit., p. 35. *Michel*, pp. 287–289 (date).

15 April 1945: *Huzel*, pp. 181–183 (date).

17 April 1945: Agoston, op. cit., pp. 55–56. *Speer-Infiltration,* p. 242 (quote).

PART V: DEFEAT AND TRIUMPH

23. Twilight of the Trolls: The Death of the Third Reich

23–24 April 1945: O'Donnell, op. cit., pp. 121–137. *Speer-Inside*, pp. 478–484 (quotes).

25 April 1945: Bergaust, *Reaching for the Stars,* op. cit., pp. 112–113. *Michel,* p. 291 (date of von Braun's departure from Sonthofen). *Ordway & Sharpe,* pp. 266–267. *Shirer,* p. 1436 (date U.S. and Russian armies met).
26–29 April 1945: O'Donnell, op. cit., pp. 152–155. *Nazi Conspiracy and Agression,* Volume VI, U.S. Government Printing Office, Washington, D.C., 1946, pp. 554–556 (Nuremberg document 3734-PS).
29–30 April 1945: *Dornberger,* pp. 271–273. *Huzel,* pp. 185–187 (dates).
1 May 1945: *Huzel,* p. 187.
2 May 1945: *Speer-Inside,* pp. 493–494. Huzel, pp. 187–190 (date; rocket team surrenders). *Ordway & Sharpe,* pp. 1–9 (rocket team surrenders). *vB&O-History,* p. 116 (Stewart's reaction).
3 May 1945: *Huzel,* p. 190 (date). *Ordway & Sharpe,* pp. 10–11 (Stewart quoted). *Speer-Inside,* p. 495 (date).
5 May 1945: *Ley,* p. 222. G. A. Tokady, "Soviet Rocket Technology," *Technology and Culture,* 4 (Fall 1936), p. 523, quoted by Walter A. McDougall in *The Heavens and the Earth,* Basic Books, Inc., New York, p. 44 (Stalin quoted).
7 May 1945: Unconditional surrender described by various sources. *Ordway & Sharpe,* pp. 271–272 (quote of von Braun). The date is approximate and inferred from this reference and *Huzel,* op. cit., p. 191.
9 May 1945: Agoston, op. cit., pp. 90–101 (date). *McGovern,* p. 203 (Version #4 as told by Dornberger). *Speer-Infiltration,* p. 244.

24. Weapons for the Next War

May 1945: *McGovern,* pp. 151–176 (primary source of information for this section). *Ordway & Sharpe,* pp. 277–286 (supplementary information).
10 June 1945: Charles A. Lindbergh, *The Wartime Journals of Charles A. Lindbergh,* Harcourt Brace Jovanovich, Inc., New York, 1970, pp. 991–993 (date). *Shirer,* p. 827.
11 June 1945: Lindbergh, op. cit., pp. 993–998.
19–21 June 1945: *Ordway & Sharpe,* pp. 285–286.
5 July 1945: Neufeld, op. cit., p. 267 (date). *Ordway & Sharpe,* pp. 319–321.
19 July 1945: *McGovern,* pp. 193–194 (quote).
August 1945: Date has been inferred from various sources. *McGovern,* pp. 193–195. Von Braun, "Why I Chose America," op. cit., pp. 15, 111 (quote), 112, 14–115. Walters, *Wernher von Braun,* pp. 93–94; von Braun wrote the introduction to this biography and presumably described to the author his meeting with Toftoy. Bergaust, *Wernher von Braun,* op. cit., p. xiii-ix lists 118 German rocket specialists, including Wernher von Braun, who were brought to the United States. The list omits Georg Rickhey who was accused of—but later acquitted of—war crimes. Tom Bower, *The Paperclip Conspiracy,* Little, Brown and Company, Boston, 1987, p. 119 (Debus). Faludi, op. cit. (Axster). Linda Hunt, "U.S. Coverup of Nazi Scientists," *Bulletin of the Atomic Scientists* (April 1985), pp. 20–21 (Rickhey and Rudolph). Clarence G. Lasby, *Project Paperclip,* Atheneum, New York, 1971,

pp. 209–211. *Speer-Inside*, pp. 504–505. U.S. Army Oberth FOI file, pp. 143, 177–178, 179 and 182 (offered services to U.S. but was rejected). *USA-vB-FOI*, p. 421 (von Braun's contract). Walters, *Hermann Oberth*, op. cit., pp. 127–128. Fritz Zwicky, "Report on Certain Phases of War Research in Germany," Headquarters, Air Materiel Command, 1947, quoted from Walters, "Hermann Oberth," op. cit., p. 128.

25. Aged Rocketeers and Astronauts

16 July 1969: NASA film, *Time of Apollo*, 1976, Cantata Communications, Houston, Texas, videotape. Norman Mailer, *Of a Fire on the Moon*, Little, Brown and Company, Boston, 1970, p. 74. *vB&O-Rockets*, p. 127.

EPILOGUE

26. Time's Vengeance on the Nazi Rocketeers

Dornberger: Current Biography, 1965, pp. 125–127; 1980, p. 453. *Oberth: Current Biography*, 1957, pp. 416–418 (quote: "All my attempts . . ."). "The Pioneers," *Time*, 1969, July 18, p. 24 (quote: "Sometimes I feel . . ."). Walters, "Hermann Oberth," op. cit., pp. 128–130, 145–149, 158–159. *Speer: Current Biography*, 1976, pp. 386–389; 1981, p. 472. *Von Braun: Ordway & Sharpe*, pp. 344–404. *Rickhey: USAvAndrae*, Depositions were submitted by Wernher von Braun (Defense Exhibit 38A), Magnus von Braun (Defense Exhibit 44A), and Arthur Rudolph (Defense Exhibit 39). Also see "National Archives Microfilm Publications Pamphlet Describing M1079." *Rudolph et al.*: Blumenthal, op. cit., pp. A1, A12. Faludi, op. cit.

Index

About the Author

DENNIS PISZKIEWICZ has been an enthusiast of space exploration since his childhood in the 1950s. In the post-Sputnik era, he chose a career in science. During his year of teaching college-level chemistry and biochemistry, he received a NASA fellowship. For the past 10 years he has been a scientist in the medical products industry, and has spent his spare time exploring the origins of rocket development and space exploration.